The Holiday Golf Guide

Haig Point (Golf Resort Marketing)

KENSINGTON WEST PRODUCTIONS LIMITED

Acknowledgements

There are a large number of people to thank for helping Kensington West Productions produce this the third edition of the Holiday Golf Guide.

We are grateful to Golf Resort Marketing for supplying us with useful information and a number of excellent photographs to illustrate the book. Numerous Tourist Boards and their agencies throughout the world have supplied essential information. Many hotel groups have also been very helpful. There are a number of excellent tour operators in the golfing market and we would like to thank them for their suggestions and comments in producing the material.

We are particularly grateful to Thomsons Holidays (Wintersun) for helping with the marketing and distribution of the guide in the last three years.

I am extremely grateful to the editors of Kensington West Productions for their time and effort in the production of this guide. The maps are once again a delight and not only are they helpful but illustrate the book perfectly.

Our typesetters, printers and reprographic workers have again demonstrated their excellence under pressure and I would like to thank them for their continued assistance.

Finally thanks to you for purchasing or otherwise reading this edition of The Holiday Golf Guide, we wish you well on and off the fairways.

**5 Cattle Market, Hexham,
Northumberland NE46 1NJ
Tel: (0434) 609933 Fax: (0434) 600066**

Front Cover : Sun City Southern Africa

Consultant Editors: Simon Tilley, Julian West, Jane Chambers
Sub Editors Sarah Mann Karen Ryan

Cartography Camilla Charnock

Typesetting Tradespools Ltd, Frome
Design Angela Burrows

Origination Trinity Graphics Hong Kong

Contents

Slaley Hall
Northumberland England

PGA National
Palm Beach Gardens Florida

Caesar Park Hotel
Lisbon Estoril

Sun City *Sun International Republic
of Bophuthatswana S Africa*

The law of supply and demand has proven a rather harsh commercial reality for golfers in recent times. Those taking up the game and looking to join clubs have generally been hit the hardest, with annual retainers often required simply to remain on the eternal waiting lists and exorbitant joining fees reflecting the strength of the golf boom. The recession has not helped either, with many new course developments falling by the wayside as companies went to the wall or simply ran out of financial backing as property values plummeted. Some say that the tide is finally turning golfers' way and that the number of courses scheduled for completion over the next few years will see an end to waiting lists and the start of clubs fighting amongst themselves for new members. We shall see.

In the meantime, if there has been any the best on the home front for golfers it has largely been at the expense of hoteliers. The last few years have not been good news for the hotel trade and to accuse hotels of making capital out of the boom in golf would not be an accurate reflection of how the sting has been taken out of green fees by the excellent value packages many hotels have put together to attract business.

The Great Britain and Ireland section of our guide features not only the pick of the tried and tested courses holiday golfers have favoured over the years, but also many top hotels which cater exceptionally well for their golfing guests. Some have their own courses, while others are ideally situated for the local clubs and all are highly recommended.

As for the situation abroad we have tried to be as practical as possible in interpreting the elements which go to make an enjoyable golfing holiday. This is not, therefore, a definitive review of the top golf courses to be found around the world, although many are included, nor by the same token does the guide seek to pass judgement on such matters as the relative merits of luxury hotel accommodation and self catering apartments. What the editorial does cover are the courses and resorts which in our opinion offer value for money in terms of both golf and accommodation available. Wherever and whenever possible we have also indicated a selection of specialist tour operators servicing the individual areas and the various options they provide, leaving the golfer free to ponder the programme best suited to his or her own preference.

The featured operators who cooperated with Kensington West in the production of this guide represent a balanced cross section of the many major and some not so major companies who are active to varying degrees in the holiday golf market. We make no apology for being unable to include operators who for one reason or another failed to supply us with information requested on their programmes prior to publication. However, we must stress that our operator listing is representative rather than selective and our international reference grid features only those operators given general editorial coverage.

In this edition readers will find mention of certain recommended destinations slightly off the beaten holiday golf track and with air fares to countries such as Australia and New Zealand beginning to tumble, we can safely predict many new courses and resorts will be included in our next edition. Till then we trust there is something for everyone between these covers, and wish golfers pleasure and success on the fairways of their choosing.

Caesar Park *Penha Longa Golf Resort*

Great Britain

Parkland Golf (Country Club Hotels)

FIVE GOOD REASONS TO STAY HERE

English Tourist Board COMMENDED

FIVE CROWN COMMENDED

One of only a handful of hotels in Cornwall with the coveted English Tourist Board 5 Crown rating. Your guarantee of hospitality, standards, services and facilities.

All 81 *en suite* bedrooms are equipped with colour TV, satellite channel, telephone, hairdryer, trouser press, radio, tea and coffee making facilities and bathroom cosmetics. We can offer you luxury three roomed suites with spa bath, four poster beds, honeymoon suites, family rooms with separate children's accommodation and luxury double and twin rooms.

The extensive facilities include luxury snooker room with full size table, indoor and outdoor swimming pools, sauna, solarium, thermal spa bath, gymnasium, games room, guest's launderette, hair salon, entertainment seven nights a week in the main season. Special children's entertainment. Fun packed Christmas and New Year programme.

Our well appointed, air-conditioned restaurant offers you experienced and caring staff, excellent food, an extensive breakfast menu, a five course multi choice table d'hôte dinner menu, a superb à la carte menu and an extensive wine list.

GOLF INCLUDED in our special seven night and five night golf holidays. A choice of ten courses to play, including the super Nicklaus course at St Mellion. We also offer stay and play golf breaks tailored to suit your requirements.

Barrowfield Hotel

OPEN ALL YEAR

RAC ★★★ **AA** ★★★

HILGROVE ROAD, NEWQUAY, CORNWALL.
TEL: (0637) 878878
FAX: (0637) 879490

WEEKLY TERMS: £168 TO £304 (HALF BOARD). SHORT BREAKS AVAILABLE ALL YEAR ROUND

Newquay and North West Cornwall

The north coast of Cornwall is perhaps more rugged than its sister to the south, but both are beautiful havens for the golfer. The following ground rules may be of some help for visiting golfers. In the low season, between October and March, golf is fairly readily available. In the high season, a game is far more difficult to find. This may seem somewhat obvious - but in some parts of the country a game at any time of the year is a battle in itself.

Working one's way up the north coast from Lands End, the first club one finds is West Cornwall (0736) 753319. The course lies fractionally beyond St Ives, at Lelant. This delightful and very natural links course is extremely popular and despite its isolated position telephone booking would be both courteous and sensible. Visitors will, on occasion, be asked to produce their handicap certificate.

Travelling northwestwards, we come to Tehidy Park (0209) 842208 - a striking course which makes much of some superb pines and rhododendrons. The course is three miles north of Camborne and a fairly testing 6222 yards in length. It has a large membershp and visitors are requested to have proof of a handicap. One of the beauties of this part of Cornwall is its contrasting countryside. There are fishing villages, beautiful coastline and in contrast Newquay, a popular and lively resort.

Newquay (0637) 872091 itself provides a fine links course with some superb seaviews. The course has over 100 bunkers and in 1990 celebrated its centenary. A week-end membership is quite good value and is ideal for those on a short break. Perranporth (0872) 572454 is a neighbouring links with similarly spectacular coastal views.

Trevose and St Enodoc

The highlight of any tour of Cornwall's north coast must of course be the near neighbours Trevose (0841) 520208 and St Enodoc (020886) 3216. These are two absolute crackers and visitors are made welcome at both though, as you would expect, they are extremely busy. St Enodoc is at Rock and green fees are available on application. The main feature of St Enodoc is its massive sand hills. The 6th hole offers the notorious "Himalayas", thought to be the highest sand hill on any British golf course. There are two courses available here: The 18 hole Church Course and the 16 hole Holywell Course. Visitors are requested to have proof of handicap for the former but not the latter.

Trevose is a larger course than its neighbour and can be found at Constantine Bay. This is the ideal place for the golfing holiday. The club offers a championship golf course of 18 holes and a further fine 18 hole course. Sensibly, and tellingly, the green fees vary with the time of year.- winter, spring, summer and autumn have different charges. Good news for juniors - they are welcomed and afforded a discount. Mindful of the course's summer appeal a fortnight's golf on the championship course can be arranged for an excellent rate. Once again sand hills play a major feature on the course and the scenery is inspiring - Booby's Bay is a marvellous sight. A stream is also a pleasant feature and the course is well bunkered. A more recent addition to the area is Bowood (0840) 213017, a first class club with a lot to offer the visitor.

South Cornwall

The wonderful thing about South Cornwall is that it houses St Mellion - one of the most recent and perhaps the finest course in Britain. The brainchild of local farmers and my, what a success they have made of it. St Mellion (0579) 50101 lies 3 miles south of Cullington on the A388. There are two courses and visitors, who require handicaps for both, are expected to pay a fairly hefty green fee, but make no mistake for golfing pilgrims it is most definitely worth it. The Nicklaus really is a must for the dedicated golfer. All the holes are superb and streams, lakes and a variety of undulation make golf not only spectacular, but also somewhat tricky. The 5th, 11th and 12th are three to savour. This course has overshadowed much of Cornish golf but there are still some thoroughly worthy courses to be inspected. Looe provides the oft windswept but delightful moorland course, named Looe Bin Down (05034) 247.

The course at St Austell (0726) 72649 is situated on the western edge of the town besides the A390. It has a mixture of both heathland and parkland and visitors are welcomed but should be club members and hold a handicap certificate. Carlyon Bay (0726) 814250 is a splendid course, and once again the views are tremendous and inspiring - and an interesting contrast to St Mellion.

Falmouth provides two tests - one a golf hotel and the other Falmouth Golf Club (0326) 311262, a welcoming club. Budock Vean (0326) 25288, is a fine test and has a superior hotel.

Our westernmost course on the south coast is located at Mullion (0326) 240276. Green fees are good value here and there is a discount for golfers who wish to take a five day membership. The course can be found on the clifftops and exemplifies much of the charm of Cornwall's array of friendly and often challenging courses.

The North Devon Coast

Royal North Devon, Saunton and Ilfracombe - a splendid trio of challenging golf. The championship links of Westward Ho! and Saunton provide the most perfect opportunity for one of those weekend breaks. The crash of the waves into craggy coves and sandy beaches, the isolation and some splendid golf. This may not of course be everyone's cup of tea but for the golfer and loved ones, it surely provides the recipe for a marvellous long weekend or fully fledged holiday. There are obvious advantages to avoiding the high season and there are similarly clear merits in visiting during the week. Although South Devon attracts more of the visitors, North Devon still has its generous share, so in the summer especially, you will be far from alone.

Westward Ho!, (02372) 473817 founded in 1864 lays claim to being the oldest links club playing over its original land. It also boasts the world's oldest ladies golf club founded in 1868. The course is laid out on common land and visitors should note that, despite the eminence of the fairways, the local sheep are perfectly at liberty to enjoy the delights of the course as well. They are enthusiastic supporters of golf and disturbances on the fairways are kept to an absolute minimum! Green fees at Westward Ho! are excellent value when compared with much of Europe and both daily and weekend badges are obtainable, although a prior telephone call is a good idea. Junior tickets are particularly cheap. The course can be approached via the A39. From Northam village follow your nose. The club house is visible from Bone Hill. The course provides a traditional out-and-back layout and the mixture of bunkers, gales and the fearsome Great Sea Rushes, provide for a stern and sometimes impossible test. Historians of the game will enjoy this course as much as any and for inspiration all golfers should know that Westward Ho! was where the great John H Taylor learnt his golf. The clubhouse is a welcome retreat and the catering together with the splendid museum, will satisfy both the tummy and the mind. Westward Ho! is a landmark in golf that should be visited by all lovers of the game.

St Mellion Golf Course (St Mellion Country Club)

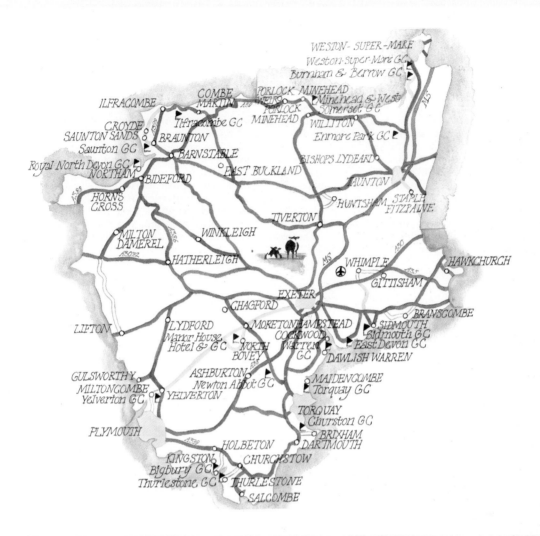

Saunton is a deceptive distance from Royal North Devon - some 20 miles, but a visit is thoroughly recommended. There are two Saunton (0271) 812436 courses, the championship East Course and the West Course. From modest beginnings it really developed its acclaim after its reconstruction in 1951. The additional 18 holes date from the more recent early 1970s. Visitors should be able to demonstrate a handicap if asked but other than that no restrictions are imposed - though once again a prior call is advisable. The charges per round vary. On the championship links the first four holes all measure in excess of 400 yards, though the 5th and 13th are fine examples of demanding short tests. The 16th is also a superb hole - a tee shot over a sand hill is the first obstacle; a huge bunker in front of the green is another. There is no doubt that Saunton is a fitting neighbour to Westward Ho! It offers delightful views, botanic delights and mountainous dunes amongst a variety of other glories for the golfer to savour - a superb course.

Our final port of call is Ilfracombe (0271) 621716. Its situation several hundred feet above the sea offers some stimulating views and while the golf is not as challenging as Saunton or Westward Ho! a visit is recommended. Ilfracombe provides a number of short par 3s, one of which measures a mere 81 yards. Marvellous, just the job for the old pins. A day's golf varies with the time of year but is pretty good value.

Exeter and South West Devon

The links of South Devon are a less vaunted but extremely playable group. To the east of the River Exe one finds our first two ports of call, namely Sidmouth (0395) 3023 and East Devon (03951) 443370 at Budleigh Salterton. Sidmouth plays along the cliffs with marvellous views, while East Devon is more akin to the downland variety with an abundance of heather and gorse. Visitors are welcome at both courses.

Moving further west one arrives at Dawlish. Here the Warren Golf Club (0626) 862255 provides splendid links golf with inspiring views over the cliffs and sea. It is a welcoming club and provides a good test for all standards of golfer. This is a lovely part of Devon and once again could be worked into a trip along South Devon's gorgeous and inviting coastline. Lovers of inland courses should not forget the pleasures of Moretonhampstead at the Manor House Hotel (0647) 40355 which offers an extremely satisfying 18 holes.

South Devon

This area is the most popular of all Devon's resorts. Golfers must therefore be a lot more organised. There are a range of splendid courses. Newton Abbot (0626) 52460 offers a real corker in Stover. Founded in 1899 the course was redesigned by James Braid in 1931 and offers an abundance of heather, a meandering brook and woods which all make for a picturesque and challenging round of golf. The course is handy for Torbay, the so-called Riviera of Devon. Churston (0803) 842751 is a spectacular clifftop course. Visitors are advised to call in advance and are required to have a handicap. Another course to note while in the area is Torquay (0803) 37471 and much the same formalities are required here.

Dartmouth is en route to our next and final cluster of holiday courses. Thurlestone and Bigbury are the two highlights. Thurlestone (0548) 560405 has an active membership and is difficult to play but, with a handicap and prior booking, a round can be arranged. You will be rewarded with spectacular clifftop views. Bigbury (0548) 810207 is only a short distance from Thurlestone and looks out across Burgh Island. The course was designed by J H Taylor and is undulating - a testing 18 holes.

The Somerset Coast

Between the busy resorts of Weston-Super-Mare and Minehead lie some first class golf courses. Burnham and Berrow (0278) 785760 is without doubt the most distinguished course and it is here that JH Taylor perfected his accurate short game. Large sand hills and small greens combine to plot your downfall. The course is set on an exquisite stretch of the Somerset coast, with views across the Bristol Channel to South Wales. The course encompasses not only massive sand hills but also flat marshland. Burnham's finishing four holes are renowned and if you score well you truly deserve a fine 19th hole, and at Burnham you find it - and a warm welcome to match.

The holiday towns of Minehead and Weston-Super-Mare also provide testing and immensely satisfying links golf. Weston-Super-Mare (0934) 621360 is the longer of the two and is well maintained. Its proximity to Bristol ensures a popular following so an advance telephone call is advisable, particularly in the summer months. The Minehead and West Somerset Golf Club (0643) 702057 is particularly susceptible to the wind due to its flat layout. It is well worth a visit and is a friendly club. People who have played on the above three courses will have enjoyed a feast of fine links golf.

The manor House Hotel and Golf Course (*Mortonhampstead, Devon*)

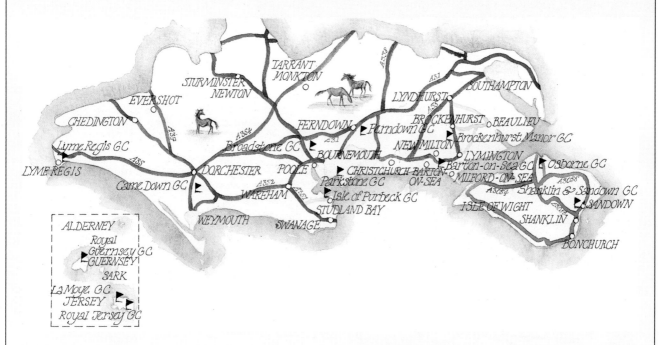

The South Coast

The Isle of Purbeck (0929) 44361 may be considered Dorset's leading course, although the choice is tricky when one considers the quintet of other delights to be found skirting the seaside towns of Bournemouth, Poole and Swanage. The Isle of Purbeck is hardly Britain's most accessible club, standing as it does just off the B3351 Studland road near Swanage, but it is surely one of the most delightful. The view from the 5th of the 18 hole Purbeck course is particularly outstanding as you tee off from the top of an ancient burial mound. The par 3, eleventh, with its backdrop of pines and two tier green, is also an exceptional hole. Visitors to the Isle of Purbeck course, as opposed to the 9 hole Dene course, must possess a handicap. With Swanage a popular holiday spot it is perhaps worth considering a short temporary membership of the club. For a golfer wishing to make Purbeck his base the fees are excellent value. The club are happy to provide details for such arrangements.

The South Coast also offers an abundance of other first class clubs, for example the 36 holes at Ferndown (0202) 874602 and the two 18 holes at Parkstone (0202) 707138 and Broadstone (0202) 692595. All are beautiful heathland courses with heather, gorse and pine trees in abundance. Ferndown is situated on the outskirts of Bournemouth, off the Christchurch Road, while the other two can be found within a couple of miles of each other just to the north of the town.

Bournemouth's two other courses - Meyrick Park (0202) 290871 and Queens Park (0202) 36198 - are both public and as a result green fees are far cheaper. Queens Park is often described as the finest public course in England.

From Bournemouth, a delightful trip through Hardy country will bring you to Sherborne, with its magnificent Abbey and cobbled courtyards, and equally marvellous golf course. Sherborne (0935) 814431, one of the country's prettiest inland courses, welcomes visitors although a prior telephone call is, as ever, recommended. The course can be found to the north of the town, off the B3145, on the edge of the famous Blackmore Vale. The journey back might wisely be broken with a quick detour to Came Down (0305) 812531. The pretty town of Dorchester stands close by as an attraction for any non-golfer.

The New Forest

The New Forest has much to delight both the golfer and his or her partner. The former will be kept well satisfied with Brockenhurst Manor (0590) 23332, a superb heathland course set amidst the splendour of the forest. It can be found after a five minute drive from Brockenhurst on the B3055. Brockenhurst Manor welcomes visitors during the week and, to a limited extent on weekends, although telephoning is again recommended. As with a number of courses in the county reduced green fees are made for those teeing off after 4.00pm.

Although not strictly in the New Forest, the clifftop course at Barton-on-Sea (0425) 615308 is well worth visiting and a worthy neighbour for Brockenhurst. It is located further down the A337 near New Milton. At 5565 yards it is not long but provides a fair challenge and also boasts splendid views across to the Isle of Wight and Christchurch Bay.

Isle of Wight and The Channel Isles

There are no fewer than seven golf courses on the Isle of Wight. Whilst Shanklin & Sandown (0983) 403217 is probably the best known and the 9 holes of Osborne (0983) 295421 the most scenic, a visit to any is appealing. All courses welcome visitors and green fees tend to compare favourably with those on the mainland.

Jersey has two courses that are particularly outstanding, La Moye (0534) 43401 and Royal Jersey (0534) 54416. La Moye, home to the Jersey Open, commands the most superb views over St Ouens Bay and is generally considered to be the better of the two. It is set high up on the cliffs and at 6464 yards, often with a stiff sea breeze to negotiate, is an extremely testing course. In addition to being a superb championship test, the course makes itself more than welcome to visitors, though to get on you must be a member of a recognised golf club.

La Moye is a privilege to play and a must for any Jersey-bound golfer. It is situated at the other end of the island, half an hours drive from La Moye. Incidentally "half an hours drive" actually means 5 or 6 miles away as 40 mph speed limits are enforced throughout the island.

Royal Guernsey (0481) 47022 can only be played on a Monday, Tuesday, Wednesday or Friday and a visit to this neighbouring island is strongly recommended.

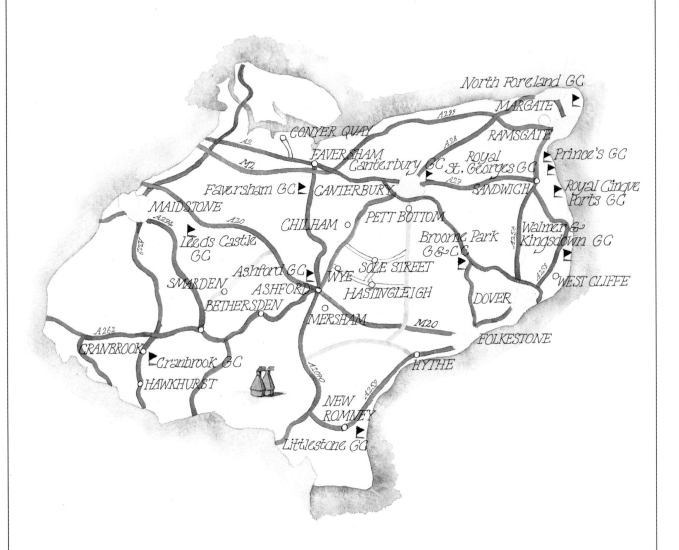

The Great Triumvirate

The major problem when considering the golf courses of Kent is where to start. With such a rich selection, it would be inappropriate to recommend Kent's striking coastal trio to anyone but the most committed of golfers.

Royal St Georges (0304) 613090 sets the scene. Gentlemen must possess official handicaps of 18 or less, ladies 15 or less before they will be allowed onto the course. The first tee is reserved daily for members until 9.45 am and between 1.15pm and 2.15pm. However, the tenth tee is usually free for golfers playing in the early morning - a marvellous time to play. St Georges is essentially a singles and foursomes club and, as a result, three ball and four ball matches are permissible only with the Secretary's prior consent. Green fees are expensive for a day's golf, though in December, January and February a lesser fee covers the day. St George's is an Open Championship course and in 1985 Sandy Lyle won - the first British champion for some sixteen years. More recently Greg Norman has won the Open here, demonstrating at the same time the majesty of his game and the quality of the course. The challenges of the course are great and the sense of history pervading this distinguished course will ensure those who are able to play, a truly memorable day.

Royal Cinque Ports (0304) 374328, or Deal as it is more commonly known, is another fabled club. There are now no weekend bookings available, but visitors to the club are welcome during the week. The wind is often a major factor when playing Deal but it is nature that has sculpted most of the course and what a first class job it has made. The outward nine are considered to be the less demanding and the course is renowned for a tough finish. Twilight golfers beware! There are some tremendous views on clear days and this has to be one of the most natural but severe courses in the country. The course has a busy and large membership and while visitors are not unwelcome, except at weekends, the prior booking routine and planning is absolutely essential. The drinks hut at the 9th in winter is a particularly crucial spot. With the tough back nine still to play you will need all the sustenance you can get.

The third highlight of this marvellous tour is, of course, Prince's (0304) 611118. Formalities once again are rigid and Sunday remains the preserve of the membership. Golf in this smart stretch of England's coast is special. Visiting golfers will no doubt appreciate this and react accordingly. No one should be put off visiting - but in this region, far more than any other in England, preparation is essential.

Royal West Norfolk G C
Hunstanton G C
OLD HUNSTANTON
HEACHAM
BRANCASTER
STAITHE
GREAT SNORING
BLAKENEY
WEYBOURNE
Sheringham G C
SHERINGHAM
Royal Cromer G C
ALDBOROUGH
King's Lynn G C
KING'S LYNN
GRIMSTON
COLTISHALL
Great Yarmouth
& Caister GC
GORLESTON-
ON-SEA
BARNHAM BROOM
NORWICH
BUNWELL
Thetford G C
THETFORD
SOUTHWOLD
Thorpeness GC
Aldeburgh
ALDEBURGH
NEWMARKET
BURY ST. EDMUNDS
OTLEY
LAVENHAM
IPSWICH
WOODBRIDGE
Woodbridge GC
LONG MELFORD
HINTLESHAM
Felixstowe Ferry GC
FELIXSTOWE

North Norfolk

The countryside of Norfolk is peaceful, the golf is excellent and there are a number of marvellous haunts in which to pitch the proverbial camp. The focus of any such trip should of course be Brancaster (0485) 210087. The Royal West Norfolk Club generally welcomes visitors, though handicaps of under 18 are required. Given the severity of the test, this is both reasonable and sensible. A days green fee is not cheap but the course is an absolute classic. Two of the features of the course are the tidal marshes, which come into play on the 8th and 9th, and its huge wooden sleepered bunkers.

Other clubs to be shortlisted in any visit include Kings Lynn (055387) 656, which welcomes visitors on all weekdays except Tuesday. The course itself, an Alliss- Thomas design, is heavily wooded and represents a pleasurable and demanding test. Hunstanton (0485) 532811 also yields a championship links and is renowned for its quite stunning beauty and excellent greens. Visitors are welcome throughout the week and at weekends.

Two other courses which complete this quite superb quintet are located at Sheringham (0263) 823488 and Royal Cromer (0263) 512884. The Lighthouse Hole at

Sheringham, and gorse and cliff views aplenty, make for an inspired march as well as, one hopes, a few fine strokes. The development at Barnham Broom (0605) 45 393 is of a very high quality. There are now some 36 holes set in 260 acres of rolling parkland. The hill and valley courses are a first class golfing combination and a round on both will certainly leave you well exercised. Green fees are not over the top for a day ticket and with Norfolk fairly close to London Barnham Broom provides a really first class excuse for a few days away.

South Suffolk

Less challenging, but thoroughly worthwhile golf can be found on Suffolk's charming coast. Thorpeness (0702) 8852176, Aldeburgh (0728) 852890, Woodbridge (0394) 3 2038 and Felixstowe Ferry (0394) 286834 provide a marvellous little quartet. This also provides golfers with the opportunity to sample some of the splendid real ales brewed in the region - good for the belly, though not necessarily the swing! Felixstowe Ferry and Aldeburgh welcome visitors throughout the week but the others keep the weekends for members use only.

The Best of the Rest of Kent

Kent has two other fine links courses in North Foreland (0843) 62140 in Broadstairs and Littlestone (0679) 63355 near New Romsey. Visitors are welcome on all days at the latter but not at weekends at the former. Green fees are available on application from both courses. Both are really worth visiting and can be tied in with a splendid weeks golf in Kent. Walmer and Kingsdown (0304) 373256 should also be thrown in for good measure - a tremendous course. If one is looking for a magnificent seventh to make up a really superb week, the golfer has a wealth of choice. Perhaps a nine holer might be in order. Leeds Castle (0627) 80467 is most welcoming and has a marvellous setting to inspire even the most exhausted golfer. Or alternatively the pleasant fairways of Faversham (079589) 561, a course which is particularly beautiful in the autumn. There are a number of courses due to open in Kent in the near future. Some will be difficult to play but others, such as Hever Golf Club (0732) 700771, will have a more welcoming approach which is good news for the holidaying golfer.

Sussex East and West

Sussex is superbly well blessed with golf and there are a number of courses which are among the very best in England. The East Sussex National (0825) 86217 is a relatively new, but outstanding addition to the fairways of East Sussex. There are two 18 hole layouts, the East and the West. The courses are both the design of Robert Cupp. Undulating landscape, mature woodlands and spectacular views of the rolling downs make this an outstanding golf-

ing experience. Greens are generally on the large side but water, effective bunkering and the Little Horsted creek will all test your golfing prowess. In order to play the course your best bet is to stay at the course's hotel, Horsted Place.

Royal Ashdown Forest (0342) 822018 is a less lavish set up but its pine and silver birch make for a glorious golf course. An ever present stream and scattered gorse and heather necessitates good golf and you will be required to show a handicap certificate before playing. All in all a first class and worthwhile golf course.

West Sussex has its own fair share of first class golf and in Pulborough (0798) 22503 it provides one of the most scenic courses in all England. The course only yields one Par 5, on the first hole, but don't be misled. With thick heather, bunkers and water hazards the course is difficult to score well at. In the main, singles and foursomes only are welcome and all visitors should contact the secretary in advance. This advice is worth following at all clubs in this part of England where demand exceeds supply and many of the courses are fairly selective!

Other courses to consider in the region include Goodwood (0243) 774968 and Worthing (0903) 60801 (which boasts two first class courses). While in Eastbourne, Willingdon (0323) 32383 and the Royal Eastbourne Clubs (0323) 29738 are both outstanding. Before we leave Sussex we should perhaps mention one of the bastions of British golf, Rye (0797) 225241. It is not merely one of the most testing and striking links in England but also fairly hard to play. A letter may do the trick - it's worth a shot for this is a splendid example of links golf at its finest and most natural.

It must be blatantly obvious to golfers and to many other people who have no interest in the game that there are too few golf courses and too many golfers. The resultant problem ensures that many golf courses are extremely difficult to play. There are, however, a number of clubs that we simply could not miss out and there are other courses that are owned by hotels and are thoroughly welcoming to visitors, especially at weekends, when some very attractive packages can be found. What follows is a quick synopsis of the premier courses and a number of celebrated hotels in which to stay.

Surrey is particularly well blessed with courses and one of its finest clubs is located at Wentworth (0344) 842201. Visitors must have a handicap of 20 or less to play these illustrious fairways which now total some 54 holes. The West Course is the most celebrated test and one of the most expensive courses in the country to play. The recently opened Edinburgh Course is a fine 18 holes of golf and the East Course will also satisfy the enthusiast. The club is constantly being modernised and is a great experience to play. Walton Heath (0737) 812380 is another celebrated club. Visitors are welcome during the week provided you make a prior engagement with the secretary. Proof of club membership and handicap are likely to be needed. There are two courses, the Old and the New, and both have a heathland character. The Old is slightly longer and the last three holes are particularly memorable.

People who are seeking to organise a company day out would be wise to consider Fernfell (0483) 268855 which is extremely welcoming and a pleasure to play. Moor Park (0923) 773146 is another extremely prestigious club. There are again two courses and both, despite their popularity, are kept in excellent condition. Green fees are on the high side and a round on the High Course is a very severe test of golf.

Arguably the finest golf course in the south of England is found at Sunningdale (0990) 20128. The Old Course and the New Course are both outstanding examples of heathland golf at its best. The green fees allow the visitor a round at each course should they have the energy. The 18th is another tremendous closing hole after what will surely have been a memorable day's golf. To organise a game phone (0344) 26064.

All the clubs we have mentioned so far hold prestigious championships and our next suggestion follows this trend. Woburn (0908) 370756 offers 36 holes of spectacular golf, The Dukes and The Duchess courses are really outstanding. A day ticket varies on the number in your party.

Collingtree Park (0604) 701202 is a first class course which is one of a growing number of pay and play courses which are so prolific and popular in the United States and France. It is thoroughly recommended for a day out and a similar recommendation can be made of Staverton Park (0327) 705911. Both courses are ideally situated in the Midlands and for people wishing to organise company golf days they are popular choices.

Abbotsley (0480) 74000 near St Neots is another course to commend. The emphasis here leans towards instruction rather than competition and for people new to the game, or for anyone who is seeking to improve their technique, one would be advised to consider a day or two here.

There are all manner of excellent courses in central England. Notts Golf Club (0623) 753225 is first class and Woodhall Spa (0526) 352511 is one of the country's most beautiful heathland courses. Woodhall Spa may be somewhat out of the way but it remains popular with golfers. Its sheer excellence is the one and only reason for this. A visit is thoroughly recommended. It goes without saying a prior telephone call is essential before visiting any one of the above clubs.

The Lancashire Coast

The Lancashire Coast

Between Hoylake on the Wirral Peninsula and Royal Lytham, less than 40 miles further up the coast, are to be found a truly formidable set of links courses. Hoylake, Birkdale and Lytham have, of course, each staged the Open on a number of occasions. The Amateur Championship has been played at both Hillside and Formby, and Southport and Ainsdale have twice hosted the Ryder Cup. Welcome to one of the finest golf locations in the world.

Visitors are welcome to play at any courses and weekdays are naturally the best times to try to arrange a visit. Green fees vary hugely, dependent on the prestige of the course, and at the more renowned courses a handicap certificate is also essential.

Those wishing to play Royal Lytham (0253) 724206 are also asked to provide a letter of introduction from their home club but subject to this requirement they are welcome on any day between Monday and Friday. Whilst advance booking is not essential it is clearly advisable. The course is a bit of an anomaly. It is a seaside links with neither sight nor sound of the sea. Bobby Jones struck one of the finest shots in golf at the 17th and make no mistake your swing will have to be in tiptop condition to register a good score. The course has many individual characteristics. It is the only Open course to open with a short hole, the only Open course where one can drive out of woods on the first three holes and the only Open course with three short holes on the front nine. It is a singular course which every enthusiast should endeavour to play. In the 1988 Open Championship two inches of rain fell within 24 hours causing the abandonment of Saturday's play and the postponement of the final round to the Monday. Still, if a day inside didn't do Seve Ballesteros any harm, then there's no reason why it should have any effect on you. Green fees at Lytham are on the high side but this is to be expected at this outstanding course. For those in search of a similar test, St Annes Old Links (0253) 723597 on the other side of town, off the A584 towards Blackpool, might fit the bill.

Moving down the coast, we come to that other famous Open Championship venue Royal Birkdale (0704) 67920. The club, host to no fewer than six Opens this century, can be found two miles from the centre of Southport, close to the main A565 road. Those wishing to play at Birkdale must be able to provide a letter of introduction from their home club and possess a handicap. Before setting off, such persons are advised to contact the secretary. In 1991 the club hosted the Open Championship for the seventh time and will therefore now prove particularly difficult to play. Don't be put off though. The course is a supreme test for the low and middle handicap player and the administration team are most friendly - provided you have the right introduction and the necessary loot! The course itself has had more than its fair share of drama - it was at Birkdale that Jack Nicklaus conceded Tony Jacklin's very missable putt on the 18th green, so tying the Ryder Cup of 1969. And it was also on these links,

eight years before, that Arnold Palmer played what he still considers to have been his best golf, in a gale that would have sent ordinary mortals back to the clubhouse well before the 18th. In the rough at the 16th there is a plaque - one of only two on our Open courses - commemorating the great man's miraculous 6 iron shot with which he somehow contrived to find the green. A shot that effectively secured his narrow victory over the Welshman Dai Rees.

Southport and Ainsdale (0704) 78000, Hillside (0704) 69902, Formby (0704) 872164 and West Lancashire (051) 924 41152 all lie off the A565, to the south of Birkdale towards Liverpool. "S and A" is the best known of the four with the famous par 5 "Gumbleys" hole its trickiest test. "S and A" allows limited play to visitors. On weekdays, you can only play as a visitor provided you submit a letter of introduction from your home club and provided you play before 4pm. After 4pm, play is only permitted if accompanied by a member. Weekends are a no go area, unless of course you know an "S and A" member. The links at Hillside and Formby apply similar restrictions.

The West Lancashire links, like Southport & Ainsdale, has also played host to the Open qualifying rounds and thus has championship status. The course welcomes visitors at all times including weekends. This most enjoyable of clubs is well worth visiting.

Royal Liverpool and others

On the other side of Liverpool, ten miles west to be precise, and 15 miles north of Chester, lies Royal Liverpool (Hoylake) 051 632 3101, the fourth oldest club in England and the first to be laid out along this particular famous stretch of coastline. Judging by the quality of some of its neighbours, what a precedent it must have set! Actually, being situated on the tip of the Wirral peninsular, Hoylake is not strictly regarded as a Lancashire course but there again in these days of sprawling conurbations nor are the Southport courses which are now in Merseyside. There are many who maintain that Hoylake remains the greatest of all England's championship links. It has only been taken off the Open Championship circuit because of its location. Its surroundings were felt to be too small to accommodate the increasingly large crowds that the event now attracts.

Rather like Carnoustie, Hoylake is renowned for its exciting final stretch. It contains two par 5s and three par 4s, any of which is capable of wrecking a potentially good score. Hoylake allows visitors but a letter of introduction or handicap certificate is required.

The Isle of Man

Say Isle of Man and most people - especially if they're bike freaks or monetarists - will mention the words "TT" or "tax haven" somewhere in their responses. Well, the golf here is good too and nowhere more so than at Castletown (0624) 822201 which sits beside the hotel of the same name. At Castletown golf is played well above sea level with views at every hole of tumbling cliffs, rocky inlets or sweeping bays. The greens are fast and true

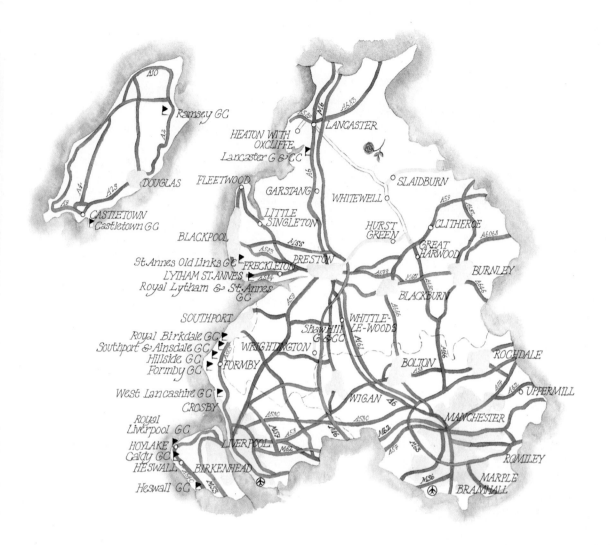

and heather and gorse border the fairways. The course has its own road hole, the 8th, which is a particularly testing par 4. The other hole which occupies the golfer's post mortem is the 17th - over 400 yards atop a cliff.

Whilst all seven courses are worth visiting, the pick of the rest is Ramsey (0624) 813365, situated to the north of the island, above Douglas. It is a 6019 yards test.

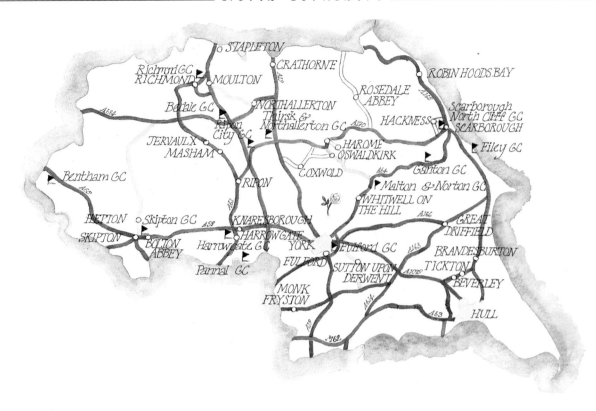

York and The Dales

York's courses are outstanding. Strensall (0904) 490304 lying approximately six miles north of York Minster, has a splendid woodland challenge designed by J H Taylor. Visitors are welcome to play at Strensall on any day of the week although it is extremely popular and a prior telephone call is essential. Green fees are priced on the high side. Fulford (0904) 413579 is York's other and better known course. Visitors are unable to play at weekends but may play during the week. Once again a fairly hefty green free is levied.

Outside the city boundaries golf perhaps plays second fiddle to some quite marvellous countryside and equally interesting country house hotels, restaurants and pubs. Of the golf clubs Pannal (0423) 871641 is perhaps the finest. The club welcomes visitors during the week. Harrogate (0423) 863158 is situated about a mile from Knaresborough. A parkland course, it's also worth a look and more modest green fees are in order here. Golfers are welcome at weekends. Despite the fact that isolated territory fills much of Yorkshire, some fairly heavily populated towns, coupled with a great love of golf, make Yorkshire courses difficult to play.

Other courses worth considering for visitors include Malton (0653) 697912, Ripon City (0765) 70041, Skipton (0756) 3922 and Richmond (0748) 2457. All these courses are playable throughout the week, but all are fairly busy so book in advance.

Ganton and The Coast

Ganton (0944) 710329 is a tremendous golf course, home for some years of the immortal Harry Vardon. It is situated nine miles from the coast, and enjoys a beautiful setting nestling on the edge of the Vale of Pickering and the North Yorkshire Moors. With gorse and bunkers aplenty, the fourth is a particularly treacherous hole. It must be played across a plunging valley towards a heavily bunkered green which is on a plateau. Golf can be

played throughout the week and all visitors should make prior arrangements with the secretary. Green fees are on the high side, but it really is a first class course.

Scarborough boasts two courses, the North Cliff (0723) 360786 and the South Cliff (0723) 374737. Visitors are welcome throughout the week, but booking in advance is advisable. One final thought is to sample the seaside course at Filey (0723) 513273, a thoroughly rewarding golf course if your game is on song - and even if it isn't actually!

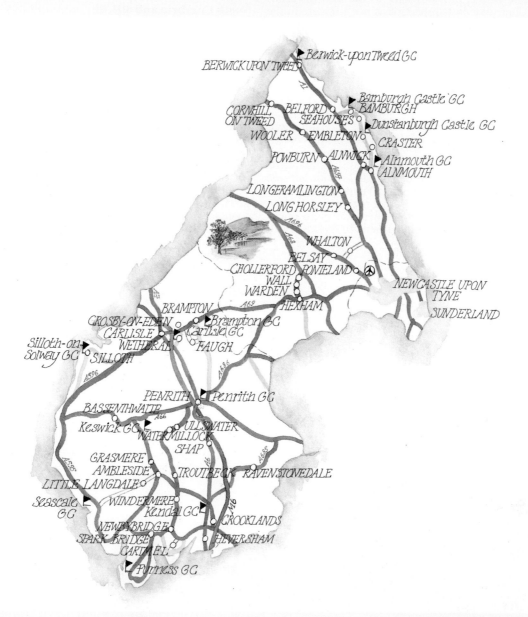

The Northumberland Coast

North Northumberland is a splendid place for golfers. Open fairways, outstanding views and some super and varied countryside. Berwick (0289) 87256, England's most northern golf course is situated at Goswick. It is an exceptionally pleasant links. The club enjoyed its centenary in 1990 and, like so many courses in Northern England and Scotland, has matured with the elements over the years.

South of Berwick, but remaining on this glorious coastline, one finds a brace of spectacular castle courses. Bamburgh (0668) 4321 is the better known and provides an absolutely glorious setting. The course is dominated by its Norman castle - an ideal diversion for non-golfers. Visitors are welcome on all days except bank holidays - when a member must accompany you. The prices at the course reflect its popularity. In the summer months green fees are almost twice the winter price. Given the severity of some of Northumberland's winter months, it is not altogether surprising that such a system is in operation. A seven day membership can be purchased in the summer months. Bamburgh is a short course but it still provides a test. Fairways which are flanked by tangling heather abound and the wind, is an important friend or foe. Other glorious views include Holy Island, Lindisfarne and the Cheviots. This really is a most beautiful course.

Embleton yields another absolute beauty. On this occasion the wonderful castle is Dunstanburgh (0665) 76562, a varied but charming and impressive edifice. As with Bamburgh, the clubhouse is practical and welcoming. Green fees are good value but a seemingly neverending demand for golf has made its mark. There are many courses suffering in this way but I would certainly not put any one off playing this fabulous links.

Before leaving this part of the country we should mention Foxton Hall (0665) 830231. Located in Alnmouth, this seaside meadowland course welcomes visitors. Green fees are more expensive than at Embleton but the course is kept in excellent condition.

The Lakes and The Northumberland Jewel

The Lake District provides some of the most gorgeous inland countryside in Europe. Golf is not a feature in the tourist board information and that's a pity! In travelling to the Lakes you may pass near to Slaley Hall (0434) 673350. This is a stunning course and although a relatively recent addition to the fairways of Britain this is a must for the lover of excellent golf courses.

The courses one should consider include Appleby (07683) 51432, a marvellously remote moorland course, where the daily green fees are great value. In Keswick, the golf course lies 4 miles east of the lakeland town. Several streams and dense woodland add to the course's natural beauty. Kendal (0539) 24079, where green fees are excellent value, has a legendary opening hole, 231 yards, uphill all the way, with out of bounds to your left and woods glaring blackly from the left. Penrith (0768) 62217 is perhaps the finest course in the region and is thoroughly recommended. Green fees here are more pricey but are still good value. Windermere (05394) 43550 is another to short list, a delightful mini Gleneagles.

North Cumbria and Silloth

Silloth on Solway (06973) 31304 is an absolute cracker. Its remote situation, 23 miles north west of Carlisle, should be no reason for not visiting. Green fees, both on weekdays and at weekends, are good value. A weekly ticket, Monday to Friday, is also available at a good price. Of the many tremendous holes, the 13th has the most stern reputation. The par five "Hogs Back" has an exceptionally narrow heather-lined fairway and a plateau green - miss it and you're in serious bother! The clubhouse is welcoming and the catering excellent. A must for all travellers of the fairways.

There are two other courses that should be considered for the Cumbrian visitor. Brampton (06977) 2255 is a beautifully maintained course, some 400 feet above sea level, affording golfers splendid views towards the surrounding hills. This moorland course contrasts with the parkland offering that makes up Carlisle (0228) 72303.

Slaley Hall

Cornwall

Barrowfield Hotel, Newquay, Cornwall. Tel: (0637) 878878

This is one of only a handful of hotels in Cornwall with the coveted English Tourist Board Five Crown rating. All of the 81 en suite bedrooms have satellite television, telephone and trouser press. The facilities available to guests include indoor and outdoor swimming pools, sauna, solarium, thermal spa bath and entertainment seven nights a week in the main season. Special golf breaks are available and there are a choice of ten courses to play, including the Nicklaus course at St Mellion.

Lanteglos Country House Hotel, Camelford, Cornwall. Tel: (0840) 213551

Long established as one of the major golfing centres in Cornwall. Situated in a secluded valley in a beautiful and unspoilt part of Cornwall and on the very edge of the Bowood Park Golf Club. The hotel provides quality accommodation, good food and friendly service in a relaxed enjoyable atmosphere.

Port Gaverne Hotel, Nr Port Isaac, North Cornwall. Tel: (0208) 880244

The proprietors of this pretty hotel on the spectacular North Cornwall coast believe in offering pleasant food, prepared from the best ingredients. The hotel also owns and runs Green Door Cottages which offer self catering accommodation for those golfers with families. Rounds of golf can be arranged at any of the 26 courses within the Royal Duchy.

St Mellion Golf and Country Club, Saltash, Cornwall. Tel: (0579) 50101

St Mellion is a modern golf and country club situated in the Caradon District of South East Cornwall, offering a superb variety of sporting facilities to both its guests and members. Guests can enjoy golf on either the Old Course or the Jack Nicklaus championship course. The hotel has everything to make the guest's stay enjoyable and comfortable. The bedrooms are attractively furnished with en suite bathroom, colour television and tea and coffee making facilities. The superb restaurant in the clubhouse serves a first class menu of international cuisine. Alternatively guests may prefer the comfort and luxury of the St Mellion Lodges, beautifully equipped and furnished with all the requirements for up to eight people.

Devon

Anchorage Hotel, Instow, Nr Bideford. Tel: (0271) 860655/860475

The Anchorage at Instow specialises in golfing breaks. Former international golfers Jon and Margaret Cann, cater for parties of up to 28 golfers with concessionary rates at Royal North Devon and Saunton amongst others. With cordon bleu cooking and a well stocked bar could any golfer ask for more?

Bolt Head Hotel, Salcombe, Devon. Tel: (0548) 843751

This is a delightful hotel set on the North Devon coast. Dining here is a pure delight and staff take care to ensure that all tastes are catered for. There are excellent leisure facilities in the area including a good golf course within a few miles of the hotel and guests are really ensured an enjoyable holiday.

Court Barn Country House Hotel, Holsworthy, Devon. Tel: (0409 27) 219

Court Barn is set in five acres of beautiful grounds amidst rolling Devon countryside. The atmosphere is one of peace and tranquillity - a place to remember. This award winning hotel and restaurant is unique for its for its personal service and relaxed atmosphere. Each of the eight bedrooms is individually furnished and decorated. There is an elegant breakfast room and the luxurious restaurant is the ideal setting to enjoy the excellent cordon bleu cuisine. Court Barn is ideally situated for Holsworthy, Bude and Launceston golf courses, each within ten minutes. Guests can enjoy special three or six day breaks which include free golf at Holsworthy.

Kittiwell House Hotel and Restaurant, Croyde, North Devon. Tel: (0271) 890247

This delightful thatched hotel dates from the 16th century and has retained much of its charm. The restaurant is distinctive with its massive stone fireplace and low beamed ceiling which give it such character. Golf can be arranged at concessionary rates and being only two miles from Saunton Golf Club and near to the Royal North Devon Club this is an ideal hotel for those who are following the fairways.

Manor House Hotel and Golf Course, Moretonhampstead, Devon. Tel: (0647) 40355

An hotel of grand tradition, the Manor revels in its oak panelled lounges, open fireplaces and wide sweeping staircases. The superb cuisine and impeccable service combine with the challenging, par 69, 18 hole championship golf course - reputed to be one of England's finest inland courses - to give you a break to remember.

The Thatched Cottage Country Hotel and Restaurant, nr Lifton, West Devon. Tel:(0566) 784224

Set in the middle of the West Country, surrounded by Bodmin

Moor, Exmoor and Dartmoor this delightful hotel nestles in two and a half acres of landscaped cottage gardens. For the keen golfer there is the challenge of approximately 50 courses in Devon and Cornwall, all within easy reach of the Thatched Cottage.

Westcliff Hotel, Sidmouth, Devon. Tel: (0395) 513252
Surrounded by superb golfing country, Devon's lanes and moors nearby, the Westcliff Hotel offers its guests an ideal base for exploring this beautiful part of Britain. There are excellent leisure facilities and the 40 bedrooms are all fitted to a very high standard.

Whitechapel Manor, South Moulton, North Devon. Tel: (0769) 573377
In the foothills of Exmoor lies Devon's only Michelin starred hotel restaurant - a tribute to the superior cooking and local Devon produce. Here you will find a part of English heritage encapsulated by this old Elizabethan manor house. For golf enthusiasts there is a choice of eight courses within 40 minutes drive.

The South Coast
Chedington Court, Chedington, Dorset. Tel: (0935) 891265

Chedington Court is a traditional country house hotel set on the edge of Thomas Hardy country in the south of England. The welcoming interior of the house creates an atmosphere of comfortable yet distinctive informality with its old Persian rugs, stone fireplaces, fine brass fittings and antique furniture. The golf course is 9 holes, par 74, built on 90 acres of parkland bisected by an ancient droveway. It measures 3425 yards and is one of the longest 9 hole courses in the country. Described as one of the best of the newer golf courses, it makes use of the natural features of the beautiful rolling countryside.

Langtry Manor, East Cliff, Bournemouth, Dorset. Tel: (0202) 553887
Very occasionally you stumble upon a rare gem of an hotel where the building, food service and history blend to form something quite exceptional, such as Langtry Manor Hotel in Bournemouth. There are about 20 golf courses in the vicinity of Bournemouth catering for all standards of player. Langtry Manor would be pleased to make arrangements for you to be able to play at most of them.

Longueville Manor, St Saviour, Jersey. Tel: (0534) 25501
The 13th century manor stands in 15 acres of grounds at the foot of its own private wooded valley and is one of the most prestigious small hotels in Europe. Exquisitely furnished with fine antiques and fabrics, the manor is a haven of tranquillity in which to enjoy fine food and wine.

South Lodge, Lower Beeding, Hampshire. Tel: (0403) 891711
An elegant country house with one of the finest Victorian rock gardens in England. The light and spacious bedrooms have fine views over the South Downs. The hotel is only a short drive from the challenging 18 hole Mannings Heath Golf Club, where hotel guests enjoy special privileges.

Kent and Sussex
East Sussex National and Horsted Place, Little Horsted, East Sussex. Tel: (0825) 750581
Horsted Place occupies an enviable setting and offers modern facilities in a delightful and elegant form. Over 1000 acres of rolling countryside have been transformed into two golf courses which present a competitive challenge. There are also fabulous practice facilities and a teaching academy.

East Anglia
Hintlesham Hall Hotel, Hintlesham, Suffolk. Tel: (0473)652334

Hintlesham Hall, originally built in the 1570s, offers the best in country house elegance and charm. Gracious living, good food and wine, attentive service and tranquil relaxation greet every guest to the hotel. Thoughtful attention to detail is apparent throughout and this includes the restaurant. Scottish salmon, Cornish scallops and Suffolk lobsters are just some of the enticements on the menu which changes seasonally. The hall is set in over 170 acres of rolling Suffolk countryside, some of which is devoted to a beautiful 18 hole championship full length golf course.

Ufford Park Hotel, Woodbridge, Suffolk. Tel: (0394) 383555
With a setting amidst Suffolk's beautiful countryside Ufford Park, provides a relaxing haven for the business visitor and the weekend guest alike. There are first class facilities including an 18 hole golf course designed to professional standards, the Cedar Restaurant and the leisure club.

Middle England
Allt-yr-Ynys, Walterstone, Herefordshire. Tel: (0873) 890307
Built in 1550 and set in magnificent surroundings this elegant hotel has kept its historical appeal and yet offers the finest of modern comforts. All bedrooms are en suite and individually furnished. Leisure facilities are excellent and if you are a keen golfer the hotel is conveniently situated for Abergavenny, Monmouth, Chepstow and Hereford courses.

Anugraha Hotel and Conference Centre, Englefield Green, Egham, Surrey. Tel: (0784) 434355
Nestling in 22 acres of glorious parkland on the edge of Windsor Great Park, this superb Jacobean style mansion offers fine hospitality and a

relaxing atmosphere. The light and spacious Orchid Restaurant provides diners with first class cuisine. Golfers are particularly well provided for but the area also has a wealth of activities for the non-golfer.

Bank House Hotel Golf and Country Club, Bransford, Worcester.
Tel: (0886) 833551

The Bank House Hotel stands in 123 acres of attractively landscaped countryside which contains a "Florida style" par 72 golf course that meanders around numerous lakes. A variety of specially tailored breaks are available for golfers and there is also a well equipped fitness centre, sauna and jacuzzi within the hotel complex. The hotel aims to provide a first class personal service and this is reflected in the high standard of the accommodation. The Elgar Restaurant offers guests a culinary delight and for a more informal atmosphere there is the beamed Exchange Bar with a wide selection of real ales and excellent bar meals.

The Cheltenham Park Hotel, Charlton Kings, Cheltenham.
Tel: (0242) 222021

The Cheltenham Park Hotel is a recently extended Regency manor house set in nine acres of landscaped gardens with a natural lake and waterfalls. The hotel has superb views over the Leckhampton Hills and the adjacent Lilleybrook golf course. The 154 luxury bedrooms include the Presidential Suite and executive rooms which command

superb views over the attractive gardens. The Lakeside Restaurant offers the best of modern English cuisine. There are two bars to choose from: the Tulip Bar with its marble fireplaces, original oak panelling and large patio overlooking the golf course, or the congenial Lakeside Bar. The hotel is next door to the well known Lilleybrook golf course and only minutes away from the Cotswold Hill golf course - a perfect golfing location.

Donnington Valley Hotel and Golf Course, Newbury, Berkshire.
Tel: (0635) 551199
Set in the beautiful countryside of Royal Berkshire and surrounded by an 18 hole golf course, Donnington Valley Hotel is a unique venue, blending charm and elegance with the luxury and personal service expected from an individually designed, privately owned, four star hotel.

Frederick's Hotel and Restaurant, Maidenhead, Berkshire.
Tel: (0628) 35934
Set in 2.5 acres of attractive gardens, this sumptuous hotel houses one of the finest restaurants in the South of England. With 37 luxuriously furnished bedrooms and award winning cuisine Frederick's is renowned for providing comfort, good food and individual hospitality. Frederick's highly accessible location is ideal for golfing at Wentworth and Sunningdale.

Hanbury Manor, Thundridge, Nr Ware, Hertfordshire.
Tel: (0920) 487722
From beamed ceilings and oak panelling to fascinating tapestries this hotel is nothing less than impressive and is to be savoured. With its huge range of facilities Hanbury Manor caters for nothing less than the civilised aesthete. Golfers can choose to play either the magnificent 18 hole golf course or the Downfield 9 hole course.

Hawkstone Park Hotel, Shrewsbury, Shropshire. Tel: (0939) 200611
This renowned golfing hotel is set in a 300 acre estate and features a fine 18 hole golf course and a 9 hole course. The hotel itself was built in 1790 and is steeped in history. It now provides a catalogue of sporting and leisure facilities. The restaurant offers traditional English cuisine and the whole ambience is one of taste and luxury.

Hutton Court, Hutton, Avon.
Tel: (0934) 814343

This is a hotel and restaurant in classic country house style that caters for every golfer's needs. The championship links of Burnham and Berrow are only 20 minutes away and golf there is available to residents by special arrangement as it is at five other courses equally as close to the hotel.

Le Manoir aux Quat' Saisons, Great Milton, Oxfordshire.
Tel: (0844) 278881
The history of this outstanding manor dates back 750 years. Set in 27 acres of beautiful landscaped gardens and woodland this is an internationally acclaimed hotel. Each one of the 19 elegant bedrooms has been individually designed and the bathrooms are equally luxurious. Le Manoir is widely acknowledged as Britain's finest restaurant and the superb cuisine is complemented by an extensive wine list.

Manor House, Castle Combe, Wiltshire. Tel: (0249) 782206
The Manor House is idyllically set in 26 acres of grounds with a trout stream and terraced Italian garden. The hotel offers five star luxury in a relaxed atmosphere with excellent cuisine. Castle Combe Golf Club is only two minutes driving distance from the Manor House.

Moore Place, Aspley Guise, Woburn, Bedfordshire. Tel: (0908) 282000
An elegant Georgian mansion with a locally acclaimed restaurant, Moore Place offers many facilities and is an ideal base for visiting local attractions such as Woburn Abbey, Whipsnade Zoo and Dunstable Downs. Woburn golf course is also nearby.

Moxhull Hall, Holly Lane, Wishaw, Warwickshire. Tel: 021 329 2056
Moxhull Hall is situated on a hill adjacent to the Old Manor, which is now better known as the Belfry. This fine country hall with beautiful grounds and splendid interior offers excellent cuisine and access to the many immediate attractions of the area.

Priory Hotel, Bath, Avon.
Tel: (0225) 331922
This well run former private residence has retained many of the early 19th century gentleman's necessities - croquet lawn, orangery, lovely furniture. There is also a wonderful and widely acclaimed restaurant. The city of Bath offers a multitude of attractions and there are numerous golf courses within easy distance.

Puckrup Hall Hotel and Golf Club, Tewkesbury, Gloucestershire. Tel: (0684) 296200

Puckrup Hall Hotel and Golf Club is set amidst 140 acres of rolling parkland between the Cotswolds and Malvern Hills, just a few minutes from junction 8 of the M5. The 18 hole par 71 golf course, with the addition of lakes to the natural water sources and astute use of specimen trees, will satisfy the most discerning golfer. The 84 luxury bedrooms, superb cuisine and extensive conference and private dining facilities are all complemented by "Generations" Leisure Club which hosts swimming pool, spa bath, sauna, solarium, steam room, gymnasium, beauty treatment room and crèche. Altogether the ideal location for a touring base, golfing break or management retreat.

Selsdon Park, Sanderstead, Surrey. Tel: 081 657 8811

Set in the rolling hills of the Surrey countryside Selsdon Park combines the ancient virtues of hospitality and courtesy with the modern attributes of efficiency and friendliness. Converted into a hotel in 1925 there are now 170 bedrooms and suites and a considerable range of conference and banqueting rooms. An outstanding asset to Selsdon Park is the 18 hole championship golf course, laid out by five times British Open golf champion J H Taylor. Covering 6407 yards this course is not perhaps for the novice, although it provides a stimulating challenge to low and high handicappers alike. After a round or two on this interesting course guests can unwind in the hotel's leisure club which has a tropical swimming pool, gymnasium, squash courts, sauna and jacuzzi.

Sodbury House Hotel, Old Sodbury. Tel: (0454) 312847

This 18th century former farmhouse is set in six acres of attractive grounds. Only 12 miles south of Bath and on the edge of the Cotswolds it is an ideal base for exploring the West Country. The hotel has been tastefully refurbished to retain its original character and all 14 bedrooms are well appointed and stylishly furnished.

Stocks Country House Hotel, Aldbury, Herts. Tel: (0442) 851341

Stocks, an elegant country house hotel in the heart of the Chilterns, dates back to 1176. Not only a peaceful house for unwinding and enjoying the delightful atmosphere and excellent cuisine, Stocks offers sporting and leisure facilities second to none, with an 18 hole golf course due to open in spring 1994.

Telford Hotel, Golf & Country Club, Sutton Hill, Shropshire. Tel: (0952) 585642

Set in the beautiful Shropshire countryside, not far from the famous Ironbridge, this hotel offers many and varied facilities - from the luxurious en suite bedrooms to delicious food served in imaginative surroundings, to the many sports activities, keep fit, ballooning, archery etc. Paramount amongst these is the nine hole golf course and floodlit all-weather driving range.

The Lancashire Coast
Inn at Whitewell, Clitheroe, Lancashire. Tel: (0200) 448222

Originally built for the Keeper of the King's deer in the 14th century, the Inn at Whitewell still retains associations with field sports. For the golfer, the splendid inland course of Clitheroe Golf Club is close by and the famous courses at Lytham and Birkdale are within easy reach. The hotel serves classic English food with an emphasis on quality.

The Stanneylands Hotel, Wilmslow, Cheshire. Tel: (0625) 525225

A handsome country house set in several acres of gardens, Stanneylands offers quiet luxury in the heart of the rolling Cheshire countryside. The hotel is ideally located for the many fine golf courses in the area including Birkdale, and arrangements can be made to play at the Mere Golf and Country Club or the Tytherington Club near Macclesfield.

North Yorkshire
Aldwark Manor Golf Hotel, Aldwark, York. Tel: (0347) 838146

This impressive Victorian manor stands in over 100 acres of mature parkland complete with its own 18 hole golf course. The beautifully furnished, individually designed bedrooms, all have en suite facilities. The restaurant offers traditional food and fine wines. Aldwark Manor combines luxury living with an atmosphere of period charm and elegance.

Feversham Arms Hotel, Helmsley, North Yorkshire. Tel: (0439) 70766

A luxuriously modernised, historic coaching inn set in over an acre of walled gardens, this hotel offers every comfort and an outstanding quality of cuisine. If you are contemplating a round of golf there are over 20 golf clubs within a radius of 35 miles, the nearest being Kirkby Moorside.

Mount Royal Hotel, The Mount, York. Tel: (0904) 628856

The hotel is the result of the tasteful blending of two beautiful William IV detached houses.

The proprietors have spent a good deal of time on restoring the former glory of these buildings and their efforts have been well rewarded. Enjoying the gracious beauty of the hotel, the style and antiquity of much of the furnishings, or slipping into the secluded heated swimming pool is the perfect way to pamper the body as well as the mind. The hotel is ideal for the small conference or private dinner party and is only a short drive from Fulford Golf Club.

Cumbria and Northumberland

**Appleby Manor Hotel, Appleby-in-Westmorland, Cumbria.
Tel: (07683) 51571**

The delights of the hotel's leisure centre and pool, together with the Lake District's breathtaking beauty, are your recipe for a splendid country holiday. There is a superb 18 hole moorland golf course set in magnificent scenery. Friendly staff, mouth watering meals, log fires and comfortable bedrooms are the extra ingredients which make it perfect.

**Burn How Garden House Hotel,
Bowness-on-Windermere, Cumbria.
Tel: (05394) 46226**

Burn How is situated in secluded, peaceful Bowness only two minutes walk from Lake Windermere. The elegant restaurant specialises in English and French cuisine using only fresh produce. Nearby Windermere golf course, now in its second century, comprises 200 acres of undulating terrain often described as a 'mini Gleneagles'.

Crosby Lodge Hotel, Crosby-on-Eden, Cumbria. Tel: (0228) 573618

An elegant country mansion combining a tasteful collection of antiques with fine furniture in both private and public rooms. The restaurant serves delicious food and is open to non residents. For the golfer arrangements can easily be made on the nearby Riverside course and on a variety of courses at Carlisle, Brampton, Penrith and Silloth.

Farlam Hall Hotel, Brampton, Cumbria. Tel: (06977) 46234

Mature landscaped gardens surround this old border house. Inside large lounges with open fires and an elegant dining room combine with 12 superb bedrooms - in which antiques and fine furniture are used wherever possible - to provide an ideal retreat at the end of a days golf. Farlam Hall is ideally situated, not just for Brampton and Carlisle golf courses, but also as a base from which to enjoy the other numerous and varied courses that are nearby. Also, if heading north to play in Scotland, the hotel's proximity to major routes makes it the perfect resting place.

Michael's Nook, Grasmere, Cumbria. Tel: (05394) 35496

A gracious stone built lakeland house overlooking the Grasmere valley. This hotel is beautifully furnished with antiques and provides memorable high quality cuisine. The hotel enjoys a close proximity to some of the excellent northern links courses and also offers special arrangements with Keswick Golf Club.

Nanny Brow Country House Hotel, Ambleside, Cumbria. Tel: (05394) 32036

The comfort and contentment of gracious country life at the Nanny Brow contrasts with challenging golf at Windermere and other courses in the locality. Michael and Carol Fletcher take the strain out of organisation and provide elegance, haute cuisine, modern comforts and spectacular surroundings for their discerning guests.

Wordsworth Hotel, Grasmere, Cumbria. Tel: (05394) 35592

In the heart of Lakeland, this first class, four star hotel has a reputation as one of the area's finest. It offers comfortable bedrooms and many leisure facilities, together with superb cuisine. For the golfer, the hotel can arrange free rounds from Monday to Friday at Keswick Golf Club.

Slaley Hall (*Northumberland*)

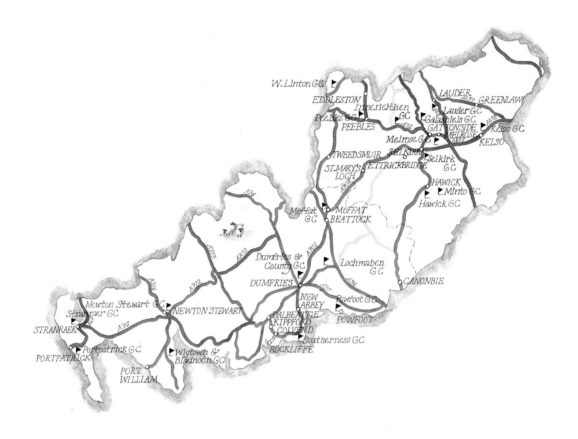

Dumfries and Galloway

The first port of call for any proposed golfing adventure in Scotland's Border country is a visit to Southerness (0387) 88677. The course is situated some 16 miles south west of Dumfries and is an outstanding test. Since its foundation in 1947, this links course has found a multitude of admirers. Visitors are always welcome and green fees are not expensive for a week's golf. The crowds may head for Gleneagles and St Andrew's but that is their mistake - Southerness is a first class course.

Powfoot (0461) 22866 is another championship course and it too welcomes visitors. It is surrounded by the Cumberland and Galloway Hills. Fees are once again attractively priced. The final thoughts for this small golfing tour are Dumfries and County (0387) 53585 and Lochmaben (0387) 810552. The former is another extremely welcoming 18 hole parkland course while the latter, no less friendly, has only nine holes. The course with its Kirk Loch setting is superb and also very good value.

Other examples of eminently visitable courses are located at Newton Stewart (0671) 2172 - only nine holes - cheap and very cheerful and the same can be said of Wigtown and Bladnoch (0671) 43354.

Portpatrick (0776) 1273 a touch further west, is also something of a gem. It contains meadowland and seaside golf and is surely one of the most beautiful courses in Scotland.

Meanwhile slightly to the north on this breathtaking peninsula one finds Stranraer (0776) 87245, a splendid parkland course designed by James Braid. Green fees are a little more pricey than at Portpatrick - which seems surprising, but it is still good value and golfers can get splendid discounts for a week's golf.

The Borders

There are few better places to start one's trip to the Borders than Hawick. Hawick Golf Course (0450) 72293 is an undulating and fairly stiff 18 holer. Five miles north east of Hawick one comes to Minto - another thoroughly welcoming 18 hole course.

Galashiels (0896) 3724 provides another hilly test. One has to be prepared for a fair amount of walking so it is essential your game is well and truly up to scratch. Green fees are great value. Kelso (0573) 23009 also welcomes visitors, the course is located within the racecourse - another excellent haunt! Our final port of call is Peebles Golf Course (0721) 20197, arguably the finest in this area.

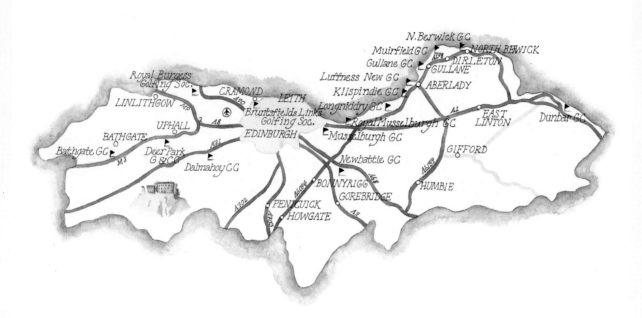

Lothian

One of the major problems with this area is managing to get on the links in the first place. Golf was invented in Scotland and it seems some of the authorities are far from keen to share the discoveries. Furthermore, many holiday-makers may be fairly keen to head northwards. This is not altogether sensible because apart from anything else, Edinburgh and its myriad of fine hotels are well seeing.

Muirfield (0620) 842123, is home to the Honourable Company of Edinburgh Golfers. The club itself has had something of a nomadic history, having moved from Leith to Musselburgh and from there some 20 miles from Edinburgh under the lee of Gullane Hill. Today, the old Tom Morris design is considered to be one of the finest tests in world golf. In order to play Muirfield, gentlemen golfers must belong to a recognised golf club and carry a handicap of 18 or less. For ladies, who may play only if accompanied by gentlemen, a handicap of 24 is required. Visitors should also note that foursomes are favoured and that four ball games will only be permitted in the mornings. All letters of introduction should be sent to: The Secretary, The Honourable Company of Edinburgh

Golfers, Gullane, East Lothian. The course is individual in that it has an inner and an outer lap. The intention of this is to prevent the golfer from playing successively with or against the wind. This is a superb course and a round here is to enjoy golf at its very finest.

This coast offers some other excellent links but the majority of travelling golfers still trek northwards. This is a pity as there is some first class golf to be found. Gullane, (0629) 842255, has three links. Visitors are welcome on all courses during the week and courses 2 and 3 at weekends. Another fine links nearby is Luffness New (0620) 843114. This is an outstanding challenge but visitors must call in advance to arrange a tee time. The views from these courses are spectacular.

Further down the road towards Edinburgh is another fine course, Longniddry (0875) 52141. The course runs along the seashore and also through parkland. Continuing eastwards is North Berwick, (0620) 2135. The course is some 23 miles from Scotland's capital and visitors are always most welcome. Green fees are considerably cheaper for a midweek game. All in all Lothian offers an excellent selection of golf courses to test the finest players.

St Andrews and North East Fife

If one had to play just one more round of golf, I wonder how many club golfers would choose to play St Andrews. The most recognisable and renowned golf course in the world. A symbol of golf itself.

The museum which glorifies the wealth of history that surrounds the course is well worth a visit during this vital golfing pilgrimage. The origins of the course can be found in a licence which dates from 1552. The public were permitted to "play at golf futeball, schuetting at all gamis with all uther, as ever they pleis and in ony time" The proprietor was also charged not to plough up any of the said land. The stomach heaves when one actually so much as contemplates the thought of the Old Course being put under the plough. In 1754 a society was formed when 22 "Noblemen and Gentlemen" formed the St Andrews Society of Golfers. In 1834 this Society became the Royal and Ancient Golf Club. All enquiries about playing the course should be addressed to the St Andrews Links Management Committee, Golf Place, St Andrews, Fife (0334) 75757. There are a total of five links at St Andrews - The Balgrove, a 9 hole course, founded as recently as 1974, The Eden Course, The Jubilee Course, and The New Course. The principal course, however, is the Old Course although the others add a pleasing variety to one's visit to the home of golf.

In order to play the Old Course, one should either have a letter of introduction or a handicap certificate. Naturally the course is far busier in the summer, but even in the spring and autumn the management committee should be contacted some time in advance. The best idea is to give a number of possible times at which you would like to play. There are many features one could discuss - numerous bunkers, huge double greens, seven in all, and some memorable landmarks which one associates with the game itself, such as the bridge over the Swilcan Burn. This is a course of champions and championships - but in many ways, like no other, it is the course of the people. Remember to think ahead as you play the course and while the fairways are often inviting positional play will determine your success or failure. There are many plans for St Andrews but these do not involve the plough. St Andrews is a developing holiday location but the Old Course remains - haunting and daunting, a challenge to us all.

For those needing respite from the links look no further than Ladybank (0337) 30814, one of Scotland's finest inland courses with pine and heather in abundance. Green fees for this excellent diversion are quite pricey and weekend mornings are best avoided. Lovers of the downland type course might wish to venture north of St Andrews and discover the delights of Scotscraig (0382) 552515. Once again visitors are welcome although prior booking should be made.

There are many other delights amidst the countryside of the Kingdom of Fife. One such beauty is Elie Golf

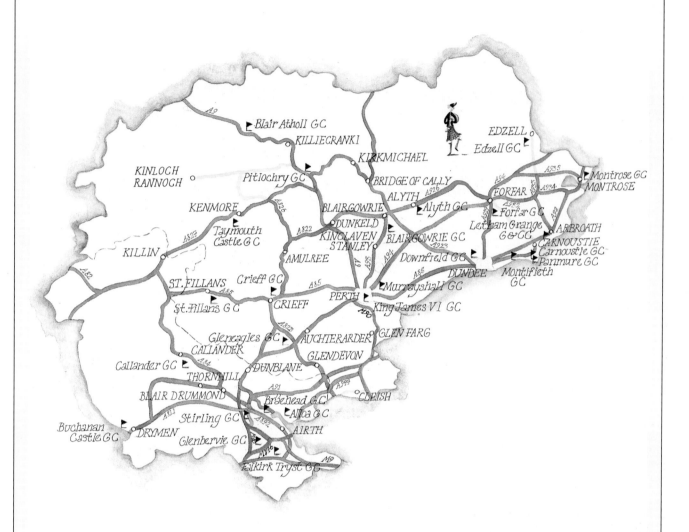

Club (0333) 330301, whose course lies 12 miles from St Andrews on the A917. Visitors are welcome. It was here that James Braid developed his golf and to follow in his footsteps along these spectacular cliffs is a true pleasure. The course is extremely busy in July and August and a ballot system is used. There are no restrictions outside these dates. The proximity of the courses to the shoreline is an inspiring sight and adds to the enjoyment of a good golfing day.

Two links that lie close together are the Lundin Links (0333) 320202, another Braid creation and the Leven Links (0333) 21390. The former welcomes visitors throughout the week and after 2.30pm on Saturdays, the latter has no general restrictions. Once again all players are urged to make a prior telephone call. Green fees at Lundin and Leven are both fairly priced and a visit is recommended.

The final outstanding links is to be found at Crail (0333) 50278. The course lies some two miles east of Crail and plays over the renowned Balcomie Links. Members and competition days always have priority, but visitors are made extremely welcome. Given the significance of the course the green fees remain good value for a round

or daily badge. A day's golf at weekends is a few pounds more expensive. The visitor is also offered short temporary membership for weekdays or a weekly or fortnightly ticket. Balcomie Castle and its friendly ghost are always watching your swing - so make sure its a 'goodun'. The course is full of character and is a relatively short 5720 yards - something the holiday golfer will relish when he has been put through the mill at the Kingdom of Fife's other outstanding courses.

Southern Fife and Glenrothes
Naturally, this area of Fife falls somewhat into the shadow of its northern limb. There are, however, a number of courses for the holiday golfer to consider while visiting this part of the illustrious kingdom. Thornton (0592) 771111, a parkland course, offers a welcome variety from the links courses of the north east coast. Further north, some 8 miles from the M90, one finds another course which provides golf at exceptional value, Glenrothes (0592) 758686. "Hells End", the course's final hole will hopefully not be a fair summary of your play. The course enjoys some fine views and is a fair test.

Central Scotland

The central region, which takes in some of Scotland's glorious countryside, is perhaps not as well known as its more northerly cousin. We start our trip at Buchanan Castle (0360) 60368 which is some way off the beaten track but is a thoroughly picturesque course. Closer to the town of Stirling one finds the duet of Glenbervie (0324) 562605 and Falkirk Tryst (0324) 562415, and the delights of Airth Castle (0328) 3411 are also well worth discovering. The courses at Stirling (0786) 84098 and Braehead (0259) 722078 are equally worthwhile - visitors should book in advance to arrange a starting time. The course provides a combination of parkland and meadowland. Callander (0877) 30090, a parkland course designed by Tom Morris, is another thought when planning an itinerary.

Perthshire

Gleneagles (0764) 62231 is one of the best known golf courses in the world. It is surrounded by the Grampian Mountains and offers a variety of colour - silver birch, a rich moorland turf and a never ending flow of heather.

The hotel for which the course is also widely acclaimed handles bookings. The course boasts the notorious Kings and Queens Courses and in 1992 a third championship test emerged. The design is the first Jack Nicklaus formula in Scotland and like St Mellion in England it will surely become a classic golf course. In order to play golf at Gleneagles you must either be resident at the hotel or a Gleneagles golf club member. The hotel is far from cheap but visitors are given the consolation of some good value green fees for a days golf.

One of the most renowned holes is the 13th on the Kings Course - a real beauty. Another of the many delights of the course is witnessed at each hole - the names themselves bring a smile - though the terrain to be covered surely delivers a shiver!

However, there are numerous other courses. You might contemplate a game at Crieff (0764) 2397 for example, where there are two parkland courses located just outside the town. Either the Ferntower or the Dornoch provide an ideal aperitif for one's future thoughts which must inevitably turn towards Blairgowrie. Green fees are exceptionally good value.

Taymouth Castle (0887) 3228, some six miles west of Aberfeldy, is a challenging 18 hole parkland course. The visitor is given an added excuse for visiting; - to see the nearby Loch Tay, though not with one's golf clubs it should be stressed. Green fees are reasonable. Blair Atholl (0796) 81274, on the A9 six miles north of Pitlochry has another pleasant setting and its flattish 9 holes are not the most arduous one will encounter. Pitlochry (0796) 2792 is a far tougher proposition. Designed by Willie Fernie of Troon, it really is a panaromic beauty. Visitors are made welcome but a prior booking is, as ever, strongly recommended.

There are a number of courses which surround the historic town of Perth, certainly worthy of a diversion. They include the aptly named King James VI Club (0738) 32460 on Moncrieff Island. The course is on an island in the centre of Perth, and one must cross the River Tay by a charming footbridge. Green fees are once again good value. Murrayshall (0738) 52784, an undulating parkland course, is also thoroughly recommended. The course was only founded in 1981 but even in that short time it has made quite a name for itself.

While these courses are most pleasing we would not be doing the visitor a service if we failed to emphasise the true beauty of Blairgowrie (0250) 2622 and its Rosemount course. One cannot praise the course too highly. Visitors to Fife or Scotland's Ayrshire coast should endeavour to play here, or if not, ensure that at least one other tour is made to Scotland to experience this distinguished course. There are, in fact, three courses at Blairgowrie. The more celebrated Rosemount and its longer and delightful brother, the Lansdowne. The trio is completed by the "Wee Course" a 9 holer with no surprises. Green fees are quite pricey but well worth the money. Holiday makers are strongly recommended to play mid-week.

Dundee and Angus

Some of Scotland's most distinctive and glorious golf courses are to be found between Dundee and Montrose. Indeed this area could in itself provide more than enough merriment for one long weekend. Before we reach the sea it is most certainly worth venturing inland to Downfield (0382) 825595, a parkland course of 6899 yards. Visitors are restricted to weekday golf , but when on holiday surely every day is a weekend.

East of Dundee one finds Monifieth (0382) 532767 which there are several good reasons for visiting. There are two courses, the Medal, and the shorter Ashludie. Visitors are welcome on all days except Saturdays and the green fees, as ever, vary. One of the many good reasons for calling at Monifieth or Panmure (0241) 53120, another seaside course, is that they both are moving us towards one of Scotlands finest links, Carnoustie (0241) 53789, described by Walter Hagen as "the greatest course in the British Isles". There are three courses - the Championship, the Burnside and the Buddon Links. Visitors are welcome but a reservation must be made. When the wind blows the championship course is perhaps the toughest in golf - and this is certainly no course for beginners. They say that one must practise and practise in order to succeed. Nick Faldo will support us here and while Carnoustie is no practice course, people endeavouring to master its challenges should perhaps purchase a weekly ticket! The length of the course is one of its striking features - even short holes are long - and when the wind gusts, as it does so often, the course can, despite its character, be a bit depressing. The final three holes, with the Barry Burn running before the 18th green, is a gruelling and harrowing conclusion to the spectacular 18 holes. Seldom will the 19th seem so welcoming.

Montrose (0674) 72634, offers two links courses, the Medal Course and the Broomfield. Montrose, like St Andrews and Carnoustie, is a public course - a fine one at that - and should be a definite part of any plans that take in this area of Scotland. Green fees are excellent value and visitors are only restricted before 1030am at weekends - otherwise there are no limitations. Once again, the course provides a tough finish but the whole course demands a high level of concentration and straight hitting. Visitors can have a weekly pass on the Medal course which is also excellent value.

Our final port of call is to be found at Edzell (03564) 235. A heathland course, Edzell allows the golfer some marvellous mountain views and challenging golf.

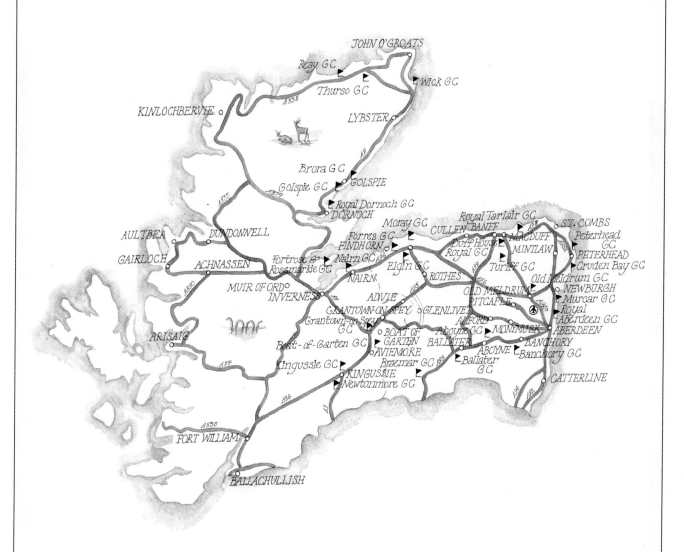

Grampian

The golfer should take a particularly well structured golf bag to Grampian. This will allow him to ferry a number of bottles of malt and enable him to drink the health of his partner when he or she misses a short putt or slices a drive. The focus of many golf tours could well be the tremendous course located at Aberdeen, Royal Aberdeen (0224) 702221. This is the sixth oldest course in the world and has been a royal course since 1903. Its location at Balgownie is now regarded as one of Britain's most demanding links. Visitors are made welcome throughout the week but not at weekends. People who are seeking a less demanding trial should consider the Balgownie short course - a little over 4000 yards. Green fees here are more modest. Balgownie has the traditional out-and-back layout. The front nine miss the shore while the back nine return on the landside towards the clubhouse. The course is not overly long but some 92 bunkers, including ten on the par 3 eigth, as well as stretches of gorse add to the course's difficulty. A number of holes stand out and the 18th is particularly memorable.   Another friendly Aberdeen course is located at Murcar (0224) 704354. Links in nature, the club is located three

miles from Aberdeen on the A92.

Golf courses cluster cosily around Aberdeen and this provides the holidaymaker with a good excuse to wander. At Banchory (03302) 2365, one finds a welcoming and interesting parkland course. Ballater (0339) 755657 is set in a large curve in the Dee with Scotland's finest scenery surrounding it. What could provide a better excuse for playing this enchanting course?

Aboyne (0339) 82328 is another undulating parkland course. The north of Scotland is becoming increasingly accessible to people from the south and motorways, high speed trains and aeroplanes all serve the holidaymaker.

One spectacular beast in golfing terms is to be found at Cruden Bay (0779) 812285. This links course is located some 23 miles north of Aberdeen and is an absolute must. The Buchan Coast is splendid while Slains Castle provides a somewhat ominous and watchful eye.

Naturally, it is important to remember that the days are longer up here allowing for a greater number of hours on the links. This is important news because we have a busy schedule. Pray continue northwards as Peterhead (0779) 72149 awaits. The course has a links make up, its green fees are great value and it is thoroughly worth visiting.

One is now presented with the option of heading north or south. Perhaps before we discuss the simply spectacular delights of Dornoch a word or two for non golfers and indeed golfers. Braemar not only hosts the Highland Games but also has a relatively short moorland course, at Braemar Golf Club (03383) 618, so it is an ideal diversion for everyone!

Elgin (0343) 812338, an 18 hole course founded in 1906, is recommended as is the Moray Golf Club (0343) 812018, where there are two links courses, the Old and the New. The scenery here is spectacular as is the golf and a visit should be on anyone's cards. Green fees vary and the higher prices are reserved for weekend players. One of the more poorly named Scottish courses is Duff House (0261) 22062 - not an encouraging omen for the visitor. The course was designed by the Brothers MacKenzie, immediately prior to their better known masterpiece, the Augusta National. The two-tiered greens are a pertinent feature of both courses. Royal Tarlair (0261) 32897, a seaside course, contrasts with the parkland course at nearby Turriff (0888) 62745.

The Highlands

The Highlands of Scotland are a place of solitude. This is an area which beckons golfers but few ever travel north of Dornoch and this is a pity. If nothing else, the green fees are incredibly cheap. Wick, (0955) 2726, is an 18 hole links where one can enjoy a fortnight's golf for tremendous value. Thurso (0847) 63807 and Reay (0847) 81288, an undulating seaside links, also offer great value golf. The golf may not be the finest in the land but you will play Britain's most northerly course - a challenge in itself.

A simply splendid golfing trio can be found by making a journey south on the A9. Brora, Golspie and the outstanding Royal Dornoch are the three in question. The drive to Brora from Wick or more likely from the south is also a dream. Sutherland's spectacular coastline is an absolute delight. Brora (0408) 21417 is stunning - the sea is ever present. The course is not long, but when the wind blows the length becomes somewhat more significant! The course is thoroughly satisfying, and with twilight running almost until dawn, one has plenty of time in which to enjoy it all. Golspie (0408) 33266 is also a rare feast. Green fees at both courses are exceptionally good value and one cannot recommend a visit more highly. And so to a highlight of any golfing tour, Royal Dornoch. At no time will a long journey be so well and easily justified. Royal Dornoch (0862) 810219 is perhaps one of the finest of Britain's courses. It has superb natural links, a backdrop of mountains and views of Dornoch Firth - a marvellous spot. The visitor is welcome at Dornoch seven days a week, 52 weeks a year although one has to be fairly prudent with one's timing. July and August are a little crowded, the winter months a little bleak. A visit in June or September may be the best answer. Now there's something to look forward to!

It is important to call in advance and ensure a tee time as the cult status is ever increasing. A day's golf is expensive for the area but this is not surprising. There is an additional eighteen holes where a lower green fee is levied. Dornoch's challenges are manifold and it is a rare treat to play.

There are other jewels in this heavily laden crown - one of which is located at Nairn, a real gem. Nairn Golf Club (0667) 53208 has had modifications from the meticulous and able hands of Old Tom Morris and James Braid. Once again one finds heather, gorse and mountainous scenery. You must surely be wondering now when a tour can be arranged. You simply must go. The course is extremely welcoming, as is the norm in this area. Green fees are reasonable for a weekday round and not over priced at weekends. A new clubhouse has recently been completed and visitors can now enjoy the delights of this as well. An altogether terrific course.

A number of courses can be found near to Inverness. Strathpeffer Spa (0997) 21219 is a welcoming parkland course - fairly short but easy to play. Fortrose and Rosemarkie (0381) 20529 is similarly welcoming and a links course.

Executive Golf

• The Executive Tour • This is a business class tour with executive car or luxury coach. The accommodation is four star, for instance the Hilton Hotel, and the Tour Manager travels with the group. Championship golf is available on the courses of St Andrews, Carnoustie, Turnberry combined with open qualifying courses such as Gullane and North Berwick.

• The Castle and Country Mansion Tour • This is a first class tour with chauffeur driven Rolls Royce limousine or luxury coach. The accommodation is in Dornoch Castle Hotel and Dalmahoy Golf and Country Club just outside Edinburgh. Championship Golf is available at Royal Dornoch, Nairn, Royal Troon, Turnberry, Dalmahoy, St Andrews, Carnoustie and Muirfield. Golf Tour Manager travels with tour.

• The Concorde Tour • Probably the best golf tour in the world! Fly Concorde to London with first class flight to Edinburgh. Transfers are by chauffeur driven Rolls Royce limousine and helicopter. The accommodation is in the Gleneagles Hotel, Turnberry Hotel and the Old Course at St Andrews Hotel. Golf on the championship courses travelling by helicopter. The tour manager will accompany the tour.

• The 1994 British Open ChamPioship Tour • This is a first class tour. Accommodation at Gleneagles Hotel with golf on the King's course. Golf at Muirfield, Royal Troon and Turnberry. Two days watching the British Open Golf. Golf Tour Manager.

• The Bells Scottish Open Tour and the Alfred Dunhill Cup Final are similar to the 1994 British Open Tour.

Executive Golf Tours tailor packages to Scotland, England, Ireland and Spain. See our 1994 Golf Tour Planner.

Please contact: Executive Golf Tours, Lansdowne Crescent, Edinburgh, Scotland EH12 5EH. Tel: 031 226 2830 Fax: 031 225 1985. From USA Tel: 011 44 31 226 2830 Fax: 011 44 31 225 1985. Ask for Ian Hepburn, Tours Director.

Agency Commission 10%

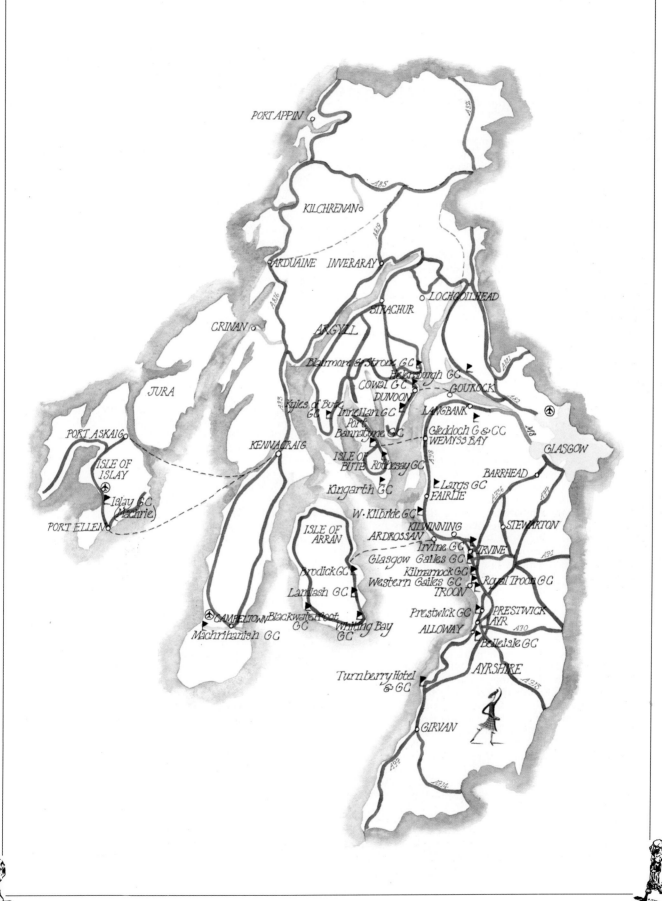

The Mainland Coast

Golf is extremely popular in this part of the world. It is essential that tee off times are booked in advance and it is also crucial to be absolutely organised. The courses are fairly restrictive and a clear plan must be made to make the most of your holiday.

It is somewhat tricky to know where to start. Troon, under the Open microscope in 1989, may perhaps provide a fitting beginning. The Royal Troon Club (0292) 311555 staged its first Open in 1925 and boasts two 18 hole courses, the Old and the Portland. Gentleman visitors are welcome to play both courses between Mondays and Thursdays, though prior arrangement is absolutely essential. The Portland course is unavailable to ladies on Tuesdays and Thursdays. All visitors must be members of a recognised club and be able to produce a handicap certificate. A fairly sizeable green fee entitles the visitor to a round on each course, while a lesser fee allows a full day's golf on the Portland course. Both courses provide a thorough test of links golf but the Old is surely one of the most challenging in golf. From Troon, it is somewhat difficult to know which way to turn. On the flick of a coin we shall head north and savour the delights of Ayrshire's southern shores at a later date.

Western Gailes (0294) 311354 and Kilmarnock (Barassie) (0292) 311077, emphasise the need to be organised. The former welcomes visitors on all days of the week except Thursdays and Saturdays and ladies are not permitted to play on Tuesdays either. The latter accepts visitors on Mondays, Tuesdays, Thursdays and Fridays. Both courses were qualifiers for Troon's 1989 Open and this indicates something of their merit. Details of green fees are available on application. Both courses are naturally at the mercy of the elements. Western Gailes, particularly well-named it seems, can be especially demanding. The Ayrshire coast, it should be emphasised, is rather the preserve of golfers than of hackers. This warning is given not only to be fair to the members of these golf courses but also for the sake of the beginner. These courses provide no easy introduction to golf.

North of these three splendid courses, but only a short drive away, one finds two further courses that served as qualifying courses for The 1989 Open - Glasgow Gailes (0294) 311347, two miles south of Irvine on the main Troon road and Irvine (0294) 75626. Both are splendid links courses. Irvine, a James Braid design located at Bogside, welcomes visitors during the week with the exception of Friday. Glasgow Gailes, founded over 200 years ago, welcomes visitors who give sufficient warning and satisfactory evidence of golfing prowess.

Two of Ayrshire's finest courses are found near to Glasgow - where, incidentally, there are a staggering number of courses. The holiday golfer should perhaps shortlist two, West Kilbride (0294) 823911 at Seamill, and Largs (0475) 873594 a mile south of the town. Largs is extremely welcoming and fair green fees can be expected. The course offers both parkland and links challenges and is recommended. West Kilbride is less easy to play. Visitors are welcome during the week but should telephone in advance to ensure a round is possible. The course itself is a real challenge with over 150 bunkers. The course is extremely well thought of in the region and with Arran and Goat Fell across the sea, the inspired views will hopefully lead to an inspired game.

Argyll

With the city behind us or in front of us, depending on our stance, there are two further suggestions of clubs to be found on either side of the Clyde Estuary. The first is Gleddoch Golf Hotel and Country Club (0475) 54304, a parkland and moorland combination. Our second, north of the Clyde, is Helensburgh (0436) 674173, a moorland course of a little over 6000 yards. The 6th hole enjoys spectacular views over the Clyde and in the distance one sees Loch Lomond. Beautiful!

Visitors to Helensburgh should note a number of additional visiting spots but most of all one should focus on a drive. No, not with a three wood but behind the wheel, for we are going on a pilgrimage to visit one of Scotlands most out of the way but outstanding golf courses, Machrihanish.

Dunoon and Cowal may not be the most immediate area to contemplate a golf tour and this is a great pity, for on the way to Machrihanish there are courses where golf is excellent value and totally peaceful. What is more you would be hard pressed to find a more beautiful location in which to play golf.

A sporting nine holes can be found at the Blairmore and Strone Course (0369) 84676 at Kilmun where green fees are extremely modest. Cowal Golf Club (0369) 5673 at Dunoon is a far greater challenge. Green fees remain good value and by now you should have warmed up quite wel. You will need to be positively hot by the time you reach Machrihanish, so two further thoughts may be of help. Firstly, Innellan Golf Course (0369) 83242 and secondly the Kyles of Bute Golf Club in Tignabruaich (0700) 811355. Neither are particularly long but both are great value and for the person happily meandering towards Arran or Machrihanish they provide a welcome break.

Some time later, through yet more spectacular scenery, one finally arrives at the glorious destination of Machrihanish (0586) 81277, located some five miles west of Campbeltown. It is a superb links with modest green fees and is surely one of the best value golf courses in Britain. There are a number of places to stay - nothing grand mind you but who really cares? A few drams, bright eyed joy at the course you've just played (and the drams you've just consumed) and a marvellous informality. That's what it's all about.

The Isle of Islay

The Machrie Hotel and Golf Course (0496) 2310 is something of a jewel. There is always something to be said for getting away from it all and Machrie, like Machrihanish, provides such a welcome opportunity. The island of Islay can easily be reached by air or sea. Loganair 041 889 3181 provide the necessary planes and a trip is really worthwhile. One can really enjoy a lot here - trout fishing, horse riding, snooker, bird watching, shooting and lots more. This is also a place to visit if you like malt whisky. A visit to one of the distilleries is an ideal forerunner to a game of golf. The hotel is a hive of fun and with self catering cottages and free golf there is a definite advantage in staying here.

The Isles of Arran and Bute

Another beautiful island setting is the Isle of Arran which is a spectacular place in which to play golf. The beauty is captivating and golf in the shadows of the oft snow-capped Goat Fell is a true delight. The best route to the island is perhaps by sea. The Hebridean and Clyde Ferry can be boarded at Ardrossan on the mainland taking you to Arran's port, Brodick. One of the features of golf in Arran is that green fees are fantastic value. There are a number of courses which please and a golfing tour is recommended. Brodick (0770) 2349 is most convenient. Telephone in advance and reserve a starting time. Three miles south one finds Lamlash (0770) 6296. Visitors are welcome, and although the course is quite short it is definitely worth a visit. Blackwaterfoot (0770) 86226 a 12 hole links course, is also in another gorgeous setting. There are no less than three 9 hole courses on the island and each has its particular attractions.

Bute is another remote isle but it boasts three courses just the same. This island is reached by the Caledonian Macbrayne Line which should be taken from Wemyss Bay to Rothesay. In Rothesay itself, only 30 minutes from the mainland, can be found Rothesay Golf Club (0700) 2244, a moorland challenge. Trees and heather are ever greedily waiting to collect your ball. There are no restrictions and green fees are once again great value. Kingarth and Port Bannatyne (0700) 2009 are the remaining courses. The former offers 13 holes, the latter only 9 holes. Once again the golf here can hardly be described as world class but a pleasant ferry ride and any number of rounds of golf will surely lift the spirit.

Turnberry and South Ayrshire

South Ayrshire provides a total contrast to the islands. Turnberry is one of golfing's finest and busiest centres. Four courses await us in our final tour. This is Burns country and it inspired many a fine poem from this richly invigorating and powerful Scottish poet. One hopes that similar inspiration lies ahead for you in your determined bid to conquer the links. Girvan (0465) 4346 is welcoming and like the others, a quality test of player and club. Reasonable green fees should be anticipated.

The Turnberry Hotel (0655) 31000 ext has to have one of the most glorious and best known golf courses in the British Isles. Here is haunting beauty, with Ailsa Craig its dominant and ever looming companion. There are a number of memorable holes including the short 6th "Tappie Toorie" and the 9th, "Bruces Castle", which is played alongside Turnberry's other noted landmark - its lighthouse. This stands dominantly on the remains of Turnberry Castle, birthplace of Robert the Bruce, King of the Scots. The 10th, "Dinna Fouter" is another challenging hole and one's drive calls for a daring shot across the bay - one of golf's most celebrated holes. Though the Ailsa is the better known course, the Arran is also a veritable test. Green fees are, not suprisingly, high but are reduced for hotel guests. These prices entitle the visitor to a round on the Ailsa and Arran courses.

A short distance north is Ayr's celebrated test Belleisle (0292) 41258, a parkland course. The course welcomes visitors and details of green fees can be found on application. Prestwick is another marvellous club which offers two courses, the Prestwick St Cuthbert (0292) 77101 and the Prestwick St Nicholas (0292) 77608. The former is a parkland test, the latter a links challenge. It was here in 1860 that it all began - it, in this case, being the Open Championship. No visitors are permitted to play at weekends, and on Thursdays no visitors are permitted after 11am. Green fees in summer are more expensive than winter and from these facts one learns an obvious lesson. The winter break may not appeal but a clear crisp day in Scotland is difficult to match. There are a number of fitting tests - the Himalayas on the 8th and the Cardinal Bunker on the 3rd which stretches the width of the fairway. Prestwick not only boasts delightful golf but also an airport which is excellent news if one happens to be a little pushed for time.

Turnberry Hotel and Ailsa Course

Southern Scotland
Cally Palace Hotel, Gatehouse of Fleet, Dumfries & Galloway. Tel: (0557) 814341

This impressive establishment offers the very best of service in a totally secluded location. The hotel grounds extend to more than 100 acres and include a private fishing/boating loch. The splendid restaurant is renowned for the excellence of its cuisine. An exclusive 18 hole golf course will be ready for Spring 1994.

Corsemalzie House Hotel, Newton Stewart, Wigtownshire. Tel: (0988) 860254

This secluded country mansion set in the heart of Wigtownshire allows guests to relax away from the rigours of city life. The surrounding area has much to offer, including a host of 18 hole golf courses. The hotel pays half guests' green fees on the 18 hole course at Glenluce.

Cross Keys Hotel, Kelso, Borders. Tel: (0573) 223303

Kelso is one of Scotland's marvellous border towns. The Cross Keys is one of the country's oldest walking inns and one of its most welcoming. This is an ideal point from which to explore the Borders and the hotel can arrange golf at nearby courses.

Lockerbie Manor Country Hotel, Lockerbie, Dumfries and Galloway. Tel: (05762) 2610

Set amidst 78 acres of park and woodland, Lockerbie Country Manor is a haven of peace and relaxation. The long tree-lined driveway gives a taste of the luxury that lies ahead. All 30 bedrooms are individually decorated and have private bathrooms, colour television and every comfort. The Queensbury

Dining Room, with its wood panelled wall, ornate chandeliers and magnificent views, is the ideal setting for a delectable meal. The cuisine is of an international nature, where Eastern flavours and cooking subtly blend with Western recipies. Golfers will love the courses in the area, offering challenges of varying degrees of difficulty. Lockerbie, Dumfries, Lochmaben, Powfoot and Moffat are nearby.

Sunlaws House, Kelso, Roxburghshire. Tel: (0573) 450331

Sunlaws House stands in the heart of Scotland's beautiful Border country and is owned by the Duke of Roxburgh. There has been a house on the same site as Sunlaws for nearly 500 years and from its beginnings it has always been a Scottish family house. There are 22 bedrooms, which include the splendid Bowmont Suite and six delightful rooms in the stable courtyard, all furnished with care to His Grace's own taste. Sunlaws is the perfect centre for a host of holiday activities. Golf is available nearby, with many Border courses boasting spectacular settings.

Lothian
Channings, South Learmouth Gardens, Edinburgh. Tel: 031 315 2226

Just a short way from Edinburgh castle is this quiet classical hotel. Channings is made up from five Edwardian town houses and has a cosy, old-fashioned club like ambience. Golfers are within easy reach of many of the famous golf courses of Scotland.

Johnstounburn House, Humbie, East Lothian. Tel: (0875) 833696

Located 15 miles from the finest East Lothian links courses (Muirfield, North Berwick, Dunbar), Johnstounburn offers the golfer comfort, fine food and drink in one of Scotland's heritage country houses, in the most peaceful and aesthetic setting at the foot of the Lammermuir Hills.

Fife
Balbirnie House, Markinch, Fife. Tel: (0592) 610066

Balbirnie House is a privately owned country house hotel and is one of Scotland's finest Grade A listed houses. Once a home to few, Balbirnie is now a home from home to many. The house itself is the centrepiece of a 416 acre park which is landscaped in the style of Capability Brown. For the golf enthusiast the hotel is ideally situated just a short chip from the first tee of Balbirnie Park golf course, a challenging and beautifully landscaped 18 hole, 6210 yard, par 71 parkland course. Locally, the championship courses of Leven Links and Ladybank offer the opportunity to sample Scottish golf at its very best.

Fernie Castle, Letham, Fife. Tel: (0337) 810381

Steeped in history, Fernie Castle is a small luxury hotel specialising in the care of its guests and the quality of food offered. Located in the heart of the historic kingdom of Fife it is the ideal base for a golfing holiday with more than 30 championship courses within 25 miles of the hotel.

Lomond Hills Hotel, Freuchie, Fife. Tel: (0337) 857498

The hotel is set in the heart of Fife in the charming village of Freuchie. Guests will enjoy the wealth of history in the area or may choose to play one of the 30 courses within easy reach of the hotel. Character and comfort combine to make a stay at the Lomond Hills extremely enjoyable.

Old Manor Hotel, Lundin Links, Fife. Tel: (0333) 320368

The Old Manor Hotel stands on a hill overlooking Lundin golf course and has panoramic views over Largo Bay. The Prince Charlie Restaurant offers classical dishes and has earned an enviable reputation and mention in several food guides. The Coachman's Grill and Ale House, in the old coachman's cottage in the grounds, offers lunch, dinner, supper and snacks. Within a short distance of this charming country house hotel are some of the finest links in the world at St Andrews, Elie, Crail, Scotscraig, and Ladybank. The Old Manor overlooks two adjacent championship courses at Leven and Lundin Links, both qualifiers for the Open. Carnoustie, Gleneagles and Rosemount are within easy travelling distance.

Rescobie Hotel and Restaurant, Leslie, Fife. Tel: (0592) 742143

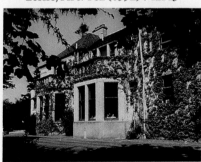

Rescobie is a 1920s country house set in two acres of grounds on the edge of the old village of Leslie. All ten of the individually decorated bedrooms have private bath or shower, direct dial telephone and colour television. The owners take great pains to run the hotel as a traditional country house and this is reflected in their personal attention to the well being of their guests, the conduct of their staff and the quality of their cuisine. Perfectly positioned for golfers in the heart of an area rich in golf courses - St Andrews, Dalmahoy, Carnoustie and Gleneagles to name but a few - Rescobie is only half an hour's drive away from Perth and Dundee and 45 minutes from the centre of Edinburgh.

Rufflets Country House Hotel, St Andrews, Fife. Tel: (0334) 72594

An outstanding country house set in ten acres of award winning gardens. There are 25 tastefully decorated bedrooms, attractive public rooms and a restaurant renowned for good food, using fresh local produce. St Andrews offers five golf courses and 16 other courses are within 30 minutes drive.

Smugglers Inn, Anstruther, Fife. Tel: (0333) 310506

With 17 courses within a 15 mile radius including the venerable Royal and Ancient at St Andrews, the no less historic Smugglers Inn at Anstruther is an ideal base for a golfing break. A traditional warm welcome, and fine food and drink await all those who pass through its doors.

St Andrews Golf Hotel, 40 The Scores, St Andrews. Tel: (0334) 72611

St Andrews Golf Hotel is a tastefully modernised Victorian house situated on the cliffs above St Andrews Bay, some 200 yards from the 18th tee of the "Old Course". There are 23 bedrooms, all with private bath and shower and all furnished individually to a high degree of comfort. The central feature of the hotel is the candlelit, oak panelled restaurant with its magnificent sea view. Golf, of course, is the speciality of the hotel, and you can either find prepared golf packages and golf weeks or have something tailored to your particular requirements, using any of the 30 or so courses within 45 minutes of St Andrews.

Tayside and Central
Altamount House Hotel, Blairgowrie, Perthshire. Tel: (0250) 873512

Just as the discerning golfer will always include the Rosemount course in his plans when visiting Perthshire, any pursuit of excellence would be incomplete without experiencing the delights of the Altamount House

Hotel at Blairgowrie.

Culcreuch Castle, Fintry, Stirlingshire. Tel: (036 086) 228

This beautiful castle has been lovingly converted by its present owners into a comfortable, friendly country house hotel. The eight individually furnished bedrooms are en suite and have full modern facilities. There is a wide range of activities in the area and golfers are particularly well catered for, with 40 courses within a 25 mile radius of the castle.

Dalmunzie House, Blairgowrie, Perthshire. Tel: (0250) 885224

Standing in its own 6000 acre estate in the Scottish Highlands, the hotel can offer turreted bedrooms, antique furnishings and even the highest 9 hole golf course in Britain. Some of Scotland's finest mountains surround the hotel and the Glen Shee ski centre is only a few minutes drive away.

The Glenfarg Hotel, Glenfarg, Perthshire. Tel: (0577) 830241

Situated amidst some of Perthshire's finest scenery, yet only 30 miles north of Edinburgh, this elegant two star hotel enjoys a well earned reputation for sporting holidays, including an array of golfing packages. The period restaurant offers an excellent selection of dishes, prepared by the hotel's award winning chef, or, if you prefer a more informal atmosphere, you can choose from a delicious range of home cooked bar meals.

The Lands of Loyal Hotel, Alyth, Perthshire. Tel: (08283) 3151

An impressive Victorian mansion overlooking the Vale of Strathmore and set in ten acres of tiered and rambling gardens. An ideal base for the ambitious golfer with 30 courses all within an hours drive of the hotel. With a highly acclaimed restaurant, the Lands of Loyal provides a complete golfing package.

Murrayshall Country House Hotel and Golf Course, Scone, Perthshire. Tel: (0738) 51171

Set in 300 acres of parkland, only four miles from Perth, the hotel has

been refurbished to portray a traditional country house style and the bedrooms offer en suite facilities, direct dial telephones and televisions. Guests dine in the Old Masters Restaurant which offers a fine range of dishes with the emphasis on good wholesome fare. The 6420 yard, 18 hole, par 73 course is interspersed with magnificent specimen trees lining the fairways,with water hazards and white sanded bunkers offering a challenge to all golfers. There are various types of membership available, including a competitively priced overseas and country membership to golfers residing more than 80 kms from Murrayshall Golf Course.

The Roman Camp, Callander, Perthshire. Tel: (08773) 30003

Standing on the banks of the River Tieth amongst 20 acres of secluded gardens, the house was originally built as a hunting lodge in 1625. At the Roman Camp you are within easy reach of many championship and picturesque golf courses and the hotel can arrange and book tee times at the local course.

Grampian and Highland

Alton Burn Hotel, Nairn, Highland. Tel: (0667) 453325

This imposing hotel stands in its own grounds overlooking the 17th tee of Nairn Golf Club. The Alton Burn offers a wide range of recreational facilities whether or not guests wish to golf on one of the many excellent courses in the area. To get away from it all and enjoy good golf, food and company there is no better choice than the Alton Burn.

Ardoe House, Blairs, Aberdeen. Tel: (0224) 867355

Ardoe House Hotel, is a Scottish Baronial style mansion set in 17 acres of its own ground with commanding views across Royal Deeside. The hotel is a popular base for golfing parties with its proximity to many leading courses, and golf packages which include de luxe room, dinner and packed lunches are available all year.

Banchory Lodge Hotel, Banchory, Kincardineshire. Tel: (033082) 2625

The Banchory Lodge is situated close to where the water of Feugh flows into the celebrated River Dee, with modern comforts discreetly enhancing its Georgian charm. The hotel retains the leisured and hospitable atmosphere of former days. The 22 bedrooms, all en suite, are individually well furnished with traditional furnishings. Log fires, fresh flowers and original paintings add to the air of relaxation and tranquillity.

Castle Hotel, Huntly, Aberdeenshire. Tel: (0466) 792696

This magnificent hotel stands in its own grounds above the ruins of Huntly Castle on the banks of the River Deveron. A family run hotel, there is comfortable accommodation and good food. Conveniently situated for several golf courses, the hotel is ideal for a golfing holiday and there are plenty of other activities for the non-golfer.

Claymore House Hotel, Seabank Road, Nairn, Inverness-shire. Tel: (0667) 453731

Situated only 300 yards from Nairn's championship golf course this hotel has everything to offer the golfer. Since being completely refurbished the hotel offers the highest standards in luxury. The speciality of the hotel is tailored golf breaks and as there are 25 golf courses within one hour of the hotel it really is ideally placed.

Craigellachie Hotel, Craigellachie, Banffshire. Tel: (0340) 881204

This celebrated hotel stands imposingly above the confluence of the Spey and Fiddich rivers in a lovely wooded valley. The hotel has

been sympathetically refurbished to retain all the original charm of a Scottish country house. Supremely comfortable public rooms and bedrooms, elegantly furnished and decorated with subtle colour combinations, combine the best traditional qualities with first class contemporary comfort. For golfing, the hotel is situated in the centre of some of the finest golf courses in Scotland. After a long day, the Ben Aigan restaurant which is noted for its excellent cuisine and wine list, welcomes you to relax and enjoy further the pleasures of this ideally located hotel for golfing enthusiasts.

Culloden House Hotel, Inverness. Tel: (0463) 790461

Historically linked to Bonnie Prince Charlie, this impressive Georgian house commands 40 acres of garden, parkland and tranquil woodland. The resident proprietors extend a warm welcome to all their visitors and are only too happy to arrange golfing, fishing or shooting activities.

Dowans Hotel, Aberlour, Banffshire. Tel: (0340) 871488

Overlooking the Spey in beautiful countryside, the Dowans Hotel has recently been refurbished. Meal times are flexible to suit the needs of sportsmen and the hotel is happy to arrange fishing, shooting or stalking by prior arrangement. There are 15 golf courses within half an hours drive of the hotel, so there really is something for everyone here.

Knockomie Hotel, Forres, Morayshire. Tel: (0309) 673146

The Moray coast is home to many courses, including links and courses at Nairn and Lossiemouth, with woodland and moorland courses at Forres and Grantown. There are 16 courses within easy driving distance. The hotel was a house frequented by Lord Cockburn and continues the tradition of a warm welcome with good food taken from the moors, rivers and seas accompanied by fine wines and whiskies. The 14 bedrooms and suites are traditionally furnished and all are en suite with direct dial telephone, welcome tray, satellite television and radio alarm. Gavin Ellis and his friendly staff look forward to welcoming both golfer and non golfer.

The Links Hotel, Brora, Sutherland. Tel: (0408) 621225

The Links Hotel has a magnificent situation overlooking the 18 hole links course at Brora. All bedrooms have a sea view and the Seaforth Restaurant offers one of the finest views in the north of Scotland. Golfers are spoilt for choice with several courses within easy travelling distance.

Meldrum House Hotel, Old Meldrum, Grampian. Tel: (0651) 872294

Set in acres of fields and gardens Meldrum House enjoys an atmosphere closer to that of a private country home rather than a hotel. Personally run by Eileen and Douglas Pearson, the house offers every comfort and high quality Scottish cooking featuring the very best of local produce which is complemented by an extensive wine list. The hotel is ideally situated for golfing parties with a great number of golf courses in the vicinity, including the top class courses of Royal Aberdeen and Cruden Bay to the east, Newmachar to the south and Royal Duff House and Royal Tarlair to the north.

Ord House Hotel, Muir of Ord, Ross-shire. Tel: (0463) 870492

Ord House is primarily a country house which offers all the comforts and amenities of a hotel. There are 12 individually designed en suite bedrooms and one even has a four poster bed. Ideally situated for the sportsman to enjoy fishing or golf, the hotel has something to offer for everyone.

The Royal Marine Hotel, Brora, Sutherland. Tel: (0408) 621252

This charming country house hotel has undergone major refurbishment recently, but great trouble has been taken to maintain the character of the original building. The hotel offers golfing breaks on the Brora links course and there are three other championship courses within 30 minutes drive of the hotel.

Stotfield Hotel, Lossiemouth, Moray. Tel: (0343) 812011

The Stotfield is situated overlooking the superb championship golf course of the Moray Golf Club - a true links course. Hotel guests playing this course can enjoy a 10 per cent discount on green fees. For the less accomplished golfer there is a second 18 hole course alongside of which is the sandy beach of the Moray Firth with the Sutherland Hills in the distance The hotel combines modern amenities with traditional charm. It has the comfortable and friendly atmosphere of a family run hotel, with 45 en suite bedrooms all equipped with colour television, direct dial telephone and tea and coffee making facilities, hairdriers. Newly refurbished superior bedrooms are front facing. (Scotish Tourist Board 4 Crowns Commended).

Argyll Islands and Ayshire Coast
Montgreenan Mansion House Hotel, nr Kilwinning, Ayrshire. Tel: (0294) 557733

Built in 1817 and set in 50 acres of secluded parklands and gardens, the Mansion House at Montgreenan still retains its Georgian elegance and splendour. The Mansion has 21 beautifully appointed bedrooms, award winning cuisine and high standards of personal service. With 35 courses within 45 minutes of the estate, including Turnberry, Royal Troon and Prestwick, the hotel offers the perfect setting in which to relax and unwind. The hotel also has its own 5 hole course, tennis court and billiard room for those with a sporting outlook, but for others roaring log fires and excellent malts are also available.

Turnberry Hotel, Turnberry, Strathclyde. Tel: (0655) 31000

This world famous resort has been extensively restored and offers luxurious accommodation for the most discerning individual. Its two championship links golf courses are for priority use by hotel guests and the Ailsa course is the venue for the 1994 British Open Championship. The Spa was opened in 1991 and is unrivalled in Britain. A new clubhouse opened in June 1993. Choice of three restaurants and five bars.

Westerwood Hotel, Golf and Country Club, Cumbernauld, Glasgow. Tel: (0236) 457171

Located 13 miles from Glasgow, the Westerwood is within easy access of both Glasgow and Edinburgh airports. The hotel has 47 bedrooms, all furnished in traditional style, many of which have scenic views over the golf course to the Campsie Hills. Set in ideal golfing country, the 18 hole, par 73 course designed by Seve Ballesteros and Dave Thomas offers an exciting challenge to all golfers. There are various types of membership available to the course including a competitively priced overseas and country membership to golfers residing more than 80 km from Westerwood golf course.

Wales

Royal St. David's (Welsh Tourist Board)

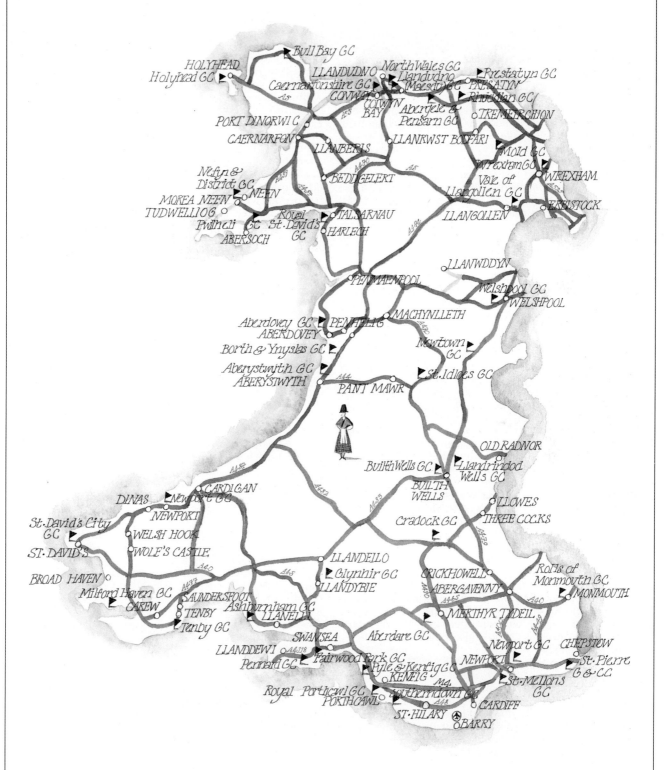

Bull Bay GC
HOLYHEAD
Holyhead GC
North Wales GC
LLANDUDNO   Llandudno   Prestatyn GC
Caernarfonshire GC   (Maesdu) GC   PRESTATYN
CONWAY   COLWYN   Rhuddlan GC
PORT DINORWIC   BAY   Abergele &   TREMEIRCHION
CAERNARFON   Pensarn GC
LLANRWST BODFARI
LLANBERIS   Mold GC
Wrexham GC
Nefyn &   BEDDGELERT   WREXHAM
District GC   Vale of
MORFA NEFN   NEFN   Llangollen GC   ERBISTOCK
TUDWELLIOG   Pwllheli GC   Royal   TALSARNAU   LLANGOLLEN
ABERSOCH   St. David's   HARLECH
GC
LLANWDDYN
PENMAENPOOL
Welshpool GC
MACHYNLLETH   WELSHPOOL
Aberdovey GC   PENHELIG
ABERDOVEY   Newtown
Borth & Ynyslas GC   GC
Aberystwyth GC   St. Idloes GC
ABERYSTWYTH   PANT MAWR
OLD RADNOR
Builth Wells GC   Llandrindod
BUILTH   Wells GC
CARDIGAN   WELLS
DINAS   Newport GC   LLOWES
St. David's City   NEWPORT   Cradock GC   THREE COCKS
GC   WELSH HOOK
ST. DAVID'S   WOLF'S CASTLE   LLANDEILO   Rolls of
BROAD HAVEN   Glynhir GC   CRICKHOWELL   Monmouth GC
Milford Haven GC   SAUNDERSFOOT   LLANDYBIE   ABERGAVENNY   MONMOUTH
CAREW   Ashburnham GC   MERTHYR TYDFIL
TENBY   LLANELLI
Tenby GC   SWANSEA   Aberdare GC   Newport GC   CHEPSTOW
LLANDEWI   Fairwood Park GC   NEWPORT   St. Pierre
Pennard GC   Pyle & Kenfig GC   G & CC
KENFIG   St. Mellons
Royal Porthcawl GC   Southerndown GC   GC
PORTHCAWL   CARDIFF
ST. HILARY
BARRY

St Pierre and South East Wales

St Pierre Golf and Country Club (0291) 5261 is as obvious a place as any to start our tour of the principality, situated as it is a mile from Chepstow on the A48 Newport road. Although there is plenty more to be considered further west, this is an outstanding first port of call for you and your partner when the trials and tribulations of the M4 will have prepared you famously for a well earned weekend of golf and good living. The club has two courses, The Old and The New, the latter only opening in 1945. It's the Old Course though, which should merit the fullest attention, as it does with all the leading pros when the European Tour comes to St Pierre for the Epson Grand Prix. Dominated by a lake covering eleven acres, this is not a course for the fainthearted.

The course's trickiest test is saved for the last 237 yards, a par 3, eighteenth, requiring a brave tee shot onto the narrow fairway, with the ubiquitous trees encroaching from one side and the vast lake on the other. Ask one Arwyn Griffiths about it. He arrived at the 18th tee with, not surprisingly, something of a spring in his step, needing to make par for a round of 63. He arrived in the clubhouse fifteen minutes later having shot a 75. Yes, Arwyn got into all sorts of trouble, but at least he had the consolation of being able to relax in one of the clubhouse's four bars. Indeed this is a golf club that boasts several 19th holes and will certainly appeal to lovers of good golf and a little of the hard stuff.

If you didn't realise already, we are actually in Gwent and the county has two more courses of note to offer the holiday golfer. Both can be found to the north of the county in the Wye Valley, both offering outstanding golf in delightful surroundings. The first is Rolls of Monmouth (0600) 715353, a newish parkland course set in the grounds of the Rolls family's country estate west of the town of Monmouth itself. The course offers a fair test for players of all standards and green fees are well priced. The Monmouthshire (0873) 2606 is located at Llanfoist, near Abergavenny, beside the River Usk. Visitors are requested to submit proof of a handicap and green fees are again good value when compared with those of the south of England. The Welsh are extremely keen golfers and in the more populated south visitors are well advised to book in advance and weekends will always be busy.

Porthcawl and South West Wales

In contrast to the rolling hills of South Wales we return to the M4 again but only for a short while. Junction 37 is our exit point for the glorious coastal strip which features Southerndown, Royal Porthcawl, and the delightfully named Pyle and Kenfig. The first you will come across between Ewenny and Ogmore is Southerndown (0656) 880476, an outstanding scenic downland course measuring a little over 6600 yards. If any was an equal for its close neighbour Porthcawl, this must surely be the course. Visitors are welcome between Mondays and Fridays and on occasions it is also possible to arrange a game at weekends.

And so to Royal Porthcawl (0656) 782251, Wales' most illustrious links and certainly one of Britain's greatest too. Actually, links is not wholly a correct description, for although much of the course is of a links nature, certain parts are more strictly downland and heathland in character. As well providing a somewhat uncompromising test, the course, like Southerndown, commands the most glorious views over the Bristol Channel towards Somerset and Devon. The green fees at Porthcawl have increased dramatically over the past two years, as so many of Britain's championship courses have, but if you really wish to test your game, especially when the wind blows, this first class course will oblige.

The great links debate is continued just down the road at Pyle and Kenfig (065671) 3093. This too sits beside the waters but is officially termed a seaside links. Like the championship courses of Lancashire, Pyle features massive sandhills which offer at least some protection from the often fierce elements. Pyle only welcomes visitors on weekdays and as ever a prior telephone call is recommended to ensure availability.

Swansea might not be everyone's idea of the perfect holiday venue they might well be right, but golfers should take note of two outstanding tests to the west of the city. Fairwood Park (0792) 203648, handy with the airport a mere four iron away, welcomes visitors at all times. Pennard (0441) 283131 operates a similar policy.

Further along the coast the championship delights of Ashburnham and Tenby can be found. For the visiting golfer these two offer rich pickings indeed. Tenby (0834) 2787 is the more famous of the two and offers a tremendously invigorating test, standing as it does beside the sea. Unusually for a course that has hosted championship after championship for countless years there is only one par 5 hole. But its par 4s are tough - very tough. Tenby offers tremendously good value and this is particularly so for people who want to purchase a weekly green fee. Visitors are welcome at all times. This is holiday golf at its very best.

Ashburnham (0554) 62466 is a little nearer to Llanelli and though weekends might be a problem, on other days is as welcoming to visitors as Tenby. It is a longer course than Tenby and at over 7000 yards is certainly not the course to choose to play your debut 18! Besides, handicap certificates are required on payment of the green fee.

Two more courses to note even further up the coast are Aberystwyth (0970) 615104, overlooking Cardigan Bay and the delightfully maintained seaside links at Borth and Ynyslas (0970) 81202, Wales' oldest club. Watch out for the road that runs alongside much of the course at Borth - a distraction many a visitor could well have done without! Green fees at both clubs are tremendously good value. Visitors are made most welcome at both.

Royal St David's and North Wales

It's actually quite a hike from our last ports of call, Borth and Aberystwth, but a true appraisal of North Wales' golfing delights must surely start at Royal St David's (0766) 780361, a course that shares the title as the Principality's greatest championship links with its southern cousin, Royal Porthcawl. St Davids provides a tricky test - measuring 6495 yards from the championship tees, it might not look at first sight a particularly daunting challenge but with two par 5s and a host of troublesome par 4s, it plays extremely long.

As an indication of its character, the course record stands at only 3 under the par 69 and many a championship has been played through the years over the hallowed turf.

Golfing challenge or not, visitors are most likely to take home with them memories of perhaps the most glorious setting to be found surrounding any fairways in Britain. On the one side stretch the blue waters of the Irish Sea in Tremedog Bay, on the other the great mountains of Snowdonia National Park. Surveying all, from its lofty perch overlooking the course, is the massive and majestic Harlech Castle, scene of many a frantic siege over the centuries, although the only battles it now bears witness to are those played out on the links. Green fees at Royal St Davids remain commendably low. Visitors are welcome throughout the week but it is perhaps advisable to make a quick call before setting out and you will also need proof of membership of a club.

Before we go round the coast to sample Nefyn's offerings, a quick detour southwards to Aberdovey (0654) 72493 is in order. Here lies another tremendous Championship links challenge designed by James Braid. Tremendous? None other than Bernard Darwin himself had this to say of Aberdovey's interesting layout, sandwiched as it is between the sand dunes on the one side and a railway line on the other.

Nefyn (0758) 720966 can be found just south of Morfa Nefyn, north west of Harlech. Actually, 'found' is perhaps taking things a little too far. This is a difficult course to find, but well worth every bit of the effort. The course, an old favourite of Lloyd George himself, measures 6335 yards from the back tees. Whilst the golf is by no means easy, it is never unfair and represents superb holiday golf. Well, that is so long as you don't dwell too long in the Ty Coch Inn, set down in a cove by the 12th green. Visitors to Nefyn must be prepared to produce a handicap certificate and be a member of a recognised club. Life is too short to miss out on this most delightful of courses. Indeed, the whole region is recommended for its solitude, friendly people and first class golf.

The seaside course at Pwllheli (0758) 612520 sits close by and was another regular haunt of Lloyd George's (when did he have time to govern?) In fact, he 'opened' it in 1909 when he was still Chancellor of the Exchequer.

Green fees are very reasonable for the touring golfer. And so to the North Wales coast, where another veritable feast of superb links golf awaits the hungry golfer. The town of Llandundo offers two particularly good tests, North Wales (0492) 75325 and Llandudno (Maesdu) (0492) 76450. The former, a seaside links course, welcomes visitors although a prior telephone call is advisable. Maesdu, a seaside parkland course, is perhaps the better known of the two and green fees are marginally cheaper here. Both command the most superb views over the adjoining Conwy Estuary, towards Anglesey.

Perhaps this stretch of coastline's toughest challenge though, is to be found at Conwy, where The Caernavonshire (0492) 593400 lies, just the other side of the aforementioned Conwy Estuary. The course plays regular host to the Welsh championships - some indication of its quality. Indeed, as far as the courses in North Wales are concerned, Conwy is generally considered to be the region's toughest, bar Royal St. Davids. Green fees are again relatively cheap. A five day membership is particularly good value.

Further along the coast, moving eastwards, Prestatyn (07456) 88353 offers yet more links golf of the highest order. Once again, visitors are made welcome, though not on Saturdays and Tuesday mornings.

Royal St. David's (Welsh Tourist Board)

Wales
The Crown at Whitebrook, Nr Monmouth, Gwent. Tel: (0600) 860254

Remotely situated one mile from the River Wye on the edge of the Tintern Forest this is the ideal place to get away from it all. The bedrooms are comfortable and are all en suite. The chef specialises in creating original dishes from fresh local ingredients and to complement these there are fine wines from the interesting cellar.

Egerton Grey Country House Hotel, Porthkerry, South Glamorgan. Tel: (0446) 711666

This 19th century former rectory is Egon Ronay's 'definitive country house hotel for South Wales'. The interior is furnished with antiques, open fireplaces, original Victorian baths and brass work, with rooms boasting mahogany and oak panelling. With Royal Porthcawl and other fine golf courses just a short drive away, this is the ideal base for the golfing gourmet.

Gliffaes Country House Hotel, Crickhowell, Powys. Tel: (0874) 730371

A thoroughly charming Victorian country house hotel, Gliffaes boasts fine gardens and parkland, situated in the National Park yet only one mile off the main A40 road. It offers peace and tranquillity as well as being easily accessible. The house stands in its own 29 acres in the beautiful valley of the River Usk. Built in 1885 as a private residence, it has been ideally adapted to provide spacious comfort in the country house tradition. There are 22 bedrooms with private bathrooms or showers and all are individual in decor and furnishings.

Lake Country House, Llangammarch Wells, Powys. Tel: (05912) 202

Complete with open fireplaces and antiques, this riverside hotel set in 50 acres of beautiful lawns and woods offers spacious and luxurious accommodation and has a splendid restaurant, which has won several commendations. For golfing enthusiasts there are four full size courses in close proximity. Builth Wells course is only ten minutes away and the hotel can organise concessionary tickets for guests.

Llangoed Hall, Llyswen, Brecon, Powys. Tel: (0874) 754525

A splendid house which was the first major commission of architect Sir Clough Williams-Ellis. Sir Bernard Ashley has bestowed similar love in its restoration and the bedrooms are simply marvellous. For the sportsman, three superb golf courses are within easy driving distance, all 18 hole with breathtaking scenery.

Penally Abbey, Penally, Pembrokeshire. Tel: (0834) 843033

Penally Abbey is one of Pembrokeshire's loveliest country houses. Ideally situated to enjoy both splendid views and the area's many attractions, not the least of which is the golf at adjacent Tenby Golf Club. With mouthwatering food and an excellent cellar, the Abbey is a haven of comfort, excellence and cheerful ambience.

St David's Park Hotel and Northrop Country Park Golf Club,
Ewloe, Clwyd. Tel: (0244) 520800 and (0352) 840440

St David's Park Hotel, is operationally linked to Northrop Country Park Golf Club and the hotel provides a perfect combination of superb modern facilities and traditional comfort. The hotel is designed in a Georgian style and offers 121 bedrooms all luxuriously furnished. A full range of golf and leisure related packages are available through the hotel and transport to the club can be arranged.

St Pierre Hotel, Chepstow, Gwent. Tel: (0291) 625261

A 14th century mansion standing in 400 acres, the St Pierre Hotel is a fine place to unwind. There are two golf courses, a lake and a leisure centre, three restaurants and a poolside bar. With a conference area and thirty executive bedrooms there are also excellent facilities for business delegations.

St Tudno Hotel, Llandudno, Gwynedd. Tel: (0492) 874411

Recent winner of the Johansens Guide 'Hotel of the Year' award for excellence. This delightful 21 bedroom hotel situated on Llandudno's seafront has to be experienced, hav ing a style and a splendour all of its own. Two AA rosettes for food. Indoor heated swimming pool. Close to three championship courses.

Trearddur Bay Hotel, Holyhead, Anglesey. Tel: (0407) 860301

Situated on the Isle of Anglesey the hotel is of distinctive character with the 31 bedrooms helping to create a lasting impression due to their panoramic views. Seafood is a menu speciality in the restaurant although all tastes and appetites are catered for. A range of sports from tennis to golf is available on the Isle.

Ireland

Ballybunion (*Irish Tourist Board*)

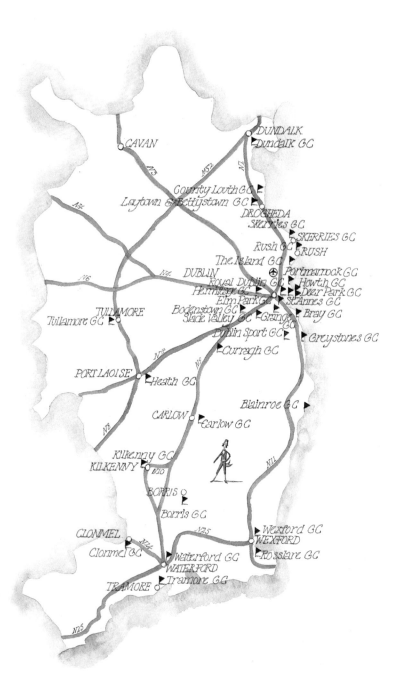

There are literally hundreds of courses in Ireland, and 60 courses are within an hour's drive of Dublin's city centre. It also has to be said that most clubs actively encourage visitors, and the welcome is second to none. Perhaps the biggest problem is where to start rather than where to go; but assuming that the golfer has arrived first in Dublin, let's make a start at Portmarnock (01) 323082, situated to the north of Dublin. This really is a testing golfcourse - 7100 yards of marvellous links golf set on a narrow peninsula and offering 27 holes. Although greenfees are expensive it is fair to say that Portmarnock is, without doubt, eastern Ireland's leading course.

The overriding feature of this course has to be the wind - you never end up playing more than two holes in any one direction, so constant assessment and re-assessment is necessary. The quality of the greens should also be mentioned - in a word "outstanding", both fast and true, so no excuses please! As with many Championship links courses, the start is deceptively easy, with three par 4s all less than 400 yards. But be prepared for a ferocious 5th hole at almost 600 yards, and a struggle all the way to the 14th and 15th holes. These are the two that most visitors to Portmarnock will remember most. The former has a stiff plateau green surrounded by bunkers, whilst the 15th, although a short hole, is an elusive little number. And so on to the 18th which again brings you to a raised green - just the right place to be to celebrate completion, although the clubhouse also beckons - a great atmosphere, delicious snacks, a pint of Guinness... ideal 19th hole.

Tearing ourselves away from Portmarnock, another course worthy of mention is Royal Dublin (01) 336346. The club was once at Phoenix Park, former home of Irish racing. The course is now at Bull Island, and has in the past hosted many major events, including the Carrolls Irish Open.

County Dublin is a county of contrasts and Greystones (01) 876624, just to the south of the city brings a mixture of heath and parkland - as well as spectacular views of the Wicklow Mountains and the Irish Sea. Also south of Dublin is the charming Woodbrook Golf Club (01) 824799, with a somewhat peculiar mix of parkland and seaside golf. Visitors are not encouraged to play the course on Saturdays. and green fees are fairly pricey.

At our next Dublin course, The Island (01) 436104, you won't be in for an easy time. Heavy rough and a discouragingly large number of blind shots will soon have you reaching for the stout again. A short drive northwards Rush (01) 437548 is well worth a potentially frustrating journey as the golf is superb and the views are really outstanding.

If you have had enough of sanddunes, you will be pleased to find the Hermitage Golf Club (01) 264549, which lies west of the city. This is a tremendous parkland affair which caters for all tastes, including those of the River Liffey: there are two par 3s at the 10th because the river has an annoying tendency to spill its banks during the winter months.

North of Dublin is Des Smyth's home club - Laytown and Bettystown (041) 27534. If you are a golfing family, this is an ideal spot to bring the children, as they are made especially welcome. Fees are a reasonable during the week and at weekends which is good to hear for this first class and challenging course.

Staying to the north of Dublin, a friendly 18 hole parkland course is found at Dundalk (042) 213179. Holidaying visitors are made very welcome on every day but Sunday. County Louth also offers the remote but utterly charming County Louth Golf Club, better known as

Baltray (041) 22329, which has greens which are considered by many to be the best in Ireland.

Ireland's Emerald Delights

Moving inland, Mullingar Golf Club (044) 48366 in County Westmeath is an absolute stunner and has extremely good value green fees, particularly when the stunning countryside is taken into consideration. Not far from Mullingar, and definitely a course to take in on a leisurely trip around south-east Ireland, is Tullamore (0506) 21439, but do be sure to book in advance. This is once again parkland in nature, and green fees are reasonable.

Further Fairways Green

Journeying southwards, we reach County Laois, and its golf course The Heath (0502) 46533. This course (actually pronounced 'Leash' by those in the know) can spring a fair number of surprises. For a start, your unsuspecting golf ball is likely to land in the midst of a herd of sheep, who are frequently to be found wandering across the fairways - which they are at perfect liberty to do! Green fees are fair on both weekdays and weekends. The club is most welcoming and friendly, so golfers from afar are sure to enjoy their game.

It is quite a long way to County Tipperary from Portlaoise, but well worth the trek when one knows that the course at Clonmel is one's final destination. Clonmel (052) 21138 guarantees an enjoyable day's golfing. Far from the horrors of crowds you may find yourself playing poetic shots, inspired by the birdsong and babbling streams. On the other hand, the attractions of your surroundings may be disastrous - accuracy and concentration are essential in order to negotiate the geographical quirks of this interesting course. Not very far away, the keen golfer can find Kilkenny (056) 22125, a course with a parkland layout and some interesting holes on slopes to catch you unawares.

Waterford (051) 74182 is worth a visit, not only for the sake of the golf course, but also for its crystal factory, which should provide a source of excellent presents for friends, family and the like. Tramore (051) 86170, is another excellent course in the same county. A lot of drainage work and tree planting on this particular patch of boggy ground had to be done before golf could be played here at all, but now it's the ideal spot for a testing day's golf while the 3 miles of sandy beaches will be welcomed by those not irresistibly drawn to the delights of the links.

Our final destination, Rosslare Golf Club (053) 32113, lies in the far south-east corner of the country, in deepest County Wexford. The course is very near the sea - good for breathing in those healthy, salty breezes, but not so good for the course itself, which suffers erosion problems. Altogether a memorable spot for an exciting and challenging round - especially if there is a strong wind blowing.

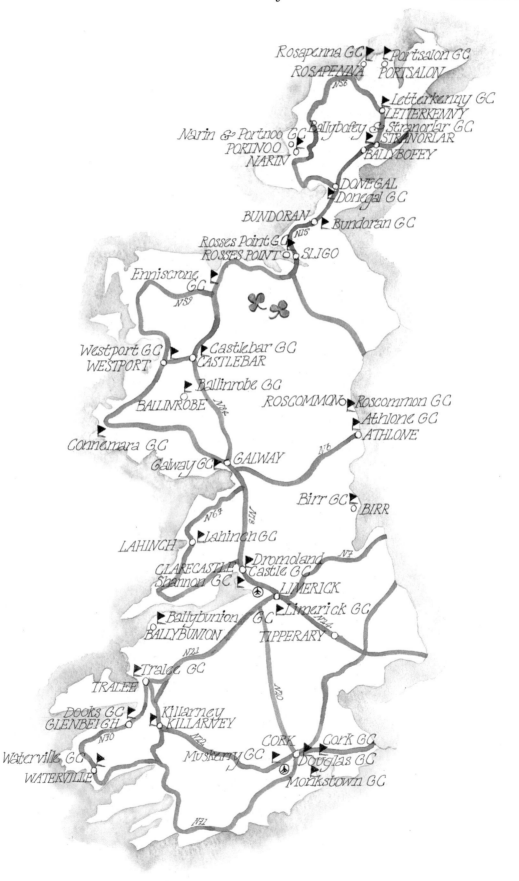

Rosapenna GC
ROSAPENNA
Portsalon GC
PORTSALON

Letterkenny GC
LETTERKENNY

Narin & Portnoo GC
PORTNOO
NARIN

Ballybofey & Stranorlar GC
STRANORLAR
BALLYBOFEY

DONEGAL
Donegal GC

BUNDORAN
Bundoran GC

Rosses Point GC
ROSSES POINT
SLIGO

Enniscrone GC

N59

Westport GC
WESTPORT
Castlebar GC
CASTLEBAR

Ballinrobe GC
BALLINROBE

ROSCOMMON
Roscommon GC

Athlone GC
ATHLONE

Connemara GC
Galway GC
GALWAY

Birr GC
BIRR

Lahinch GC
LAHINCH

Dromoland Castle GC
CLARECASTLE
Shannon GC
LIMERICK

Ballybunion GC
BALLYBUNION

Limerick GC

TIPPERARY

Tralee GC
TRALEE

Dooks GC
GLENBEIGH
Killarney GC
KILLARNEY

Waterville GC
WATERVILLE

Muskerry GC
CORK
Cork GC
Douglas GC
Monkstown GC

County Kerry

There are many places in the world to play golf, but this neck of the woods is one of the very finest. All manner of golfing goodies can be found, ranging from rugged links set in savage and exciting dune country to the well ordered parklands to be found in the more sedate inland. Our first tour will take in County Kerry. Take a deep breath for this is one of the most outstandingly scenic places in the world.

Perhaps Killarney Golf and Fishing Club (064) 31034 should be our first port of call. The course is situated on the edge of the Killorglin Road, on the edge of the town. This is a place to lighten your darkest hour. The New Course, the design of Sir Guy Campbell, opened in 1939. A second 18 was created in the 1970's. Both courses, Mahony's Point and Killeen, enjoy a near perfect setting beside the shores of Lough Leane, which in turn is guarded by the stunning splendour of the Macgillicuddy Reeks and the Carrauntoohill Mountains. Mahony's Point is the better known of the two courses but when a championship is held here a combination of both courses is made, indicating the merits of both courses. Water abounds and if your game fails to find inspiration we thoroughly suggest you row into the aforementioned Lough - and release your clubs to its grasping depths! Green fees vary and at weekends prices are higher. So if you visit at weekends it is perhaps best to play only one round and leave the rest of the day for a bit of gallivanting. Speaking of which, a new clubhouse has recently been completed. A cool million was spent on the project - should be a cracker as they say in these parts.

There are two great courses to the south east of Killarney. The Dooks Golf Club (066) 68205 is situated three miles from the alarmingly named Gorey. The course is an unassuming combination of links and downland. It also enjoys superb mountain and sea views. The course is absolutely beautiful and a visit is highly recommended. Green fees are more modest but the golf is marvellous.

Slightly further afield one finds another majestic course, Waterville (0667) 4102. The course is situated on the famed Ring of Kerry some 50 miles from Killarney - a journey that will once again inspire the most wretched soul. Tom Watson once said, "Waterville is magnificent. In particular I will never forget the par 3 holes. As a group they must be the greatest in Europe, possibly the world." The par 3 17th, known as Mulcahy's Peak, features a tee which towers above the landscape. This is a legendary course, which must be seen and played to be believed. Green fees are reasonable, and this will be money well spent. A time at last to put life in perspective, forget the doctor, bank manager, accountant and anybody else who happens to be bending your ear at the time. This is a time for reflection.

Although the above trio provide something spectacular, it would not be unrealistic to suggest that they are overshadowed by Kerry's best known golfing links, Ballybunion (068) 27146. Indeed perhaps one could go so far as to say that the Old Course, Ballybunion represents the ultimate links test. This, however, is only half the story, for the Old Course has a younger and phenomenally gifted brother, the New Course. The wildness of this isolated corner of Kerry is something to behold. From the medal tees both courses stretch 6500 yards. There are a whole host of breathtaking holes and the 7th, which runs along the shore, is enough to bring the fear of God to the most gifted player. If by chance the hero or heroine is not affected by the 8th tee, the 11th will truly make the grip a little warmer than usual, to put it mildly. The

Atlantic waves lie beneath you and sand dunes group menacingly from your left hand side. The New Course is also visually stunning; if you feel you are something of a golfer then you must visit the mighty links of Ballybunion. If you meet its challenge, you can die happy. If you don't succeed you can die contented, but if you never visit you will never know - and another lonely soul will wander the sand hills of Ballybunion. In short Ballybunion is a course on which many golf architects should play and live before they build golf courses. The architect of the New Course, the indisputable master Robert Trent Jones, said of its 10th hole "There is no more natural golf hole in the world, an outrageously beautiful stretch of God-given terrain." The 19th is handily placed between both courses and My Lord you will need a drink or two. Shannon is the course's nearest airport and this lies some 60 miles away.

Some 40 minutes south of Ballybunion one finds another stupendous links challenge - a large breakfast is an absolute must. The course is Tralee (066) 36379 - visitors are welcome on every day but Sunday. The course lies at the entrance of the Dingle Estuary. Don't bank on having the best complexion at the end of this particular trip - the salt and the wind are bound to conspire, wrinkles I'm afraid are inevitable and the turf has taken a battering as well - but this remains a fine course and one that should not be missed.

County Limerick and County Clare

North of Kerry one finds Limerick -
"There was an old golfer who said,
While crawling straight out of his bed,
Please give me my balls and my clubs,
For I'm anxious to keep out of pubs."
Not much of a limerick, but the point is this is a jolly place - fun, smiles and laughter - what a fabulous part of the world. Limerick Golf Club (061) 44083, lies three miles south of Limerick and provides a parkland test - trees and shrubs will be a welcome change to the sparse links of Ballybunion. The course is not playable at weekends except in the later afternoon.

Lahinch (065) 81003 is perhaps another one of south west Ireland's great courses. Located only 30 miles north west of Shannon, it is nicknamed the Irish St Andrews and is similarly inextricably associated with the town. The renowned Dr Alister Mackenzie, who had a short time here before completing Cypress Point, helped construct the course and commented, " Lahinch will make the finest and most popular course that I, or I believe anyone else, constructed". He should know - he was something of a master - he went on soon afterwards to build the Augusta National in association with Bobby Jones. The course is full of charm and the 6th is the ultimate in golfing nightmares - a blind par 3. The only clue you have is a white rock which is relocated every time the holes are repositioned on the green. Make no mistake, south west Ireland may have its remote parts but Lahinch Golf Club is generally not one of them. It is supremely popular - so much so that from 1975 the Castle Course was increased from 9 holes to 18. Both courses are superbly maintained and a visit is thoroughly recommended.

North Western Ireland

In Galway, The Galway Golf Club (091) 22169 is another splendid example of the brilliant design skills of Dr Alister Mackenzie. The course runs essentially inland, though some holes wander close to the ocean. The course is situated about two miles west of Galway in the holiday resort of Salthills. At Connemara, (095) 21153, the elements can be particularly savage and a good score is something of an achievement. The last six holes are especially daunting so save some energy - or perhaps take a whiskey with you for consumption on the 13th tee! This is once again a thoroughly recommended golf course. Just off the coast one finds Inishbogin Island - a particularly pleasant place to visit - a thoroughly worthwhile trip which takes in Lough Corrib which has some 365 islands - one for each day of the year if you are planning a more long term holiday.

Westport (098) 25113 enjoys spectacular views over Clew Bay and also has splendid mountain views of the Holy Mountain, Croagh Patrick. Of the many excellent holes the 5th is perhaps the highlight. It features a long carry from the tee over an inlet of Clew Bay. We recommend that golfers think of the aforementioned Holy Mountain before playing the drive - one will need all the help one can summon. Enniscrone (096) 36297 is another links to visit. It lies alongside Killala Bay and is an ideal warm up before the trials of Westport.

As we move northwards into County Sligo, we move into the romantic heart of Ireland which includes Yeats' Lake Isle of Innisfree, Lissadell House and of course County Sligo Golf Club (071) 77134, otherwise known as Rosses Point. Known as the home of the downhill drive; four holes feature this tricky characteristic, but despite this, it is still the best course in this area of the Republic and remarkably uncrowded. What is more, the green fees are very reasonable for a championship course.

Bundoran Golf Club (072) 41302 is only about 25 miles north of Sligo and should definitely be taken in on a golfing tour of this area. It is owned by the hotel adjoining it - the Great Northern and is a friendly club with visitors welcome at all times. The wind is a vital factor, as the course is exposed to the elements, but you are bound to feel elated after conquering this mixture of links and parkland golf.

The great beauty of the Blue Stack Mountains in County Donegal now beckon, and with them the Donegal Golf Club (073) 34054, which is situated about a mile off the Ballyshannon to Donegal Town road, and is a stern test of golf at 7271 yards. Again the visiting golfer will be welcomed with true Irish charm and will certainly not feel robbed with green fees set at a very reasonable price, depending on the day of the week. The coastline here is beautifully rugged, but sadly there is a dearth of first class hotels in the area. Perhaps the best recommendation is to include Donegal in a trip up the coast, encompassing Rosses Point and Bundoran, where the accommodation is undoubtedly of a higher standard.

No golfing trip to Ireland would be complete without a visit to Rosapenna Golf Club (074) 55301. Set in the far north of the country, the course is steeped in tradition - another of 'Old' Tom Morris' creations, it is hardly surprising that it is so highly regarded. Particularly enjoyable are the holes that run parallel to the ocean, but all are a stern test of golf, aided and abetted by the fact that bunkers often loom mid fairway. This area is a paradise for the angler as well as for the golfer, and Ireland's most northerly point, Malin Head is not far away. It is on the Inishowen Penninsula where motorists can take the 100 mile drive round the 'Inishowen 100', or visit Fort Dunree which is perched above Lough Swilly.

Around Cork

From one extreme to another, or put another way, from north to south. A mention here for that most beautiful of Irish cities, Cork, which is also home to Cork (Little Island) Golf Club (021) 353451. This is a marvellous, undulating course with immaculate greens, where green fees are reasonable on week days, and at weekends. Also worthy of note is Mallow Golf Club (022), also in County Cork, and equally reasonable as far as green fees are concerned.

--- *Northern Ireland* ---

Royal Portrush and the North Coast

We shall start our tour of this marvellous golfing country with a true gem in the north - Royal Portrush (0265) 822311. There are two championship courses here, The Valley and Dunluce Links. For both, the green fees are very reasonable and exceptionally tempting, when one considers the illustrious footsteps that have trodden the greens before.

The views as one makes one's way around the Dunluce Course are quite spectacular. It really is one of the finest links courses in the world, with the crags of Dunluce Castle and the pounding waves of the Atlantic echoing below. The 5th hole has taken a battering from the same bashing, and almost disappeared into the sea 50 years ago. Keen golfers and club members with a particular fondness for this testing hole managed to raise enough cash to build a retaining wall to save it. When you play the hole you appreciate why such a generous effort was made.

It is important not to get side-tracked by the drama of the surroundings because the course demands that you are on top form from start to finish. There is a punishing rough and each approach shot requires a different form of attack the 14th is not called Calamity Corner for nothing! Careless golfers have been forced in the past to play their next shot from the bottom of a huge ravine 50 feet below the hole, so it is best not to sample the excellent dining and bar facilities until the rigours of the course have been conquered.

Do spare a few hours when playing Royal Portrush for the Giant's Causeway, either a geological freak or the work of one Finn McCool, depending how superstitious you are. It has to be seen to be truly appreciated. The story goes that Finn was such a romantic giant that when he fell in love with a lady giant who lived on an island in the Hebrides, he simply had to build a road across the sea so that she could be with him in Ulster. This is typical of the romance of the country, alive with stories and remnants of the past. After playing this course you too will have your fair share of tales.

Just to the east of Royal Portrush, along the A2, you will find Ballycastle Golf Course (02657) 62536, which is equally good value and again ferociously lashed by the Atlantic. It is impossible to move on from here without talking about Jimmy Kane's Special. This is not a hole but one of the many whiskies available for tasting at Bushmills Distillery. Visitors can see the whole process from water to whiskey, and for more information, call (0265) 731521.

However, if you are planning to travel westwards from Royal Portrush then Portstewart (026 583) 2015 and Castlerock (0265) 848314 are a dynamic duo. Portstewart is a pretty fishing village, and the course can boast one of the most fantastic opening holes in links golf. Castlerock consists of a series of challenging holes where any lapse of concentration might spell disaster. Again, both are superb examples of links golf at its best, with green fees fairly priced.

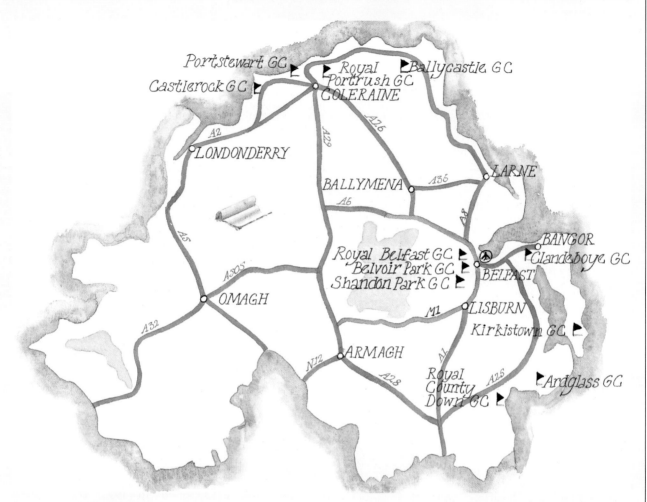

Belfast's Capital Golf

Belfast may sound a somewhat unlikely venue for holiday golf, but rest assured - three courses here are well worth a visit. The Royal Belfast Golf Club (0232) 428165 can be visited and played at weekends and during the week. It also has the added attraction of being the oldest club in Ireland. The excellent golf in Belfast continues at Belvoir Park (0232) 641159, with good value green fees. Shandon Park (0232) 701799 is slightly cheaper still.

Royal County Down and Seaviews

Head south and you will find yourself driving down the Ards Peninsula - well worth your attention when heading for Kirkistown Castle Golf Club (02477) 71233 whose green fees are extremely good value. An American whose passion was to find the world's best golf course felt that he had finally reached Mecca when he saw this course. The holes are testing, but the views over the Irish Sea are spectacular.

When St. Patrick came to Ireland in AD 432, he landed in County Down. If the golf course at Ardglass (0396) 841219 had been there he would no doubt have enjoyed many a game for he decided to stay in the county until he died. Golfers might not want to end their days here but a good game is there for the taking. It has a craggy setting and in typical Northern Irish mode the 2nd and 11th holes are dangerously near the water's edge. Unwary golfers take heed.

We shall end our tour of this delightful land with a game on that most spectacular of courses Royal County Down (03967) 23314, which has a splendid reputation and rightly so. The course is situated in Newcastle, and is well worth

the green fee during the week or at the weekend. Mondays, Tuesdays and Fridays are particularly easy for visitors to play.

Starting with history, 'Old' Tom Morris was imported for the task of designing the course back in 1889. Sand dunes and rough are a particular feature of the course, as well as narrow fairways that will have you gritting your teeth in determination or even desperation. It is a beautiful and very natural test of links golf and makes few concessions to the wayward hitter. The course consists of two distinct loops of nine, and you will probably need a breather after tackling the first half. A gentle start at the first, a par 5 often aided by the prevailing wind, is succeeded by two stiff par 4s, with sandhills and pot bunkers to contest. The 4th may prove somewhat distracting as it faces the Mountains of Mourne, but perhaps they will provide inspiration. By the time you reach the 9th you must have your wits about you as the drive is uphill and very difficult to gauge - skill and luck are both required to hit the green with your second shot.

The second nine holes are something of a relief, but still far from easy. The 12th is the easiest hole, but the 15th again provides stiff challenges, demanding precision if the awkward green, cut into a dune, is to be reached in two. All in all, the visiting golfer will take home many memories of Royal County Down and will no doubt have improved his golf immeasurably in the process. Well, that's the intention anyway!

If you are looking for some of the finest golf in Europe, Northern Ireland must feature in your calculations.

Northern Ireland

Blackheath House, Coleraine, Co Londonderry. Tel: (0265) 868433
The house, which dates from 1791, is set in two acres of gardens and has a fascinating history. It also offers individually styled bedrooms and a fine restaurant which makes the most of freshly grown produce. Blackheath has special rates with local golf courses.

Magherabuoy House Hotel, Portrush, Co Antrim. Tel: (0265) 823507
Located in natural golfing country the famous fairways of the championship course of Royal Portrush are barely five minutes from the hotel. The house incorporates the period home of the former Minister of Home Affairs and has been carefully restored and extended, providing modern comforts in a majestic setting.

Dublin and South East Ireland

Aghadoe Heights, Killarney, Co Kerry. Tel: (010 353 64) 31766
With its unique location and breathtaking panoramic views of the lakes and mountains, the Aghadoe Heights is recognised as one of Ireland's finest hotels. With 60 luxuriously furnished bedrooms, a superb leisure centre with indoor pool, plus the acclaimed Frederick's Rooftop Restaurant offering outstanding cuisine, the Aghadoe Heights provides the perfect base for playing Kerry's championship golf courses, exploring South West Ireland or just rest and relaxation.

Hunter's Hotel, Newrath Bridge, Rathnew, Co Wicklow. Tel: (010 353) 404 40106
Hunter's Hotel is one of Ireland's oldest coaching inns, established for 200 years in the beautiful county of Wicklow. The hotel has been run by the same family for five generations and is justly famous for its high standards of accommodation, cuisine

and service. Golf can be arranged at a number of fine courses in the area.

Marlfield House, Gorey, Co Wexford. Tel: (010 353 55) 21124
A fine 18th century mansion set in 35 acres of woodlands and gardens and only 80 kilometres from Dublin. Accommodation is in 19 superb rooms all decorated using period furniture. The award winning restaurant serves modern French cuisine making use of freshly grown produce. There are a variety of sports available and the hotel is only two kilometres from a golf course.

Mount Juliet, Thomastown, Co Kilkenny. Tel: (010 353 56) 24455

Mount Juliet is set in 1500 acres of unspoiled parkland and is one of Ireland's premier hotel and sporting estates. The hotel offers several types of accommodation including the Hunter's Yard which is just a two minute walk from Mount Juliet House. Designed around a traditional courtyard this is the centre of Mount Juliet's sporting activities. In the clubhouse golfers can meet friends in the Spike Bar, unwind in the President's Bar or enjoy the relaxed surroundings of The Loft Restaurant. The rustic ambience of the 13 courtyard bedrooms is popular with golfers and conference delegates alike. Guests can make the most of the Leisure Centre at Hunter's Yard by enjoying a leisurely swim in the pool or easing away tensions in the steam room. The Spa also provides a full range of body therapy treatments. The 18 hole Jack Nicklaus signature golf course, home of the Irish Open in 1993 and 1994, takes full advantage of the natural beauty of the estate. As of 1st May 1994 the David Leadbetter Golf Academy, the first and only in Ireland, will open at Mount Juliet. Golfers of all handicaps will be able to take advantage of the expert tuition that will be on offer.

Nuremore Hotel, Carrickmacross, Co Monaghan. Tel: (010 353 42) 61438
Originally a Victorian country house, the Nuremore has been skillfully converted and extended into a magnificent country hotel, beautifully situated within 200 acres of woods and parkland. Guests are offered an unrivalled range of sports and leisure facilities - for instance in 1992 the Nuremore was the venue for the PGA Ulster Open professional championship.

Rathsallagh House, Dunlavin, Co Wicklow. Tel: (010 353 45) 53112
This large comfortable farmhouse is situated in 500 acres of peaceful parkland, surrounded by some of the most beautiful countryside of eastern Ireland. The atmosphere is happy and relaxed in this hotel with its huge variety of diversions. Guests can choose from tennis, golf, driving range, practice holes, putting or archery among others.

Slieve Russell Hotel, Golf and Country Club, Ballyconnell, Co Cavan. Tel: (010 353 49) 26444
The Slieve Russell Hotel, Golf and Country Club opened its doors on 1 August 1990. The hotel stands in 300 acres of parkland which encompasses gardens and two natural lakes. Opened in 1992, the 18 hole championship standard golf course blends well with the typical Cavan drumlin and valley landscape.

Waterford Castle, The Island, Ballinakill, Co Waterford. Tel: (010 353 51) 78203
Set on a private 310 acre island and reached by ferry, this 18th century castle is beautiful
ly tranquil and impressively decorated inside with stone walls, old panelling and a gorgeous ribbon plastered ceiling. The castle also boasts its own leisure club and 18 hole championship golf course.

West of Ireland

Coopershill, Riverstown, Co Sligo. Tel: (010 353 71) 65108

Coopershill is a fine example of a Georgian family mansion and is only two miles from the village of Riverstown and 13 miles from Sligo. Five of the seven bedrooms have four poster or canopy beds and all have their own private bathrooms. Guests can relax in front of a log fire in the large and comfortable drawing room. Dinner by candlelight with family silverware and crystal glass adds to the special atmosphere. There are several golf courses within easy driving distance, including the County Sligo Golf Club at Rosses Point.

Downhill Hotel, Ballina, Co. Mayo.
Tel: (010 353 96) 21033

The Downhill Hotel is a family owned and managed Grade A *** established over 55 years. Situated one mile outside Ballina, on the famous salmon fishing river Moy, in close proximity of four magnificent golf courses - Enniscrone, Rosses Point, Belmullet and Wesport - all within 35 miles radius of the Downhill.

Luxury accommodation • Health & Leisure Centre • Entertainment in Frogs Piano Bar • Knock and Sligo airports both 30 minutes drive from the hotel.

Glin Castle, Glin, Co Limerick.
Tel: (010 353 68) 34173

After 18 holes on one of the most challenging links in the world, at Ballybunion, it is a soothing respite to return to the peace and comfort of Glin Castle on the banks of the lordly River Shannon. six double bedrooms, with dressing rooms and bathrooms, on the first and second floor and an enfilade of 18th century reception rooms, decorated with style and grace, are at your disposal downstairs. Family retainers welcome you and serve your dinner in the dining room under the envious eyes of the rows of portraits of the former Knights of Glin. Your drinks are in the smoking room by the cosy log fire as you sink into the comfortable sofas and armchairs. After a piping hot bath and change, crystal glasses of Irish whiskey, or silver goblets of cocktails, precede a delicious dinner cooked from all the fresh ingredients grown in the walled garden, and conversation invariably flows at this outpost of comfort in the middle of its beautiful green demesne. One hour's drive from Shannon airport the castle can be rented by the week or overnight stays arranged.

International Best Western Hotel, Killarney, Co Kerry.
Tel: (010 353 64) 31816

Right in the heart of Killarney within minutes of the lakes. Ideally located for touring, entertainment and shopping. The hotel has 88 rooms with bath/shower, television, radio and direct dial phone. There are three restaurants with entertainment nightly in season. Nearby are Killarney's two 18 hole championship golf courses.

Longueville House, Mallow, Co Cork.
Tel: (010 353 22) 47156

Resting in a 500 acre cattle and sheep farm, this substantial Georgian hotel has a very relaxed and informal atmosphere, with a fine collection of antiques to decorate the interior. There is horse riding at nearby stables and golf at a dozen courses close by, including premier championship courses at Killarney, Ballybunion and Tralee.

Newport House, Newport, Co Mayo.
Tel: (010 353 98) 41222

This is a superb ivy- clad, bow-fronted Georgian mansion encircled by mountains, lakes and streams. The hotel is famed for its hospitality and there is a rare feeling here of continuity and maturity. The discerning golfer has the pleasure of the 18 hole championship course at Westport as well as the more relaxed 9 hole course near Mulraney.

Rock Glen Hotel, Clifden, Co Galway. Tel: (010 353 95) 21035

A converted shooting lodge first built in 1815, the Rock Glen is now a 29 bedroomed, cosy, family run hotel, nestling in the heart of Connemara. The hotel is renowned for its exceptional cuisine and traditional hospitality. Connemara's 18 hole championship course is just a 15 minute drive from the hotel.

Waterville House and Golf Links, Waterville, Co Kerry.
Tel: (010 353 66) 74102

Built in the 18th century, Waterville House presides serenely on the shores of Ballinskelligs Bay. All 10 bedrooms have wonderful views and in addition to warm hospitality and fine cuisine guests can enjoy a heated pool, sauna, steam room, snooker and billiard room and of course, for golfers, the world class Waterville links.

Getting a round in Northern Ireland.

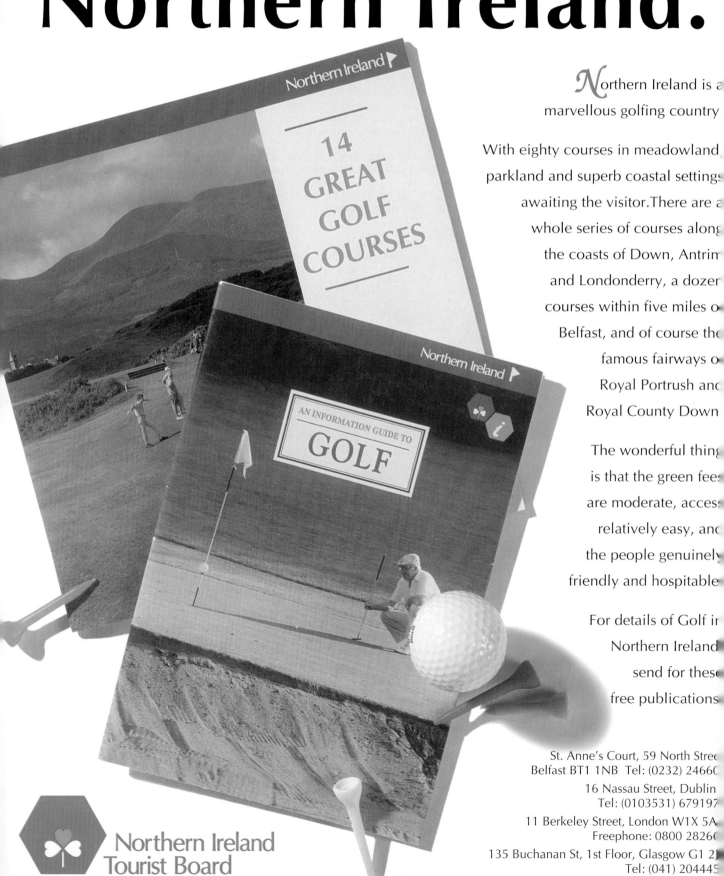

Northern Ireland is a marvellous golfing country

With eighty courses in meadowland, parkland and superb coastal settings awaiting the visitor. There are a whole series of courses along the coasts of Down, Antrim and Londonderry, a dozen courses within five miles of Belfast, and of course the famous fairways of Royal Portrush and Royal County Down.

The wonderful thing is that the green fees are moderate, access relatively easy, and the people genuinely friendly and hospitable.

For details of Golf in Northern Ireland send for these free publications.

St. Anne's Court, 59 North Street Belfast BT1 1NB Tel: (0232) 24660

16 Nassau Street, Dublin Tel: (0103531) 679197

11 Berkeley Street, London W1X 5A Freephone: 0800 28266

135 Buchanan St, 1st Floor, Glasgow G1 2 Tel: (041) 204445

Northern Ireland Tourist Board

America

Grand Cypress *(Golf Resort Marketing)*

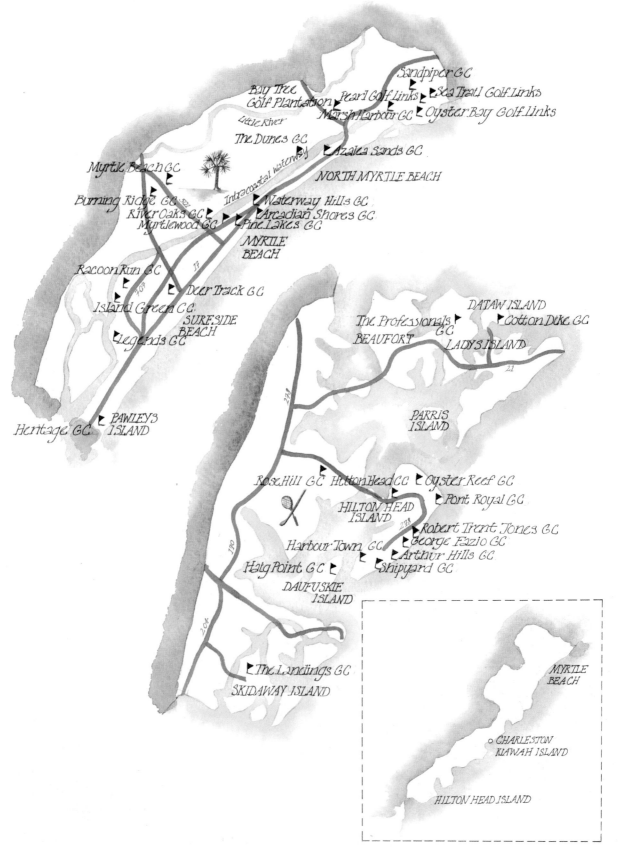

Sandpiper GC
Bay Tree
Golf Plantation
Pearl Golf Links
Sea Trail Golf Links
Marsh Harbour GC
Oyster Bay Golf Links
Little River
The Dunes GC
Azalea Sands GC
NORTH MYRTLE BEACH
Myrtle Beach GC
Intracoastal Waterway
Burning Ridge GC
Waterway Hills GC
River Oaks GC
Arcadian Shores GC
Myrtlewood GC
Pine Lakes GC
MYRTLE BEACH
Racoon Run GC
Deer Track GC
The Professionals GC
DATAW ISLAND
Cotton Dike GC
Island Green CC
BEAUFORT
LADYS ISLAND
SURFSIDE BEACH
21
Legends GC
PARRIS ISLAND
Heritage GC
PAWLEYS ISLAND
Rose Hill GC
Hilton Head CC
Oyster Reef GC
Pont Royal GC
HILTON HEAD ISLAND
Robert Trent Jones GC
George Fazio GC
Harbour Town GC
Arthur Hills GC
Haig Point GC
Shipyard GC
DAUFUSKIE ISLAND
The Landings GC
MYRTLE BEACH
SKIDAWAY ISLAND
CHARLESTON
KIAWAH ISLAND
HILTON HEAD ISLAND

Myrtle Beach

With over 80 courses on and around this 60 odd mile stretch of Carolina coastland, known as the Grand Strand, there is really nowhere else in the world offering holiday golfers such a concentration of quality golf and accommodation. Although the first course, Pine Lakes International, was built back in the 1920s, The major era for course building did not begin until the 1960s when the area as a whole grew in popularity as a tourist resort. For golfers the mild winters in this area are a bonus, making it an attractive proposition the whole year round.

While the number of courses in itself is sufficient to prevent them generally becoming overplayed and overcrowded, the region's clubs, hotels and the tour operators cooperate in an efficient tee reservation service which more or less guarantees satisfaction providing courses have been selected in advance. This is, of course, the tricky bit and with the territory comes the choice of accommodation otherwise more time may be spent in the hire car than on the course.

North Carolina

As a point of reference the courses to the north of the Grand Strand are the furthest from the airport at Myrtle Beach, and the golf and the accommodation to be found here set the standard for the whole region . As may be expected, various authorities on the game of golf have their particular favourites and the tour operators themselves are selective in those they feature in their programmes. Equally there is not space here to do justice to all the courses in the north let alone the whole collection to be found the length and breadth of the Grand Strand.

If there is one course, however, which captures the essence of holiday golf in the enjoyment it provides then it must be Sandpiper Bay and it would be worth the drive north from the airport just to experience this course alone. The beautiful natural surroundings with plenty of water and tall trees are typical of the region and well preserved, while the golf is played on generous wide fairways and large elevated greens with the championship tees providing a challenge for low handicappers seeking that little bit extra from the course.

The major golfing complex in the north is the Sea Trail Plantation which is featured prominently by Sovereign and Destination Golf. There are three courses here and set amongst the fairways, lakes and towering forests of oak and pine is luxury accommodation in villas and apartments with leisure facilities to match. Each course is the creation of a leading American golf architect and bears his stamp and name accordingly. Dan Maples, Rees Jones, and Willard Byrd are the three designers.

Notorious for its design is Carolina Shores, the creation of Tom Jackson. The lush fairways here are lined with tall pines and the greens are exceptionally well protected. This is not a noticeably long course, however, and the premium is on accuracy.

Still to the north and still in North Carolina are two more clubs with courses of special interest. The Pearl Golf Links has attracted its fair share of accolades over the years, though some of the compliments paid, as the name suggests, tend to the obvious. There are two courses here with a mile and a half of marshland frontage and the area abounds with wildlife. Both 18s are played through spectacular scenery and offer challenging golf for high and low handicappers.

The Marsh Harbour course rises naturally above its saltmarsh setting to provide some spectacular views and a test of golf which places the course deservedly amongst the top 25 public courses in America.

Accommodation to match can be found suitably close by at The Winds complex situated on the ocean front. Eagle Golf Tours and Leisure Link both recommend the fine apartments and spa houses here as an excellent base from which to explore the golf in the north as well as the nightlife.

South Carolina

Still in north Myrtle Beach but across the line in South Carolina, the influence the Scots exert on the game of golf manifests itself at Heather Glen, a club and course where the desire to emulate the best traditions of Scottish golf is not a well kept secret. From the layout of the 27 holes to a clubhouse with its origins in an 18th century Scottish design everything about Heather Glen is inspired by a respect for the game's rich heritage. The course, as one might expect, has won its fair share of awards and is one of only seven or eight courses to be mentioned in dispatches by all the tour operators, although under the circumstances this is understandable.

More traditional Myrtle Beach style golfing fare is, however, never far away and one of the courses ranked by Condotel patrons in their favourite five, Cypress Bay, is close by. Condotels, privately owned condominiums let by the owners, feature in The Flying Golfer programmes and offer a very high standard of accommodation throughout the Myrtle Beach region. As the name suggests, the course of Cypress Bay has a lot of water and a good many trees to negotiate before reaching the safe haven of the beautiful clubhouse.

Back on the coast itself with magnificent views over the intercoastal waterway and saltwater marshes from its seaside peninsula setting is Tidewater. A relatively new course and a winner in the Best New Public Course polls in 1990, it enjoys Hale Irwin's seal of approval. The layout of the 18 holes follows the natural terrain with the result that nine holes play along the coast and nine through forest and around lakes.

At River Hills, Tom Jackson has created another course to provide something of a traditional test in the Scottish style. One other noticeable feature is the rather undulating layout which is in marked contrast to the majority of courses in the area.

No tampering with nature was needed by Rees Jones to create a real challenge at Gator Hole, where oak trees majestically line the rolling fairways. While the general prevalence of water and trees on Myrtle Beach courses demands a fair degree of accuracy, this is a course which punishes poor club selection as much as a par shot.

The final three holes at Eagle Nest will not provide much solace either for the wayward golfer. Considered by many to have the toughest finishing stretch to be found anywhere on the Grand Strand, this popular course is also regarded as one of the most scenic, which considering the competition is fair praise indeed.

Whole World Destination Travel recommend the Golf Colony Resort at Bay Tree Golf Plantation as a suitable base for north Myrtle Beach. The only problem here is forsaking the attractions of the three Bay Tree courses for others.

The accommodation takes the form of one or two bedroom villas, which are spacious and well appointed, overlooking the tenth fairway of the Silver course and only ten minutes drive from Myrtle Beach's other attractions. Each of the three courses at Bay Tree, the Gold , Green and Silver, has its own distinctive character and collectively they offer the most consistently testing golf in Myrtle Beach.

Further inland at Buck Creek, golfers select their own

degree of difficulty on this 27 hole development opened in 1990. Tucked away amidst towering hardwoods, and with the Waccamaw River meandering its length and breadth, the tees are appropriately labelled 'stag', 'buck' 'fawn' and 'doe' offering players of all abilities the chance to enjoy their own game to the full.

Scaling the same heights of popularity amongst the tour operators as Heather Glen is Long Bay, though this time the cachet is due to its creator, Jack Nicklaus and deservedly so. Be warned though that this is a course for proficient golfers on top of their game, and a good deal of concentration is required when plotting a route away from the deep bunkers and water hazards to the small elevated greens.

By way of complete contrast and known as 'The Friendly Course' is Possum Trot, whose generous fairways invite all golfers to play to and below their handicaps. A recognised neighbouring championship course, Beachwood, also presents a fair challenge to high and low handicappers alike, while a third course in this immediate area, Azalea Sands, is very much a manmade test of golf but none the less enjoyable or challenging for it.

It is from this point south on the Grand Strand that most quality recommended accommodation is to be found beginning with Ocean Creek, a 57 acre resort nestling between Myrtle Beach and North Myrtle Beach. Longmere and Whole World Destination Travel both make much of the wide range of accommodation available here from lodges and villas set amongst oak trees to apartments in the high rise ocean-front towers, while residents can take full advantage of the many sporting and leisure facilities. The complex boasts an excellent restaurant, the Four Seasons, and there is a dedicated team of golfing staff to assist and advise holiday golfers.

Select World Golf and Leisure Link join with Whole World Destination Travel in promoting the Myrtle Beach Hilton as alternative conventional hotel accommodation just down the coast. Set on the ocean front , the hotel has its own nightlife, a selection of bars and restaurants with gourmet continental cuisine on offer in Alfredo's and a rooftop nightclub to dance away the calories. Another advantage of the Hilton is the hotel's proximity to it's own top ranking golf course, Arcadia Shores, where the terrain's natural features have been moulded into a contemporary design with lakes, oak-lined fairways and strategically placed bunkers.

Direct competition to the Ocean Creek resort and the Hilton comes in the form of the Radisson Resort, set in the 145 acre Kingston Plantation and featured by British Airways, Select World Golf, Destination Golf and Eagle Golf Tours. The resort has over a mile of private beaches and features a 255 room hotel with villas set around the estate, which is effectively one huge sport and leisure centre. For those who tire of the resort's nightlife, Myrtle Beach's very own 'Restaurant Row', complete with bars and nightclubs, is only five minutes away.

Exceedingly popular with the tour operators are the Sands Ocean Front Resorts, comprising the Ocean Dunes and Sand Dunes as well as the Ocean Forest Villa Resort. While the properties may not match the Radisson Resort for setting, this is still quality, with a choice of hotel or self catering style accommodation, and the appropriate sports and leisure facilities to match. Longshot, Longmere, Leisure Link and Sovereign all find a place for one or all of these properties in their programmes as do Whole World Destination Travel, Eagle Golf Tours and Destination Golf.

One further course to be aware of before moving onto the attractions of the southern half of Myrtle Beach, is Waterway Hills, and not just for the unique access afforded by overhead cable car. The glass gondola does, however, provide excellent views of what lies in store for the visiting golfer - rolling fairways surrounded by forests of oak, pine and chestnut interspersed with lakes and a ravine. Waterway Hills has 27 holes and whatever combination chosen the scenery is superb and the golf fun and relaxing.

Ideal for the Pine Lakes course (known as 'The Grandaddy' around these parts) and appropriately situated at the centre of all the golfing activity is Sea Island, a

Spectacular Golf, Myrtle Beach (*Carolina Fairways*)

small family run hotel commended by British Airways and Destination Golf . Personal attention, elegantly furnished spacious rooms and a dress code for dinner give Sea Island its own unique charm which has endeared it to the legions of golfers who return year after year.

At the Pine Lakes Club, great store is also set by traditional values. The club prides itself on the hospitality proffered to visiting golfers. It will come then as no surprise to learn that if there is one course which manages to rise above the generally magnificent condition of all the other courses in the area, then this is it.

Further inland still from the beach are the River Oaks and Wildwing clubs which merit inclusion in any Myrtle Beach golfing schedule. River Oaks lives up to its name with water featuring on 14 of the 18 holes which cut through forests of oak. The emphasis here must be on accurate shot making if a good score is to be returned, but generous fairways invite confident play and should make the experience an enjoyable one.

Wildwing benefits from two exceptional Willard Byrd designed courses, the Hummingbird and the Woodstork, and some would say, the best greens in Myrtle Beach. Each course offers a different challenge. The Hummingbird has an open feel to it as it follows the natural contours of the land, while the Woodstork's water hazards call for precise play.

Almost sandwiched between River Oaks and Wilding but unlikely to be missed is the Myrtle Beach National complex, which figures prominently amongst the courses featured by tour operators. The design concept which called for an enjoyable test of golf to match the beautiful surroundings has not been compromised over the years. The courses call for proficiency with every club in the bag and the standard of the greens is such that the claims of Wildwing's sup-

porters must be treated with caution. For those golfers with time and inclination to attempt only the championship test, this can be found on the North course along with the distinctive 'SC' (South Carolina) bunkers.

Another complex close by which enjoys a prestigious reputation is Legends, which now boasts three excellent courses. Of the three, the Heathland is justifiably considered the most authentic and the most challenging of all America's 'Scottish links' designs. The Moorland with its serious rough comes a close second, while the latest addition, Parkland, marks a return to the trees and is undeniably American in its layout.

The two course at Burning Ridge may not ask as many questions as their more illustrious neighbours, but they are certainly as popular, and, probably by virtue of the West Course, Burning Ridge ranks in the Condotel top five. The attractions here are the broad fairways and large greens although plentiful water hazards demand some precise play.

Also ranked in the Condotel top five and given favourable reviews by a number of operators is Quail Creek, another club exhibiting all the characteristics that make Myrtle Beach such an attractive proposition - superb scenery, Southern hospitality, an immaculately maintained course, and an enjoyable but not overtaxing round of golf.

The Witch may not sound quite as inviting but it is equal to any of the other courses in this central group away from the beach. Spread over 500 acres of unspoilt forest and wetlands, a network of bridges spanning literally thousands of yards is required to transport golfers over the 18 holes.

While the choice golf may be away from the ocean, the pick of the accommodation on offer remains on or by the beach, and by far the most popular amongst the tour operator selections is the Sea Mist resort,

 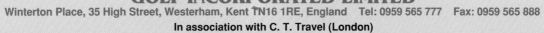

which caters for golfers right down to a complimentary hat. The rooms here are well equipped and have kitchenettes. An ocean-front setting of some ten acres includes a wide range of sports facilities with practice nets and a sand trap for the dedicated golfer. Other recommendations include The Breakers, from the British Airways and Longmere programmes, which offers accommodation in spacious, comfortable rooms over two sites, the Resort Hotel and North Tower, side by side on the beach. Whole World Destination Travel promote the Dayton House Best Western which, although not on quite such a grand scale as some of the self catering orientated resorts, still enjoys a beach front setting and provides its residents with suitable diversions.

For upmarket luxury hotel accommodation, Longshot, Longmere, Golf Holiday International and Sovereign all recommend the Myrtle Beach Sheraton which will not disappoint golfers looking for five star comforts and associated amenities.

Sovereign offer a three star alternative in the Comfort Inn which offers a practical but basic package to golfers, while the Swamp Fox Ocean Resort's wide range of accommodation makes it another favourite with those looking for budget accommodation on the ocean front. It can be found in the Longmere and Whole World Destination Travel programmes.

The next collection of courses to note lies to the south of the airport in the Surfside Beach Garden City area. Heron Point is very typical of Myrtle Beach golf with its tree-lined fairways, water hazards, and strategically placed bunkers making for a memorable days golf. A fun day too should be guaranteed at Island Green, a 27 hotel complex, which is pleasant on the eye and not too taxing.

Much more challenging are two courses closer to the ocean which make up the last two spots in Condotel's top five, as featured by The Flying Golfer. Indian Wells is an exceptionally picturesque course with some 15 acres of water in play especially on the par 5s where a clear head will be needed for decision making. At Indigo Creek, Willard Byrd has turned an old plantation into one of his golfing masterpieces, threading wide lush fairways through tall pines and creeks.

Gary Player also excelled himself at Blackmoor, the first course he designed on the Grand Strand, where oak trees and lakes have been incorporated into a discernibly superior creation.

Dan Maples is known to regard his Willbrook design as one of his best, and this is a course which has only recently dispensed with its members-only tag. Some visitors confronted by the awesome first hole may be inclined to wish the club hadn't bothered, but this is truly a course to savour as it winds its way around oak trees, marshes and rice fields, demanding accurate play at every turn.

The Willbrook is one of three courses in the Litchfield by the Sea complex, which together with the Litchfield Country Club and the River Club make up 'the Triple Crown'. This 4,500 acre country club resort lies some 20 miles south of Myrtle Beach centre and offers a wide range of first class accommodation, from hotel suites to cottages and villas on the ocean front and all the assorted sports and leisure facilities one would expect. British Airways, Longmere, Whole World Travel and Destination Golf all feature the resort.

Of the two other courses, the Tom Jackson designed River Club tends to attract more of the plaudits for the way the architect created the wealth of water hazards and blended them with wide fairways and large but well protected greens to provide a demanding test of golf. Litchfield's fairways are much narrower and only occasionally punctuated by sand and water, but this is still regarded as one of Willard Byrd's classic designs and is a

treat to play.

Just south of the Litchfield complex on Pawley Island is the appropriately named Pawley's Plantation, a resort which in its time has played host to history in the form of George Washington, Winston Churchhill and the like. The resort now revolves around its Jack Nicklaus designed golf course which has been built amongst the swamp, saltmarsh and hardwood. By incorporating the natural hazards into his design, Nicklaus has created, as was his intent, a course where precision rather than power is rewarded, as are golfers with the foresight to take a camera to record their round in one of golf's more memorable settings. Equally unforgettable is the standard of accommodation in the fairway villas which are spacious and luxuriously appointed right down to the jacuzzi in the en suite bathrooms. Programmes including Pawley's Plantation Country Club are offered by Longshot, The Flying Golfer and Sovereign.

Two courses which should not be overlooked before pondering alternative holiday golf some distance south, are the Heritage and Sea Gull courses. The Heritage is another championship test to spring from an old colonial rice plantation and bears testimony to the sterling work Harry Young has done in developing Myrtle Beach golf. Sea Gull is the farthest south of the Myrtle Beach area courses below Pawley's Plantation and provides typical pleasure for high and low handicappers alike, with inviting fairways and large greens compensating for the length of this beautiful course.

A final word of caution when it comes to booking a golf holiday to Myrtle Beach. Do check the status of the courses you wish to play vis a vis the programme offered by the tour operator. While packages may be promoted as including free golf on a daily basis, a surcharge is payable at certain courses. This may vary depending on the accommodation selected, so it is advisable to consider all the options open when budgeting the holiday, bearing in mind that a surcharge does not always mean a better course in this part of the world.

Kiawah Island and Charleston

Some two hours drive south from Myrtle Beach lies the historic city of Charleston. Positively ancient by American standards with buildings dating back over 300 years, Charleston offers culture and recreation, sandy beaches to relax on and the chance to slip back in time. For golfers, the history of the region is tied up with a much more recent drama which unfurled some 21 miles south at Kiawah Island in 1991. The very fact that the events of that final day of the Ryder Cup are indelibly printed on the consciousness of millions of golfers is in itself sufficient to guarantee Kiawah's golfing Mecca status and it is therefore something of an added bonus that the island boasts three other superb courses and miles and miles of unspoilt coastline with beautiful safe beaches.

Any average club golfer harbouring the notion that he might tame Pete Dye's now legendary Ocean Course is in for a severe shock to his system. Not for nothing does it rank as America's most difficult resort course, and for most golfers the score returned will be very much a secondary consideration compared with the thrill of facing the challenge.

More manageable in most respects are the three other courses, each designed by a leading golf architect. In its 14th, 15th and 16th holes Jack Nicklaus's Turtle Point Course has three of the most spectacular golf holes to be found anywhere in the world, and provides such a test of judgement, especially over the closing stretch, that it does not come as a surprise to find it ranked among Carolina's top ten courses.

Fans of Gary Player designs will not be disappointed with Marsh Point. Water hazards figure on 13 holes and

Hilton Head

Despite some rather obvious claims, Hilton Head Island does not feature with the majority of operators offering golf packages to the USA. The three days allocated by British Airways on their Classic Golf Tour are barely enough to do justice to the Palmetto Dunes courses let alone the other 16 on or just off this small island. Measuring twelve miles long and five miles wide, Hilton Head is one of America's, if not the world's, most popular holiday golf destinations and a sporting paradise in its own right. The island's development to cater for tourist demand has not compromised its natural appeal and the courses themselves accordingly make full use of the local terrain.

Longmere, Whole World Destination Travel, Eagle Golf Tours, Destination Golf and Golf International do organise programmes including Hilton Head and one of the favourites amongst these operators is The Westin Resort. This is the top rated luxury hotel on the island, affording magnificent views out over sandy beaches and the Atlantic from its situation on the north end of the island. The service and facilities here are of the highest quality, while guests are well placed for three of the island's best courses at the Port Royal Club, each offering a unique challenge.

Robbers Row, designed around an old civil war fort, has wide, inviting fairways but scores are made by finesse around the greens. Planters Row also offers generous fairways but good judgement and precise play are needed to reach the greens on this Willard Byrd championship rated course. Things get really tight at the Barony with its small greens and although the fairways are accommodating, position from the tee is all-important.

A fourth course in the Port Royal Plantation group is The Shipyard which lies toward the centre of the island. The 27 holes created here by George Cobb and Willard Byrd are regarded by some as golfing heaven, running through the old plantation's forests of oak and around the 'alligator-infested' lagoons.

Also located in the 800 acres of the Shipyard Plantation is Marriot's Hilton Head Resort, which comes highly recommended by Whole World Destination Travel and offers accommodation and facilities to the high standard associated with the name.

The opportunity afforded by British Airways to enjoy the courses at Palmetto Dunes under the guise of a Classic Golf Tour is no overstatement. All three courses have won their fair share of awards in the "Best......"polls which abound on this side of the Atlantic.

The George Fazio course is considered as Hilton Head's truest championship test and provides an exhilarating challenge with little or no respite, especially on the par 4 holes. The Robert Trent Jones course follows the lagoon system so water does come into play a lot, especially on the par 3s, while the design of Arthur Hills follows natural contours and displays all the characteristics of a Scottish links with water hazards adding to the level of difficulty when this seaside course is at the mercy of the elements.

While British Airways favour the Harbour Side 111 property, other accommodation on the 2000 acre Palmetto Dunes Plantation comes recommended in the shape of the Hyatt Regency and the Hilton Resort. Longmere feature both while Destination Golf promote the Hyatt, and Whole World offer the Hilton. Neither can really be faulted for their service and facilities. The Hyatt is very sport orientated and offers guests plenty to keep them occupied off the golf course, while the Hilton preaches leisurely self indulgence.

Guests of the Hyatt are also well placed to enjoy another Arthur Hills design in the relatively new course at Palmetto Hall which immediately ranked as one of the top three on the island. Again the course follows the natural contours closely and the layout is such that all golfers should find the challenge entertaining.

At Sea Pines there is another Pete Dye course to be found and one which ranks among his best. His Harbour Town design includes probably the best known hole on the island, and definitely one of the most intimidating, in the shape of the 18th with the Harbour Town lighthouse in the background.

Two George Cobb designs complete the trio of courses at Sea Pines. Ocean Course was the first to be built on the island and provides a typical Carolina test of golf with plenty of water, trees and well protected greens. Sea Marsh does not present quite the same challenge, but lagoons and marshes do come into play and the course is none the less enjoyable.

Longmere and Whole World both commend the accommodation options at the Sea Pines Resort to golfers looking for the ultimate self catering holiday, especially those with families in tow. From apartments overlooking the harbour to ocean-front condominiums, all the accommodation is spacious and well equipped and the resort boasts extensive sport and leisure facilities as well as a five mile stretch of beach to enjoy. The Longmere and Eagle Golf Tours programmes both include a number of private properties spread throughout the island.

There are other courses of a very high standard to also consider when preparing a golfing schedule. The Rees Jones design at Oyster Reef is the longest on the island and is noticeable for the thick forests which line the fairways, the number of doglegs and tiered greens. Gary Player has produced another superb golfing challenge with his Hilton Head National design. Just off the island, Old South is a very natural course with a sting in its tail and a trip 20 minutes north up the road to the Country Club of Calawassie is a must for those golfers determined to confront Carolina's top courses.

Hilton Head, Island Resort (*Marriott Hotels*)

the undulating greens are well guarded, while the fairways are lined by marsh.

At Osprey Point, Tom Fazio has made use of the local terrain's undulating nature and semi-tropical vegetation to create links style fairways in foreign surroundings.

Accommodation on the island itself is best found at the Kiawah Island Inn and Villas, which can be found in the programmes offered by Eagle Golf Tours, The Flying Golfer, Destination Golf and Golf Holidays International. The resort also features in British Airways, Classic Golf Tour itinerary which takes in golf at Myrtle Beach, Kiawah Island and the courses further south at Hilton Head.

The resort of Kiawah Island is famed for its peace and tranquillity but residents of the Inn or Villas should find plenty of diversion away from the courses, while the accommodation comes complete with all the amenities necessary for an enjoyable stay. Whole World Destination Travel elect for accommodation south of Kiawah at the Seabrook Island Resort which has the added attraction of courses designed by Robert Trent Jones and Willard Byrd amongst its 2200 acres.

One programme which seeks to combine the best of the golf to the north and south of Charleston is offered by The Flying Golfer and is based at the Omni Hotel at Charleston Place. Longmere recommend three hotels in Charleston as ideally situated for both golf, sightseeing and relaxing. Of these the Hampton Inn is a modern functional city centre development, while the Lodge Alley Inn is at the heart of the old town and has spacious, elegantly furnished rooms as well as one of the City's top restaurants. This rich vein of traditional southern hospitality and decor also extends to the Holiday Inn Mount Pleasant.

The best golf to the north of Charleston is found at the Wild Dunes Complex, a 1600 acre development which boasts two championship courses. The resort comes very highly recommended and ranks accordingly both for golf and the facilities provided, with Wild Dunes Golf Links considered among the World's top 100 courses, while the Harbour Course provides a rather unique challenge across the harbour itself. Eagle Golf Tours feature the resort's villas in their programme, and the standard of the accommodation here, together with the extensive sports facilities, justifies the five star rating.

Kiawah Island (Carolina Fairways)

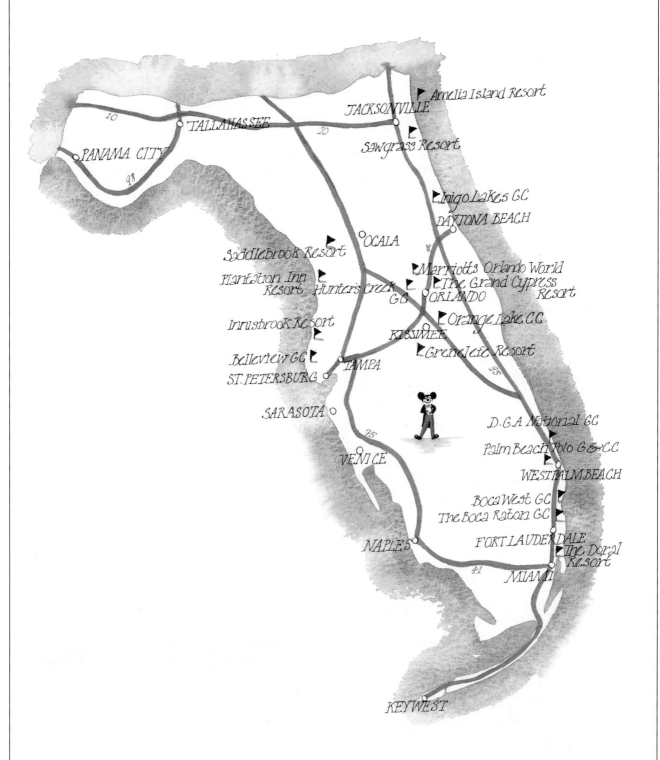

Amelia Island Resort

JACKSONVILLE

TALLAHASSEE

10

10

PANAMA CITY

98

Sawgrass Resort

Inigo Lakes GC

DAYTONA BEACH

OCALA

Saddlebrook Resort

Plantation Inn Resort

Hunters Creek GC

Marriotts Orlando World

The Grand Cypress Resort

ORLANDO

Innisbrook Resort

Orange Lake CC

KISSIMEE

Belleview GC

ST. PETERSBURG

TAMPA

Greneleje Resort

95

SARASOTA

D.G.A National GC

Palm Beach Polo G&CC

VENICE

95

WEST PALM BEACH

Boca West GC

The Boca Raton GC

NAPLES

FORT LAUDERDALE

The Doral Resort

41

MIAMI

KEY WEST

63

Time was when British golfers planning a holiday to America would more often than not look no further than Florida. For a variety of reasons this is no longer the case, but the state remains exceedingly popular and the holiday golfer has a wide selection of excellent courses and resort accommodation to choose from, not to mention tour operator programmes.

In and around the Miami area, golfers electing to play and stay on one of the prestigious resort course complexes will find themselves secluded in tranquillity and luxury, surrounded by splendid scenery and remarkable facilities. Just eight miles from the international airport is a prime example in the Doral Resort and Country Club with its six courses including, of course, the Blue Monster on which the Doral Ryder Open is played annually, while the Red, Gold, White and Silver courses all merit championship status. Instruction facilities here are second to none, while those who like to combine a spot of fishing with their golf need look no further. Other sport and leisure facilities are amongst the finest in America and the spacious hotel rooms and suites are superbly appointed. The Doral Resort is featured by Destination Golf and Whole World Destination Travel.

Anyone with a passing knowledge of American football will have no difficulty placing Don Shula's Resort and Golf Club. Formerly known as the Miami Lakes and Inn Golf Resort it is now, for what it is worth, the official hotel of the Miami Dolphins and finds a place in Whole World's programme. The resort features a floodlit 18 hole executive course as well as one of the best championship courses in the South of Florida, Miami Lakes, with tight tree-lined fairways and water hazards aplenty on the back nine. Accommodation can be found in either contemporary surrounds or a more 'olde worlde' setting and there is no shortage of entertainment to be had locally.

Turnberry Isle lies 20 minutes to the north of Miami and this Gold Coast resort and country club with two PGA rated Robert Trent Jones courses is justifiably ranked amongst the best Florida has to offer. Elegant Resorts, Eurogolf, Golf International and Whole World Destination Travel all include this magnificent sport and leisure complex in their programmes, and golfers looking to really indulge themselves will find suitable opportunity in the luxuriously furnished rooms, bars, restaurants and clubs.

The Turnberry Isle courses are both of championship standard and the famous island green on the South Course is typical of the target golf nature of their challenge. The design and setting of these courses, however, is such that they appeal to all golfers and can be enjoyed by high and low handicappers alike.

Golf in this part of the world is all about position and precision and another fine example of this kind of challenge is found to the south of Miami at Key Biscayne which plays host to the Seniors tour and is worth a visit, not simply for a demanding round of golf but to marvel at the lush tropical location.

Returning north and bypassing Fort Lauderdale which is not devoid of good golf and accommodation as Whole World Destination Travel do point out, the next premier resort to enjoy almost universal recognition is Boca Raton. Golfers can take their pick from programmes offered by Destination Golf, British Airways, Sovereign, Elegant Resorts, Eurogolf and Golf International if they find the golf and accommodation on offer here sufficiently appealing.

Boca Raton dates back to the 1920s and the architecture has a dramatic effect on guests approaching the palm tree-lined Camino Real drive. The estate is as renowned for its flora, fauna and wildlife as it is for its two championship golf courses. The original 18 hole layout also goes back to the 1920s and was the work of a certain Sam

PGA National Resort and Spa

Palm Beach Gardens, Florida

Home to the PGA of America, and boasting five championship golf courses designed by the likes of Jack Nicklaus, Arnold Palmer, and the Fazio brothers. Try your luck in the "Bear Trap", the spectacular finishing holes of the championship course, venue for several major tournaments including the PGA Seniors Tour and the 1983 Ryder Cup matches. The PGA National Resort & Spa is a complete holiday destination. A world class health spa, tennis club and fitness centre, not to mention pools galore, sailing lake and beach for children's activities in the summer months. There is also a host of restaurants and bars, from the casual ambience of the 19th bar to gourmet dining in the critically acclaimed Explorers Restaurant.

PGA National can be found at the heart of Palm Beach County, renowned for its year round climate, shops, beaches, big game fishing, golf and a wide selection of evening entertainments. There are waterfront restaurants, such as Harpoon Louie's, overlooking the historic Jupiter Lighthouse, not to mention better Italian restaurants than you will find in Italy!

With a choice of accommodation from two bedroomed / two bathroomed club cottages to the 335 rooms and suites of the 4 Diamond Hotel, the PGA National has the flexibility and welcome to accommodate your every need, be it a family holiday, intensive golf, a retreat to winter sunshine, golf schools or the ultimate in conference and business incentives.

For fully inclusive packages and tailormade stays, brochures and resort video please contact:-

Michael Holmes
Director of Marketing
PGA National Golf Club UK Office
Summer Lane
Beaulieu
Hants
SO42 7YS
Tel & Fax: (0590) 612575

Snead. Like Turnberry, this is Florida golf at its best with accurate play required around the palm trees and lakes of both courses.

Offered a choice of accommodation, golfers should elect to take rooms in the recently refurbished Cloister unless they prefer panoramic views from the high rise Tower. Cloister rooms are spacious and the whole complex has a mediterranean ambience. With a fitness centre, watersports and fine cuisine also in its favour there can be no surprise that this resort enjoys international acclaim.

From Boca Raton it is not a million miles inland to another Florida favourite, the PGA National, which boasts no less than five championship courses including The Champion Course, venue for the 1983 Ryder Cup which proved the springboard for Europe's future success. This, however, had nothing to do with Nicklaus being called in to redesign the course in 1989. The General Course, named after its designer Arnold Palmer, falls into the American style Scottish links category and will no doubt suit those golfers seeking a change from the more typical Florida fare. All the courses here are suitable for high and low handicappers, providing the former are not too ambitious in their tee box selection.

Golf and accommodation packages at the PGA National can now be arranged through its own UK marketing office headed up by Michael Holmes. The excellent value to be had at this resort, with its exceptional sports and leisure facilities which the whole family can enjoy, is also evident in the options offered by Destination Golf, Leisure Link and Whole World Destination Travel.

Leisure Link also feature a Best Western Hotel, the Palm Beach Lakes in West Palm Beach, which is ideally situated for the course of the same name. Palm Beach Lakes is one of the most established courses in the area and its layout is relatively undemanding compared to some contemporary developments. Water features on only six of the 18 holes and problems are posed in the traditional shape of doglegs making this an excellent course for a relaxing round. The hotel itself has well appointed rooms, an outdoor swimming pool and is close to the nightlife as well as many other good courses.

On the coast again and north of Palm Beach is the Indian River Plantation which is featured by Longmere, and is another self sufficient resort complex with accommodation ranging from deluxe hotel rooms to apartments and ocean-front villas. All manner of sporting and leisure diversions can be found to keep guests occupied and the resort boasts its own private 18 hole course.

Orlando and the surrounding area may be better known for Disney World and the Epcot centre, but it is nevertheless one of the prime destinations for holiday golfers, and one of the more popular resorts is Grenelefe, situated 40 miles drive south of Orlando. The Grenelefe Golf and Tennis Resort enjoys a lakeside setting covering some 1000 acres and recent renovation has made the resort one of Florida's best. It comes duly recommended by Destination Golf, British Airways, Golf Holidays International, Leisure Link and Whole World Destination Travel.

The high standard accommodation includes self catering options in suites and villas and the recreational facilities on and around the lake are second to none. Equally impressive is the Robert Trent Jones West Course here which has consistently figured at the top of the Florida ratings for the last ten years and is memorable for the strategic bunker emplacements around small elevated greens. Of the two other courses here, the East Course designed by Ed Seay and Arnold Palmer is considered to be one of the most challenging in Florida and accurate play is called for around the narrow fairways. The third course and most recent developed creation of Ron Garl

Grenelefe Resort (*Golf Resort Marketing*)

and Andy Bean may be shorter but the plentiful water hazards and sand traps together with tricky greens call for a fair degree of skill.

Close to Orlando airport and closer still to Disney World is the Grand Cypress Resort set in a spectacular 1500 acre estate around Lake Buena Vista and featuring one of America's leading hotels the Hyatt Regency, Grand Cypress. As may be expected both the hotel and the villas here feature in the Elegant Resorts programme, and Destination Golf and Longmere also include this resort as one of the finest in Florida. The hotel accommodation and facilities leave nothing to be desired and the magnificent atrium never fails to impress. The villas come in all shapes and sizes but are consistently appointed to a very high standard and enjoy their own leisure facilities.

There are 45 holes of golf, with the three original loops of nine now joined by the New Course, an 18 hole design of Jack Nicklaus which brings the spirit of St Andrews to the USA with its pot bunkers and double greens. As to whether Nicklaus has succeeded in his grand design, it should be noted that Greg Norman has nothing but praise for the the resort and its Academy of Golf which offers unparalleled instruction and practice facilities.

Another resort to enjoy the commendation of Destination Golf and Longmere is Orange Lake, which provides recreational fun for all the family and offers accommodation in functional well appointed villas. Orange Lake has a respected golf school, and the three 9 hole loops as designed by Joe Lee typically favour accuracy rather than power.

Orange Lake and the Marriot course and resort at the Orlando World Centre are both only minutes away from Disney World, and while Orange Lake may be for families, the Marriot resort offers sophisticated entertainment and facilities more in keeping with Florida's premier golf resorts. The Joe Lee designed course is to championship standard and is one where the relatively short yardage belies the hazardous nature, including water on 16 holes.

Accommodation at Marriot's Residence Inn takes the form of villas with self catering although there are centralised restaurants and the whole complex is recommended by Longmere and Whole World Destination Travel .

Golf Holidays International offer programmes in the Orlando area using the Golden Key Inn, Radisson Hotel and The Stouffers Resort. While the Golden Key is as far removed from the resort and country club norm as any city centre property can be, it does offer excellent value and is well situated for the attractions of downtown Orlando. Both Radisson and Stouffers are located in the International Drive area and a suitable budget choice can be made between the two. Stouffers is more highly rated in terms of facilities but would not necessarily give overall value for the seriously committed golfer who is likely to be out and about on the fairways all day long.

Longmere's programme here includes two of the top ranking Disney courses, Palm and Magnolia, which are well maintained and tight without too much water - well at least not on every hole. This is more the style of Cypress Creek, which does compensate with some generous fairways. Kissimee Bay, like Cypress Creek, is a Lloyd Clifton design and though new and rather open it provides an acknowledged championship test with plenty of water to avoid. Another course to be enjoyed now, before it goes private, is Windermere set in an exclusive area of Orlando. The 18 holes are maintained to a very high standard and visiting golfers have to be on top of their game to return a good score.

In this area there are a host of other quality hotels and courses recommended by the tour operators. Some resorts like the Sheraton World feature with more than one operator, in this case Sovereign and Whole World Destination Travel, while British Airways, Leisure Link and Select World Golf also have their own favourites. Without delving too much into the influence of budgets and travelling companions on the planning of a golf holi-

Grand Cypress Resort *(Golf Resort Marketing)*

day, Orlando has courses and accommodation to suit any golfer's pocket and enough attractions to keep the whole world happy.

One final resort to merit mention in the Orlando area, 50 minutes from the airport, is the Mission Inn Golf and Tennis Resort, which can be found in the Longmere and Eagle Golf programmes. This is another exquisite resort with elegance, charm, first class service and a superb setting to provide golfers with another glimpse of heaven, which may be a trifle over the top as an observation, but should convey the right impression. Depending on which of the polls you read, the course ranks in either Florida's top 20 or top 40, and its location amongst the rolling hills and orange groves to the north west of Orlando adds to the enjoyment to be derived from a round on this magnificently maintained course.

Back on the Atlantic Coast, an hour and a half's drive from Orlando is Daytona. This lags somewhat behind in popularity with British golfers but British Airways, Golf Holidays International and Longmere feature the area in their programmes.

British Airways recommend two first class hotels on Daytona beach, the Marriot and the Hilton which conform admirably to the high standards anticipated, with slightly cheaper but still elegantly furnished accommodation at the Casa Del Mar. The Holiday Inn, again on the ocean front, is comfortable and welcoming, well placed for the centre of Daytona, and British Airways are joined by Longmere in recommending this hotel as a base for the Daytona and Palm Coast areas. Longmere offer further budget style accommodation at the Seagarden Inn and Daytona Inn as do Golf Holidays International at the Howard Johnson Plaza. It should be noted that the term 'budget' hardly does justice to the quality of the accommodation, facilities and settings which is far superior to the image usually created in the mind of British tourists.

Courses selected by the tour operators as part of their programme in the immediate vicinity of Daytona Beach include the Indigo Lakes Hilton Course which has been subjected to some extensive renovation and now provides an excellent test over 18 holes which are surrounded by forest and often protected by water as would be expected. Cypress Head is very similar in layout and accurate play to the sloping fairways is necessary to avoid a watery grave. Pelican Bay incorporates a number of doglegs which again call for accuracy off the tee, and some power will be needed to par the monster 616 yard par 5. At the Halifax Plantation, deep forest made way for the golf architect's design. The end result proves exceptionally picturesque and not without its fair share of challenges.

Visitors to Daytona will also find plenty of golf some 15 minutes to the north in the Palm Coast area, but any decision on a holiday base for the whole area must take into account the new Sheraton Palm Coast Resort which lies between St. Augustine and Daytona Beach on the intercoastal waterway. As at Mission Inn the emphasis here is on service and the provision of first rate facilities in a suitably picturesque setting. The accommodation meets Sheraton's high standards and the cuisine is a match for any restaurant in Florida.

While the Sheraton itself does not have its own course, tour operators such as Destination Travel, British Airways, Golf Holidays International and Whole World Destination Travel are quick to point out the various first rate courses which can be enjoyed in this locality.

Top of the schedule should be the Hammock Dunes Links Course, a private club where guests of the resort enjoy playing privileges. The course here is considered one of Fazio's masterpieces and has attracted the usual array of accolades from the pollsters. With oceanside greens and fairways open to the elements, oak trees and marshes, the course combines the best aspects of golf in the old and new worlds.

Any Gary Player design tends to be a favourite with holiday golfers and Cypress Knoll, the latest addition to the area, has another attractive blend of the old and new. The area's first course, Palm Harbour, is similar in character to Cypress Knoll with fairways meandering through tree-lined avenues, while the Ed Seay and Arnold Palmer creations at Matanza Woods and Pine Lakes are more typical of Florida and long irons into island greens are more the norm than the exception.

Near Jacksonville and the furthest north of the resorts featured on the Atlantic Coast is the Amelia Island Plantation which finds particular favour with Destination Golf, deservedly so as it ranks among the top twelve American golf resorts according to Golf Magazine. The setting overlooking four miles of white sandy beaches, massive dunes and lagoons is spectacular and the 27 holes of golf reflect a remarkable cooperation between man and nature. Local attractions include the restored Victorian resort of Fernandina Beach which dates back some 400 years and now provides visitors with fine shops and restaurants.

A word briefly on another holiday golf option to be found on the Atlantic Coast, some 40 miles north of Palm Beach. Here at St Lucie can be found the Club Med Sandpiper Village which lays great store by the golf facilities it provides and the proximity of two championship courses where all the instruction and practice can hopefully be put to good effect.

On the Gulf of Mexico, the most northerly of the golf resorts featured by tour operators, The Plantation Inn at Crystal River ranks as the most popular selection, with British Airways, Destination Golf, Eagle Golf Tours, Sovereign and Golf International all commending it. The resort lies two hours away from Orlando and is set in a most tranquil area as famous for its fishing as its golf, and there is a casual feel to the resort which sits admirably with the genuine warmth of the hospitality. Watersport facilities are understandably very popular with residents, although differing opinions can be heard from those negotiating the course. All told there are 27 holes here and the championship layout has played host to ladies Tour events. However, the resort is probably best known for its Golf School which has an impressive track record of success.

From this luxury base camp of villas and condominiums, golfers can also tackle a choice selection of other courses such as Glen Lakes and Seville, which both call for precise play, as does Twisted Oaks, a newish course with tighter fairways and smaller greens than most. Rainbow Springs has a mature feel to it and is magnificently maintained, while the style of Citrus Spring has led to comparisons with some of the best golf to be found in Carolina. Slightly more forgiving with a rather open layout is the Lakeside Golf and Country Club and the course is also not unduly long.

To the south and inland from the Gulf coast is the resort of Saddlebrook, which lies only 25 miles north east of the airport at Tampa and remarkably features only with Destination Golf. The resort covers 480 acres of woodland and there is no shortage of water to punctuate the scenic fairways as they wander through the tall pines. The two courses, Saddlebrook and Palmer, were both designed by Arnold Palmer and are designed to bring out the natural ability of every golfer in these most picturesque and enjoyable surroundings.

Accommodation at the resort has been the subject of recent refurbishment, and the hotel rooms and suites are now on a par with most of the top Florida resort complexes. Sporting facilities are varied including fishing, which may be a more acceptable pastime for weary golfers than the jogging trail.

Another of Florida's premier resorts featured only by

Destination Golf is Innisbrook at Tarpon Springs, a 40 minute drive north west of Tampa airport. Like Citrus Springs but in many respects totally unlike Citrus Springs, the golf here has been likened to the style of the Carolinas and is amongst the finest to be found in America, let alone Florida. The 63 hole layout comprises the Copperhead, ranked as the championship course, the Island, which qualifies as one of the top 50 resort courses in the USA, and the Sandpiper, which accounts for the other 27 holes, played in any combination requires a proficient long and short game.

The accommodation at Innisbrook is very much of the deluxe self catering variety with three excellent restaurants on hand if required.

Whole World Destination Travel do provide in their programme an insight into accommodation and golf in Tampa itself. The Holiday Inn and the Quality Suites Hotel in the Busch Gardens area are well situated for both golf and nightlife, which may prove a decisive factor for some golfers. Courses of note include two American-style Scottish links creations at Summerfield and the Links of Lake Bernadette, while those who have come for the target golf will not be disappointed by Hunter's Green, and the Golf Club at Cypress Creek, a leisurely 40 minute drive south, will be enjoyed by high handicappers, providing they are not too ambitious.

Destination Golf also extol the local golf attractions to be found south of Tampa and propose Shorewalk Vacation Villas as an ideal self catering base to explore the 50 or so courses in the Bradenton and Sarasota region. Leisure Link offer an alternative in the Timberwood Vacation Villas which are well situated for courses and local shops, bars and restaurants, and have all the mod. cons. including remote controlled garage doors.

Undoubtedly the pick of the golf resorts in Sarasota is the Longboat Key Club, and Destination Golf are joined by Longmere in recommending the championship course, with water very much to the fore again, and the accommodation which varies from standard hotel rooms to deluxe suites. Longboat Key is considered one of Florida's more sophisticated resorts and there are gourmet restaurants and good shopping to be enjoyed. Longmere also promote the attractions of the Holiday Inn on the Lido beach at Sarasota, which is one of the top hotels in the Holiday Inn group, as well as the delights of Dunedin, a rather quaint resort which is home to the Best Western Jamaica Inn and the exquisite cuisine provided in its Bon Appetit restaurant.

The South Sea Plantation on Captiva Island may only have a 9 hole course but it is one of the most beautiful and challenging in Florida. Golf though, will probably not feature high in the list of priorities for guests here in what is aptly described as "Florida's Tahiti" by Elegant Resorts. Destination Golf also stress the alternative attractions of this luxury resort.

When it comes to the Ritz Carlton in Naples, Elegant Resorts do draw attention to the golf available at Pelican's Nest where mother nature has not been unduly disturbed by Tom Fazio's layout, which features natural forests, marshlands and God-given lakes and rivers.

Destination Golf, British Airways and Whole World Destination Travel all recommend a more traditional style of golf holiday at Naples Beach Hotel and Golf Club which enjoys magnificent views out over the Gulf of Mexico and is well placed for the beach and the shops. Accommodation in the hotel varies from standard to deluxe, and watersports including deep sea fishing can be arranged.

The course dates back to the 1920s but was redesigned at the end of the seventies by Ron Garl, and further work on the layout took place in 1992. The strategic deployment of hazards has over the years conspired to make this one of the more demanding championship courses in Florida.

The last word on Florida goes appropriately enough to Destination Golf who propose the Registry Resort as the ideal base for the neighbouring Pelican's Nest course. While the rooms here are well appointed it is more the spectacular setting of the Registry that has earned the accolades, although there are some who will judge the resort entirely on the strength of Garrett's, the resort's nightclub.

Saddlebrook (*Florida Tourism*)

Golf Arizona

Myrtle Beach, Hilton Head and Florida may well be favourites of British and European golfers, but a 'new kid on the block' is making people sit up and take notice - Arizona.

An average of 306 sunny days a year provide a perfect backdrop for the increasing numbers of golfers travelling to Arizona to experience the wide variety of courses. Indeed, the Phoenix, Tucson and Scottsdale areas are fast becoming recognised as the golfing Mecca of the United States.

Golfers of all ages and abilities can play on a wide variety of courses ranging from the lush oasis setting to the challenging target style courses similar to those found at Kiawah Island in South Carolina.

Famous golf course architects Pete Dye and Robert Trent Jones have displayed some of their best work in Phoenix and Scottsdale, not to mention professional golfers, Jack Nicklaus, Arnold Palmer, & Tom Weiskopf who have also helped build championship courses throughout the aptly named Valley of the Sun.

To complement the near perfect weather and superbly conditioned golf courses are some of the nation's finest resorts. Three properties in the Phoenix and Scottsdale area earned the AAA Five Diamond rating: The Boulders Resort, The Marriot's Camelback Inn and the Scottsdale Princess. Only 40 of the 37,000 AAA inspected sites in the US in 1993 were rated as Five Diamond properties.

This distinction, combined with the beauty of the Sonoran desert, spectacular mountain views, plentiful sunshine and a wealth of championship golf courses, has added to the popularity of this unique state.

There are a variety of other activities for the whole family to enjoy. One of the seven wonders of the world - the Grand Canyon - can be found in the northern part of the state. A four hour drive leads to views and breathtaking panoramas, the like of which cannot be seen anywhere else in the world. Desert jeep tours, balloon rides and horseback riding are just some of the attractions to be enjoyed along with the golf.

It must be noted that with the average daytime temperature rarely dipping below 70° the winter months are, of course, the high season, as golfers try to escape the winter's wrath in other parts of the USA and northern Europe. But now the message is getting out about the terrific advantages and benefits of summer golf in Arizona. Vacationers will find the higher temperatures surprisingly tolerable at this time of year due to the very low levels of humidity and savings over the high season rates make the conditions even more bearable.

Kelken

Kelken Golf Tours offers an open invitation to visit Arizona. With the added advantage of being based in Scottsdale, the local British staff have both expert knowledge of all the world class resorts and championship golf courses in the Valley of the Sun and an understanding of the specific needs of the British golfer.

With June to September being the low season, tourists can take advantage of as much as 70% savings on accommodation and golf. In addition, unlike Florida where afternoon thunderstorms often interrupt the day's golf, the extremely low levels of humidity make Arizona an ideal alternative for the British and European traveller.

The unique target style desert courses are an added attraction, with shots having to carry expanses of natural terrain to reach grassed fairways and island greens. There are however, numerous traditional style golf courses suitable for golfers of all levels.

So for those golfers wanting to experience golf of the highest quality while relaxing in sophisticated and elegantly furnished resorts and hotels, Arizona is waiting to be discovered at a very competitive price.

Arizona

For specifics on the courses, resorts and programmes available to British golfers in Arizona, Kelken have a UK office in Glasgow which can provide details of their operation and assist with reservations and travel arrangements. Golf Inc. are also in a position to select a suitable holiday golf package for interested parties from the Kelken, Whole World Destination Travel and Destination Golf programmes.

Two of the resorts to receive the prestigious Five Diamond rating feature with all the operators, namely The Boulders Resort and The Scottsdale Princess and both offer 36 holes of quality golf.

The Boulders lies 33 miles to the north of Phoenix, close to a village called Carefree in the tranquil beauty of the High Sonoran Desert. Luxury accommodation is provided in adobe style casitas which blend perfectly with the desert surrounds. The golf course was designed by Jay Marrish of Jack Nicklaus' Golforce and in many ways represents a triumph of man over nature, although some would argue that it is the very setting itself which should attract the accolades.

At the Scottsdale Princess, Tom Weiskopf and Jay Marrish collaborated on the two course layout. The TPC Stadium plays host annually to the Phoenix Open and as the name suggests it has been designed with both golfers and spectators in mind. Visiting golfers can also not fail to be impressed by the Desert Course which offers a real test of target golf from tee to green. Equally impressive is the Mexican colonial style architecture of the resort which houses guests in spacious luxuriously appointed rooms.

Whole World Destination Travel and Destination Golf also feature another Scottsdale resort, The Phoenician, which is also very highly rated and adds a touch of European elegance to the desert surrounds. The front nine holes here are more tropical in style than desert, with a lush feel to the fairways and lakes and palm trees, which may be easy on the eye but are hard on the golf. This is another championship rated course, which may also be enjoyed for the spectacular views on the back nine around Camelback Mountain.

Another way of enjoying the golf in Arizona is to participate in Golf Links, Arizona World Pro-Am! This annual tournament is part of a two week programme organised in the Scottsdale area by Golf Links and serves to introduce some other outstanding courses. Competition takes place over the Pine and Palm Courses at McCormick Ranch, which are well suited to the demands of Pro-Am golf, although the programme also includes events at other courses such as a Texan scramble played with members of Karsten Solheim's Moor Valley Club on the superb par 73 course. Optional tournaments take place daily in the warm up to the main event including one on the TPC course and one at Tatum Ranch, another fine desert course and one where golfers can relax slightly and let fly to some rather generous fairways. Few golfers will pass on the Troon North option, which is Jay Marrish and Tom Weiskopf's most internationally acclaimed creation and ranks among the top American courses.

For accommodation, Golf Links use the Valley Ho Resort and the Regal McCormick Ranch itself. Both offer excellent accommodation and facilities, with the Valley Ho's location ideal for those with an inclination to be as close as possible to downtown Scottsdale, while the Ranch enjoys a more scenic and secluded location on the golf complex and is a short drive away from the nightlife.

Bermuda &
The Caribbean

Wyndham Rose Hall (Barclay Sratton)

Six hundred miles off the east coast of America, and one thousand miles to the north of the Caribbean lies Bermuda, an island in the Atlantic with eight golf courses to its 22 square miles. Year on year, the popularity of Bermuda as a holiday golf destination grows and there is certainly no shortage of tour operators to service the increasing demand. Unlike the Caribbean islands, Bermuda's situation leaves it subject to temperatures as low as the low 60s between November and March and, although this is still perfect for golf, visitors should take note that this is officially the off-season.

During the off-season, prices fall but unfortunately certain restaurants and leisure facilities do have to close due to the decline in the number of American tourists visiting the island. No doubt, this will not deter the dedicated golfer.

Given the size of the island, all the courses are easily accessible although not every golfer will be inclined to take the grand tour. Most tour operators opt for programmes including golf and accommodation to the west of the island.

Furthest removed from the airport and the most westerly of the group of four courses favoured by the operators is Port Royal, a Robert Trent Jones design offering spectacular views out over the Atlantic Ocean. This is a long course, magnificently maintained with lush undulating fairways and manicured greens well protected by bunkers.

Port Royal may not enjoy the same international renown as Bermuda's other championship course, Mid Ocean, but it certainly provides an exacting challenge in a most beautiful setting and is far more accessible to visiting golfers than its illustrious rival.

Just five minutes from Port Royal are the Mediterranean style cottages of the Lantana Estate. Featured in the Elegant Resorts programme, this 20 acre estate is as lovingly maintained as the Port Royal course and provides its guests with superb accommodation, first class cuisine and a wide selection of watersports.

The Pampano Beach Club also enjoys an exquisite setting adjacent to the Port Royal course and the delights of this relatively small family run hotel are endorsed by Caribtours and Whole World Destination Travel. There are three standards of accommodation within this hotel but all are spacious, well appointed and afford splendid views out over the Atlantic. The hotel has its own small private beach where guests can enjoy the numerous watersport facilities available.

Slightly removed to the north and set on its own 25 acre peninsula is one of the world's most famous resorts, Cambridge Beaches, whose elegantly furnished cottages and suites are more reminiscent of stately homes than hotel rooms. The main house provides all the charm and sophistication of bygone days with its lounge and library, not to mention the fine timbered bar. The cuisine here is considered the most tempting on the island and can be enjoyed in either informal or formal surroundings. With first class sport and leisure facilities, guests of Cambridge Beaches do not lack for entertainment night or day and discerning golfers will find the resort featured by Silk Cut, Caribtours and Elegant Resorts.

By way of contrast the most economical form of accommodation available to golfers throughout Bermuda are the guest houses, apartments and small hotels which make up Bermuda Small Properties. All rooms are en suite, some have self catering facilities and there are beach properties available. Silk Cut, Caribtours, Whole World Destination Travel and Golf Holidays International all feature these properties, a prime example being the Whale Bay Inn which overlooks Port Royal and the Atlantic Ocean.

Moving east along the coast we find the Southampton Princess, another luxury resort but one which in many ways contrasts sharply with properties such as Lantana and Cambridge Beaches. Not only does it stand six storeys high, affording views of the South Shore to one side and the Atlantic to the other, the whole ambience is much more highly charged with a larger volume of guests availing themselves of the extensive facilities which include seven restaurants and a fitness complex and sports amenities that are on a par with anything else to be found on the island. Silk Cut and Elegant Resorts both feature the Southampton Princess which is also remarkable for its 18 hole par 3 golf course.

This is no pitch and putt course. With the shortest hole over 100 yards and the longest over 200, set amidst palm trees and tropical shrubs, this is a unique challenge in magnificent surroundings.

Also on the South Shore is another of Elegant Resorts' recommendations, The Reefs, where accommodation is perched high on clifftops overlooking the private secluded beach. The Reefs, in keeping with the standards set by the other properties featured by Elegant Resorts, offers luxury accommodation, a high standard of service and cuisine as well as the usual array of leisure facilities, especially watersports.

Other golf in this area includes Riddels Bay on a northern peninsula jutting into the Atlantic. While this course may be one of the shortest on the island, it is very similar in design to many in Florida with narrow fairways and tight greens making for a challenging round, doubly so when the breeze whips up from the Atlantic.

Close by, almost completely surrounded by the waters of Salt Kettle Bay is the Glencoe Harbour Club which comes highly recommended by Caribtours for its fine cuisine, friendly and efficient service and luxuriously appointed rooms.

However, there are many golfers who will look no further for accommodation and recreation than the Belmont Hotel Golf and Country Club, part of the Forte Group and also featured in the programmes of Longshot, Golf International, British Airways, Select World Golf, Whole World Destination Travel and Golf Holidays International. 114 acres of beautifully landscaped grounds provide an admirable setting for the pastel pink buildings of the hotel, whose rooms are all distinguished by their elegant Queen Anne furniture adjacent to the largest swimming pool on Bermuda lies the golf course.

Though again no monster, only some 300 yards longer than Riddels Bay, it poses questions of its own and a fair degree of local knowledge needs to be acquired before a good score will be returned. The problems are mainly associated with the elevated double tiered greens which are often only reached by a blind approach and with some of the greens best described as narrow, golfers really do have to know their way round this scenic parkland course to return a good score.

A particular favourite amongst the tour operators when it comes to suitable accommodation for golf in this area is the Harmony Club at Paget on the south coast where it should be noted there can also be found some of the best Bermuda small properties. Silk Cut, Longshot, Caribtours, Golf International, British Airways, Select World Golf and Whole World Destination Travel all include this sophisticated hotel which does not accept children. Holidays at the Harmony Club are taken on an inclusive basis which adds to the private club atmosphere. Use of all leisure facilities and entry to the entertainment are provided as well as cocktails and house wines as part of an exceptional package.

As for the golf on the eastern half of the island, it is important not to, and highly unlikely that anyone would, mix up the Ocean View and Mid Ocean Golf Clubs. While both boast some very beautiful and challenging holes one has only nine holes and is barely known outside Bermuda. The latter's 18 holes, on the other hand are considered on a par with the best in the world. To play this magnificent course requires an introduction but, in keeping with the spirit of hospitality found on the island this can be arranged more often than not. This may depend, however, upon the influence or contacts of the management at the resort of your choosing, so if a round at Mid Ocean is a must then it would be advisable to check this element out before booking.

A near neighbour of Mid Ocean is Castle Harbour which does not lag very far behind, at least as far as green fees are concerned. This is a Charles Banks and Robert Trent Jones joint venture whose undulating fairways reflect the natural terrain with numerous strategically placed sand traps adding to the degree of difficulty. It would, however, be unfair to imply that average golfers would not derive pleasure from a round at Castle Harbour.

The course is part of the 200 acre Marriot's Castle Harbour complex which boasts a 402 luxury bedroom hotel with views out over Castle Harbour and Harrington Sound as well as the hotel's own tropical gardens and beaches. The choice of restaurants includes a Japanese steak house and there are three bars in which to unwind, a swimming pool and for the more energetic, a tennis court and a health club. The hotel features in the British Airways programme.

More traditional accommodation at this end of the island can be found in the cottages of the Ariel Sands Beach Club which is recommended by Caribtours. The club's situation is most picturesque with green lawns leading down to a white sandy beach. While the range of facilities may not be as extensive as in some resorts, this is still a highly commendable option which is popular with families, and the bright lights of Hamilton are not far away.

Finally, on the eastern tip, a Robert Trent Jones course with a difference. The difference this time being that the layout contains nine par 3s and the score returned will bear more testimony to the elements than to any artificial tinkering with the terrain perpetrated by the great man.

Castle Harbour (Golf Resort Marketing)

The Bahamas

Where the Atlantic Ocean meets the Caribbean Sea, the Bahamas are not as yet a major focal point for the British holiday golfer, but this is not to say that there is no golf to be had on these islands. The Bahamas Princess Resort and Casino boasts two especially fine championship courses, The Emerald and The Ruby, at Freeport on Grand Bahama.

The Emerald, designed by Dick Wilson, has a spectacular par 5 hole in its 532 yard ninth which is probably the best on the island, and typifies the long and accurate play required off the championship tees to the well protected greens if this course is to be mastered.

Water comes much more into play on Joe Lee's Ruby course which is very picturesque with fairways lined by Arrawak pines and approximately 200 other species of flora.

Both courses are maintained in excellent condition the whole year round, and with the magnificent facilities of the Bahamas Princess Hotel on hand, the resort merits serious consideration. Operators such as North America Travel Service and others who specialise in the Caribbean will be able to provide details of a programme including golf at the Bahamas Princess, which with its casino, clubs, bars, restaurants and sports facilities is one of the largest and most celebrated resorts in the Caribbean.

Jamaica

Undoubtedly the island with the highest golfing profile in the Caribbean yet, like Florida, Jamaica has earned an unenviable reputation as a thieves and muggers paradise. While it would be naive to suggest that the capital, Kingston, does not have problems, the resorts and courses are sufficiently removed from the trouble spots for visitors to enjoy the breathtaking beauty and natural hospitality of the people without having to exercise anything other than normal common sense and caution.

Courtesy of the Johnnie Walker World Championship, the course now very much in the spotlight is fittingly one of Jamaica's oldest and most established, Tryall. While the medium of television has brought the course to the living room of millions of golfers around the world, nothing can quite compare with the reality awaiting those teeing off. The famous view from the championship tee, on 18, of water wheel and aqueduct is just one of many stunning backdrops to be found on this former sugar plantation. But appearances can be deceptive, as any golfer who has strayed off line here will confirm, and the murderous rough does not offer any second chances.

Naturally, the Tryall Golf, Tennis and Beach Club is very much in vogue as a holiday golf destination, and the accommodation and facilities here leave nothing to be desired. The Tryall Great House has 52 luxuriously appointed rooms, individually furnished in the old colonial style, as well as some splendid villas dotted throughout the 2200 acre estate. The days and nights are passed in an atmosphere of relaxed informality, with no shortage of entertainment, and golfers with a penchant for watersports will certainly not be disappointed. The resort features in programmes to Jamaica operated by Caribtours, Elegant Resorts, British Airways, Eurogolf and Golf International, and there are numerous options available when it comes to accommodation packages.

Of course, there may be golfers for whom the very idea of jumping too obviously on the Tryall bandwagon may be sheer anathema. These golfers (and any who find Tryall fully booked) will not be disappointed by the resort's near neighbour at Montego Bay, Round Hill. If anything the Round Hill Hotel and Villas is even more elegantly appointed and colonial in style than Tryall, and plays host to a very fashionable clientele. Demand for this property is very heavy, particularly during the winter. Interested parties are always advised to book early and to bear in mind that golf at Tryall is always available but not included in the package prices quoted for Round Hill by Elegant Resorts and Caribtours.

The Montego Bay area is also home to another of Jamaica's exceptional resorts, the Half Moon Beach Club, which boasts a typically spectacular Robert Trent Jones course. The club, which is highly recommended by Elegant Resorts, Select World Golf, Eurogolf and Golf

Tryall *(Barclay Stratton)*

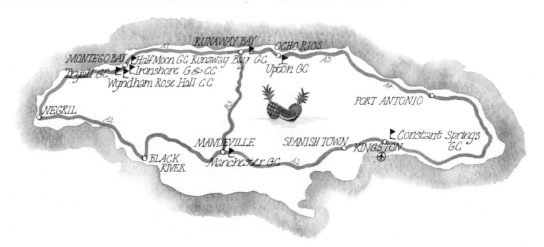

Jamaica

International, enjoys a delightful setting amidst 400 acres of tropical estate, although it is the magnificent crescent shaped beach which for many is the jewel in the resort's crowning attractions. Accommodation options at the Half Moon are numerous, with all manner of rooms, suites and villas to select from. The sports and leisure facilities are no less diverse and equally as impressive, while the cuisine is of the highest standard.

As for the golf, there are those who might argue that Robert Trent Jones could not fail to come up with a masterpiece given the material he had to work with, and the final product definitely does justice to the surroundings. The undulating fairways have a natural feel to them as they follow the subtle contours of the land through hosts of coconut and palm trees. The panoramic ocean views are as spectacular as from Tryall and the rough is equally dangerous.

Golfing couples, of the mixed foursome variety, may care to take note of the various Sandals resorts on Jamaica, all of which include golf at the Sandals-Upton course in their inclusive packages for couples only. Guests of Sandals do not want for anything when it comes to luxury accommodation, entertainment, sports and leisure facilities, and the golf course 2 miles out of Ocho Rios and set 700 feet above sea level is a veritable green and pleasant land with stately trees and dramatic views out to sea.

The two closest Sandals properties to the course are Sandals Ocho Rios and Sandals Dunn's River, and the clubhouse doubles as a gourmet restaurant for residents of the Ocho Rios Complex, whose facilities are also easily accessed from Dunn's River. Sandals resort holidays can also be booked through operators such as Caribtours, and British Airways feature Dunn's River in their golf programme.

Equally well placed to enjoy the golf at Sandals-Upton are those literally carefree guests of the Sans Souci. Another of Elegant Resorts' highly commended properties, the Sans Souci impresses on many fronts, not the least of which is the impressive facade of this spa hotel. A total air of relaxation pervades the atmosphere of this luxury resort with no irritating engine buzz from waterskiers offshore to disturb the peace and quiet.

British Airways includes a much more golf orientated programme out of Jamaica Jamaica, a good quality hotel with well appointed rooms. The inclusive package extends way beyond free golf at the Runaway Bay golf course, covering tennis, watersports, horseriding and much much more. Golfers can also take advantage of free lessons every day from the club's qualified teaching professionals, Monday through Friday, and the video camera is always on hand to monitor progress.

Runaway Bay itself is another of Jamaica's championship courses, the creation of the British naval commander James D Harris, and is renowned for its sand traps. Presumably the naval commander chose to steer clear of water.

A final word on Wyndham Rose Hall, a course which visitors to Jamaica should make an effort to play. Lying just to the east of Montego Bay, the 18 holes follow an imaginative design around the historic estate and contain one of golf's more celebrated holes in the par 4, eighth hole, "Chinaman's Reef".

The Cayman Islands

The very mention of the Cayman Islands conjures up pictures of waving palm trees, mile upon mile of sandy beaches, blue seas and colourful reefs. But the Cayman Islands as home to a true test of championship golf? Surely not. After all this is the home of the Cayman ball.

While the Britannia Golf Club still thrives at the Hyatt Regency where the unique concept of a three in one course designed by Jack Nicklaus used to be the only golf on the island, 1994 has seen the opening of a genuine championship test of golf in the links at Stonehaven. And not without something of a struggle, as a great deal of technical ingenuity went into literally growing the course on this 280 acre estate and some 5 million gallons of desalinated water are required each month to maintain its immaculate condition. Know then that the water hazards are not just for show.

But it is not just water posing questions at Stonehaven Links. The name given to the course reflects the nature of the challenge which is dominated by the prevailing sea breezes, first helping then hindering. The design is very much in keeping with the traditions of links golf, lush rolling fairways following the natural terrain and some large but undulating greens. Some 4000 trees indigenous to the Cayman Islands adorn the course, including mahogany, mahoe and coconut palms with a liberal sprinkling of tropical plants, so this is most definitely a Caribbean version of links golf, but one which can be enjoyed by all golfers with a choice of five different tee boxes.

The Stonehaven complex has all the usual practice facilities

AFTER PLAYING OUR NEW CHAMPIONSHIP COURSE YOU COULD END UP UNDER WATER

The Links at SafeHaven, a brand new 18–hole par 71 championship course, is the latest pride and joy of the Cayman Islands. 6,525 yards long, it is reminiscent of a traditional Scottish links layout, except for the weather!

Indeed this golfer's paradise is fringed by a turquoise sea and typically bathed in Caribbean sunshine. Exotic tropical plants adorn the fairways and the lush greens are built to the most stringent USGA standards. While lakes and warm trade winds present their own special challenge.

Equally irresistible to beginners and experts alike is Grand Cayman's first golf course, the Britannia.

Architected by the maestro himself, Jack Nicklaus, it can be played in three ways: as a 9–hole championship course, as an 18–hole executive course and as an 18–hole Cayman Ball course. In fact it is the first course in the world designed for this revolutionary ball, which flies half the distance.

But quite apart from world class golf, this friendly British Crown Colony in the Caribbean offers world class diving - with instruction for all levels.

Swim with the turtles. Commune with the friendly Stingrays at the world's best 12ft. dive.

Or stretch out under a nodding palm tree on the powder white sand of Seven Mile Beach. There are fine hotels, apartments, guest houses and restaurants for dining out under the stars.

And Cayman Airways fly there direct from Miami in just 70 minutes.

To find out more about golf and other exciting activities where the weather won't handicap you, contact us now.

BROCHURE HOTLINE
071-581 9960

Cayman Islands Department of Tourism.
Trevor House, 100 Brompton Road, Knightsbridge, London SW3 1EX
Telephone 071-581 9960 · Fax 071-584 4463

CAYMAN ISLANDS

including a driving range with a difference. Land being at something of a premium, golfers use floating range balls to fire at targets in one of the lakes.

It is planned that the resort will ultimately comprise a 350 room hotel, and 600 condominiums with extensive sport and leisure facilities including a marina. The first phase of condominiums was completed before the course opened, but golfers planning a holiday will for the time being have to look around for hotel accommodation.

Not that this should prove too difficult given the course's location on Seven Mile Beach, where most of the island's prestigious hotel and apartment complexes are to be found. The major golf hotel, of course, continues to be the Hyatt Regency, which is unquestionably the most complete resort in the Cayman Islands. It is featured by Elegant Resorts, North America Travel Service and Thomas Cook, all of whom can be prevailed upon to offer a golfing programme. The accommodation at the Hyatt is set in a series of low rise colonial style buildings and there is a wide variety of luxuriously appointed rooms to select from, excellent water sport facilities to enjoy and fine cuisine to savour.

Elegant Resorts also feature The Colonial Club with its magnificent ocean-front apartments which include everything and the kitchen sink, while the sport and leisure facilities are a match for any on the island. North America Travel Service recommend the modern spacious apartments of the Britannia Villas complex which is surrounded by the Britannia course, while Thomas Cook promote the Holiday Inn, a near neighbour of the Stonehaven complex and one of the most lively hotels on the island featuring an English Pub. The Safehaven Apartments themselves are well appointed and enjoy a pleasant setting in landscaped gardens with a swimming pool.

There are more than 20 properties to be commended in the Seven Mile Beach area, and now that Stonehaven is up and running it is to be expected that many if not all will have an arrangement at the course for their guests. This can be easily determined by checking with the numerous general tour operators who feature the Cayman Islands or by contacting specialists such as Golf Inc. for a tailormade holiday.

Antigua St Kitts and Nevis

Antigua falls very much into the fun category when it comes to golf. It is a shame the game is not taken more seriously in these parts and one can only bemoan the fact that such gifted athletes as Ritchie Richardson and Curtley Ambrose have been obliged to divert their talents into cricket.

Nevertheless the island does boast one 18 hole and one 9 hole course, and its situation is ideal for golf on St Kitts and Nevis. Viewed from this perspective Antigua could be the base for an island hopping Caribbean golf holiday with a difference.

Elegant Resorts rate Curtain Bluff in Antigua as one of their top three featured properties in the whole of the Caribbean and it is easy to understand why. From the setting itself to the decor and furnishings, everything about the resort exudes class and guests are similarly expected to follow dress codes. The resort is a sportsman's paradise, so much so that 18 holes at the Cedar Valley Golf Club may suffer by comparison with other leisure facilities.

Caribtours promote another course bearing the Half Moon name, only a 9 hole course but testing nevertheless and with some spectacular views. At the Half Moon Bay Club the golf is part of an impressive range of sporting facilities located on the 150 acre estate, and guests will also be impressed by the idyllic setting above a long crescent shaped sandy beach. Accommodation is in spacious well appointed rooms and the hotel provides a variety of entertainment for guests in the evenings, when jacket and tie are considered appropriate for the restaurant.

St Kitts

A volcanic island with dark sandy beaches, and tropical vegetation. The pace of life may be slow but things can be positively lively here compared with some of the neighbouring islands. Eurogolf and Golf International fea-

Stonehaven *(The Cayman Islands)*

ture the Jack Tarr Village on the eastern coast, where the rooms of this luxury resort overlook Lake Zuliani and the estate's own magnificent gardens as well as the championship rated course of St Kitts. This is golf at its most picturesque with views from the course over the Atlantic to the north and the Caribbean to the south and seven lakes in play.

Other watersports available include scuba diving which will always come in handy for retrieving lost balls. The resort has plenty of activities and entertainment to keep guests diverted on this quiet island, and the fashionable casino is well frequented.

Quiet sophistication is more the order of the day at The Golden Lemon, where golf can be arranged for those who tire of doing nothing all day. This is one of the smaller hotels featured by Elegant Resorts with an atmosphere all of its own and a typically tropical setting.

Nevis

If neither Antigua nor St Kitts fits the bill as the ideal base for a golf oriented holiday in these parts, then the long white sandy beaches, the championship Robert Trent Jones course, and the celebrated Four Seasons resort will certainly tip the scales in Nevis' favour.

Featured by Elegant Resorts, Eurogolf and Golf International, the Four Seasons ranks as one of the Caribbean's premier resorts and boasts some rather august patrons, including royalty. The golf course is in keeping with the high standards of the hotel itself, with the added bonus of being able to claim justifiably that some of its holes are as impressive as the surrounding scenery. The lush fairways and towering palms of the course surround the hotel on three sides, with the sands of Pinney's Beach on the fourth. This stretch of the coast enjoys a sheltered location and watersports facilities here are amongst the best and most impressive in the Caribbean. The same can be said of the accommodation. Each room or suite has its own large veranda, and there are also cottages available in the grounds of the 350 acre estate. Central to all activities is the Great House, which houses two gourmet restaurants behind the magnificent old plantation style facade.

Renowned for its own plantation style charm is the Nisbet Plantation, which comes highly commended by Elegant Resorts as an alternative to the Four Seasons for golfers who prefer something approaching more the ambience of a country house. Accommodation is in cottages around the estate and the Great House here dates back to the 18th century. While the Nisbet Plantation may be smaller, guests lack for nothing in terms of facilities and can enjoy their own half mile stretch of pristine white sand beach.

Martinique

The experience of playing the excellent Robert Trent Jones Golf de la Martinique course is one that all P & O golf theme cruise participants should definitely enjoy. Also any golfers planning a Club Med holiday at Les Boucaniers on this island would be well advised to remember their clubs.

The golf course has a marvellous green feel to it, with palm trees sprinkled all around, and the often elevated greens are well protected by bunkers. There is also no shortage of water to add to both the magnificence of the setting and the difficulty of the golf, with inland lakes, a river and the sea all coming into play, most noticeably over the closing holes. The fifteenth is a par 3 played dramatically out to sea, while on the par 5 sixteenth golfers play from the tee to an island fairway. Each hole on this course presents an exhilarating challenge and the clubhouse is a suitably magnificent place to retire for a well earned drink.

Accommodation on Martinique in the Port de France area comes in the form of luxury hotels all very closely situated to the club and linked by courtesy shuttle minibus. The Bakoua-Sofitel comes very highly commended as a favourite with golfers visiting the island, and Golf Inc can be relied upon to provide advice on a suitable package to this paradise in the Caribbean.

St Lucia

Another Caribbean island to exhibit considerable French influences, but where English is spoken, St Lucia is one of the most spectacular with its dense tropical jungles and towering Pitons. The island may only boast one 9 hole course at Sandals La Toc, but the course is set in some of the most picturesque surroundings on this island and by definition in the whole of the Caribbean. The course may not win many prizes for design but the tree-lined fairways have a challenging par of 32 and the golf here is an integral part of the island's magnificent portfolio of sports and leisure amenities.

Golf de la Martinique

Set in the beautiful, natural bay of Fort-de-France, Golf de la Martinique was conceived in 1976 and designed by the famous golf architect Robert Trent Jones. It is steeped in history, being situated on land once owned by the parents of the Empress Joséphine, wife of Napoléon Bonaparte, and there is a museum close by which chronicles her incredible life.

Nothing has been left to chance in this truly unique location - rivers, trees, bunkers and other such hazards have been skilfully employed in the creation of a challenging 18 hole course. Golf de la Martinique offers golfers an exciting and fulfilling game on one of the most beautiful courses in the Caribbean. Once played it will never be forgotten. At the pro shop, visiting golfers can buy or rent from a selection of the latest in golf club technology. Practice facilities within the grounds of this luxurious country club include a 250 metre driving range, sand traps and a putting green.

After a round of golf, or a game of tennis on one of three courts, guests can relax on the terrace of the bar-restaurant in the clubhouse. Hotels such as the Méridien, Bakoua-Sofitel, PLM Azur and Pagerie are situated close by and the club provides a courtesy minibus shuttle service for all resident golfers.

Golf de la Martinique 97229
Trois-Ilets Martinique
Tel: (010 596) 68 32 81
Fax: (010 596) 683897

Couples may enjoy the Sandals resort itself which is the latest addition to the group's properties in the Caribbean, and thrives on the same winning formula of rest and recreation in luxurious surroundings.

British Airways, Silk Cut and Caribtours all feature the Sandals resort in their programmes to the Caribbean, but Silk Cut and Caribtours have alternative accommodation on offer at Le Sport and Windjammer Landing. Both resorts offer packages inclusive of golf at Sandals, in addition to their own sporting facilities.

Le Sport is a concept resort where the goal is to help guests reach peak mental and physical condition through relaxation, health and beauty treatments, and plenty of sporting activity. The all-inclusive nature of the programme takes away the immediate burden of carrying cash around the resort as guests simply don't need it and the facilities provided for guests in active pursuit of this fitness ideal cannot be faulted.

Windjammer Landing, unlike Le Sport, is well set up to cater for children, and though it has many fine leisure facilities available to guests, there is a relaxed "take it or leave it" atmosphere which sums up the spirit of freedom here. Accommodation in the villas and suites dotted around the 55 acre hillside estate is to a very high standard and the resort has a village feel with a central bar and restaurant area.

Barbados

P&O golf theme cruisers on the Canberra who took advantage of the opportunity to play Golf de la Martinique are equally advised not to miss out on a round at Sandy Lane, one of the Caribbean's premier courses and another to spring from an old sugar plantation.

The eighteen holes wend their way through a bravura display of tropical flora and fauna, and the first nine are played through the Sandy Lane estate itself where some of the most beautiful mansions on the island are to be found. While the par 3 seventh requires a controlled shot to a green set some 80 feet below the tee box, it is on the back nine played over higher ground where the undulating terrain does come into play, although good position from the tees is not that difficult to find. By far the most memorable aspect of the back nine though will be the magnificent views over the countryside and the Caribbean.

Forte consider their Sandy Lane Hotel and Golf Course to be the Caribbean's finest resort and there are many who will agree. Tour operators offering their services to golfers interested in Sandy Lane are almost too numerous to mention with Silk Cut, Caribtours, Eurogolf, Golf International, Elegant Resorts, British Airways and Select World Golf all in on the act.

Suffice it to say that the accommodation comprising 91 rooms and 30 suites can only be described as deluxe, the facilities are outstanding, and the service first class at this hotel which stands amidst lush tropical gardens on a glorious stretch of white sandy beach in its own 380 acre estate.

It is in many ways almost churlish to suggest alternative accommodation, but then again Sandy Lane is very popular in the winter months. Elegant Resorts and Silk Cut offer some very fine properties, including Glitter Bay and its sister hotel the Royal Pavilion, which are both outstanding in terms of accommodation and the range of sport and leisure facilities provided for guests. Another of their recommendations, the Sandpiper Inn is less than a mile away from Sandy Lane and inspires a devoted following amongst those who have enjoyed the privilege of staying there, which in itself is a tribute to the management, service and generally magnificent standards of this small hotel.

Sandy Lane *(Barbados)*

LONGSHOT

LE TOUQUET • NORMANDY • BRITTANY • BORDEAUX

GOLF ™

PARIS • LOIRE • VENDEE • BIARRITZ • LANGUEDOC

HOLIDAYS

PROVENCE • COTE D'AZUR • RHONE • ALPS

IN

FRANCE

1994 • 1995

P&O European Ferries

AIR FRANCE

Le Grand Golf

France

Barbaroux *(Golf Resort Marketing)*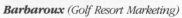

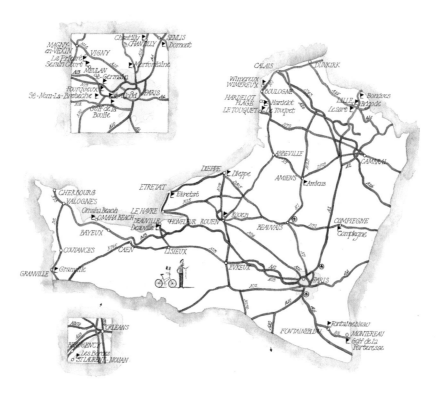

Pas de Calais

It is perhaps no coincidence that this, the most accessible region of France for the British golfer, is also considered by many to hold some of the finest French courses.

The two at Le Touquet, namely La Mer and La Foret, certainly do rank with the best, with La Mer a links course of championship standard, and La Foret a slightly less demanding and shorter course which meanders through picturesque woodland.

Le Touquet features in the programmes of all the tour operators offering packages to golfers after more than just a day trip to Boulogne. The accommodation included in this resort is, like the golf, of a very high standard and Le Manoir is one hotel which has for many years catered exceptionally well for both the sporting and gastronomic tastes of its guests. Equally as popular with the tour operators is the Hotel Westminster, a four star hotel with excellent facilities, as is the new Grand Hotel featured by BDH, Leisure Link and French Golf Holidays. These latter two operators along with Homecavern also recommend the three star Hotel Le Bristol for its comfort, charm and friendly staff. Another four star hotel worth noting is the Picardy - a modern sporting development, which comes highly recommended by Eurogolf as well as Leisure Link and Homecavern. Accommodation worth noting of two star rating can be found at the Red Fox and Openfield hotels, although most of the operators covering this area have a selection to suit any budget.

Slightly north of Le Touquet, lies Hardelot with its Les Pins and Les Dunes courses, each with their own clubhouse, and each worthy of comparison with the challenges at Le Touquet. Les Pins has noticeable similarities to The Berkshire, sharing as it does the same designer in Tom Simpson. Les Dunes, despite the name is also a parkland course, albeit a very hilly one, and in the opinion of

some will one day surpass its elder brother in reputation.

While many will be tempted to make base camp for the whole area at Le Touquet, there is an excellent alternative on the courses at Hardelot in the Hotel du Parc, which is featured by most operators to the region.

Further north still is the typically testing links course at Wimereux where the prevailing wind dictates playing conditions. For those inclined to take cover at the first hint of a channel breeze, a trip inland to St Omer may be the answer. This is, however, no easy option covering undulating terrain with a challenge worthy of any great golf course in its last four holes.

As for accommodation in these parts, there is a wide variety from which to choose. In Wimereux itself, Homecavern and French Golf Holidays both recommend the two star Hotel Paul et Virginie. However, further inland there are some fine chateaux to be found in the Cresta programme, namely the Chateau Tilques and Chateau de Cocove, classics of their kind, while French Golf Holidays offer the Hotel-Chateau Clery at Hesdin L'Abbe.

A word, finally, on two other courses to consider if planning a prolonged stay in the region, or fresh fields for the seasoned campaigner. The Belle Dune links course south of Le Touquet is particularly recommended by Cresta. They also include nearby Golf Nampont St. Martin in their programme, an enjoyable test in very pleasant surroundings with a 15th century clubhouse, and this course is also featured by Eurogolf and Homecavern.

Chantilly, Versailles, Paris

Although there are some quite exceptional courses and magnificent chateaux-hotels to be found in this area, it is not one serviced by a large number of tour operators. The widest selection can be found in the Longshot and

French Golf Holidays/Play & Stay programmes which feature in Chantilly Vineuil a perfect parkland course rated as one of the best in Europe. The sister course, Chantilly Longeres, also boasts some fine holes and the nearby Domaine de Chantilly with its water hazards and wooded surrounds is equally demanding. Recommended accommodation includes the four star Golf Hotel de Chantilly, on the Domaine course and the purpose built Hotel du Griffon which overlooks its own 18 hole course. Magnificent chateaux-hotels at Gouvieux and Bazincourt-Sur-Epte feature in the French Golf Holidays programme. Other recommended courses include the two at Le Prieure, the recently designed John Jacobs course at Apremont and the manicured splendour of Rebetz.

Eurogolf also offer a programme including the Golf Hotel de Chantilly and surrounding courses and, like all operators promoting the Golf Nationale west of Paris, they extol the attractions of Yvelines and the two courses at La Vaucouleurs with their tree-lined fairways.

BDH, Leisure Link and A Golfing Experience also include the Golf National in their programmes. The L'Albatros course at just over 7000 yards is the venue for the French Open, and the many water hazards make for a round which demands consistently good shot making. The second course, L'Aigle, is shorter and certainly more 'fun'.

The three star Novotel San Quentin is favoured by Longshot, Eurogolf, BDH and A Golfing Experience, and this modern hotel is ideally situated on the course. However, for those enamoured of the more classical tradition of French accommodation, Hotel Abbaye des Vaux de Cernay is four star refinement featured by French Golf Holidays and Leisure Link, while Longshot commend the prestigious Trianon Palace.

Normandy

There are many who consider that Normandy has in Deauville and Omaha Beach courses to match the standards set up the coast at Le Touquet and Hardelot. Yet it is a third course, Golf Champs de la Bataille which is presently rated as the Number One course in Normandy. Set in the grounds of a magnificent Louis XIV chateau south of Rouen, it is well off the beaten golfing track but found in most tour operators' programmes. A slightly mundane opening hole leads to some of the most spectacular golf holes to be found in France, and unquestionably the most beautiful natural surroundings.

Rouen makes as good a base as any for those golfers keen to play Champs de la Bataille and then head off towards Chantilly and Paris. One local hotel for golfers to consider is the Hotel Mercure Champs de Mars in Rouen from the Eurogolf and French Golf Holiday programmes, with more golf to be enjoyed just north of the city at the Mont St Aignan Club where there are some difficult holes to be negotiated on this well established hilly course.

The attractions of Normandy for most golfers though are to be found on or near the coast, and Deauville is the pick of the resorts. The original 18 holes here are another Tom Simpson parkland creation from 1929, while a further nine were added in the 1960s courtesy of Henry Cotton. Although Deauville is not memorable for its length, tight fairways and well bunkered greens call for accurate shot making on the exceptionally well maintained course. The views from the course out over Deauville and Trouville are magnificent, and these two resorts are popular holiday destinations in their own right.

Justifiably popular with tour operators and golfers alike is the four star Hotel du Golf, Deauville, which elegantly complements its golfing surroundings and is matched in quality only by the Hotel Royal and Hotel Normandy. For those seeking slightly less refinement there is still excellent value to be had in the area, at the Orion Apartments featured by Touralp and Cresta. The latter also has good three star accommodation at P&V Hotel le Beach, Trouville where French Golf Holidays also recommend the Hotel Mercure.

The other course on the coast where golfers, critics and tour operators are united in their approbation is the Omaha Beach. The course comprises three loops of nine holes, each of individual character. La Mer is considered the most spectacular offering the best views out over the D Day beaches, La Bocage runs through the valley and groves of apple trees, while L'Etag is renowned for its water hazards.

Omaha Beach is about an hours drive from Deauville and accommodation is not as plentiful, although there is an excellent three star golf hotel at the centre of the complex which is featured by effectively all the tour operators servicing this area.

Golfers looking to explore more of Normandy's golfing attractions are well served by the tour operators, and comprehensive programmes have been put together by Longshot, BDH, Eurogolf and Brittany Ferries. Others, slightly more selective in their choices, include A Golfing Experience, French Golf Holidays and Cresta, while the likes of Leisure Link and Select World Golf concentrate on the big three courses.

There are certainly many others well worth playing. Etretat, a links course perched on a cliff top is one of the more spectacular and the Golf Hotel Dormy House there is recommended by Eurogolf.

Around Caen, where the three star Hotel Friendly lives up to its name according to BDH and Brittany Ferries, there are two inland courses to note, Golf de Clecy and Golf de Caen, as well as the links course Cabourg-Le Home.

Closer to Deauville are the recently developed courses at St Gatien and St Julien which come into the "well worth a visit" category if only for the clubhouse at the latter. Golf d'Amiraute, designed by a Scotsman in American style, is often compared favourably to the Golf Nationale and has a modern three star hotel close by also known as L'Amiraute, which is highly recommended by French Golf Holidays and Eurogolf.

Le Golf (Golf Resort Marketing)

Situated on the heights of Mont Canisy, in the middle of the vast green expanse of the golf course, the Hotel du Golf dominates the Touques valley and the Seine estuary, the sea and Deauville's famous beaches. Where does the expression "green baize" come from - from the casino or from the Hotel du Golf!

A resort hotel with all the essential elements to make your stay unforgettable: 175 rooms, ten of which are suites, are fully equipped.

For active guests, nothing has been forgotten: 27 golf holes, a practice ground and putting green, a private swimming pool, two tennis courts, sauna, fitness gym and a fun park for children.

It is a combination of luxury, rest and relaxation. A paradise for golfers and for those who enjoy the good life.

Needless to say, fine cuisine has not been overlooked either. From your table in the restaurant 'La Pommerai', you can enjoy the finest view in Deauville. Lunch at the hotel is served in the clubhouse and at the poolside barbecue.

You can even work in the twelve seminar rooms.

But the Hotel du Golf is also in Deauville, with its casino and many other attractions and special events.

Choose a 'Golf Getaway' or any other type of holiday and take full advantage of all of these facilities and services.

Stay and play in a haven of peace, a dream image in a cameo of Impressionist greens.

The Hotel du Golf has a soul. Come and discover it for yourself.

INFORMATION AND BOOKING: (010 33) 31 88 19 01

LUCIEN BARRIERE
Resorts, Hôtels & Casinos
Deauville · Trouville

HOTEL DU GOLF

Brittany

If there is one area of France which British tour operators service well, then this is it. As can be divined from the names of companies such as Brittany Fairways and BDH (Brittany Direct Holidays), not to mention Brittany Ferries, there are specialists to consult whose very involvement in the golf industry stems from the attractions of this area.

In many respects the inland course and club at La Freslonniere near Rennes typifies the high standard of golf, excellent facilities and fine cuisine awaiting the golfer visiting Brittany, yet like Champ de la Bataille it is set inland and away from the more obvious seaside resorts. Nevertheless this excellent course, carved from woodland and with more than its fair share of water hazards, features in most tour programmes. Other courses of merit in this area include the Golf de Rennes St Jacques, Golf de Cice Blossac and the Golf des Rochers. Eurogolf recommend the converted water mill, Ar Milin at Chateaubourg as an ideal base for golfers visiting this region, although in Rennes itself there is plenty of excellent accommodation to be found.

For most golfers, though, these courses will be played as an excursion south from the delights of St Malo, Dinard and Dinan. Of the many courses in this region,

the Golf Club des Ormes has over the years become the most popular. A classic parklands course in the grounds of a 16th century chateau, it wends its way through woods and lakes and is a most attractive challenge. The golf here, as one would expect, features in nearly every tour operator's programme and the majority plump not surprisingly for the Golf Hotel des Ormes as the most suitable accommodation nearby. As an alternative to this modern, well appointed creation there exists the Hostellerie Abbatiale, Le Tronchet, an abbey dating back to the 16th century which stands on the banks of Lake Mirloup and is deservedly featured by Brittany Ferries, Leisure Link, Eurogolf and BDH.

The abbey stands on Le Tronchet course, one of the better new courses and is almost as popular with tour operators as Des Ormes itself.

For a testing piece of links golf, the course at Dinard is the one to try, with views as breathtaking as the prevailing wind which gives this rather short course its bite. An elegant place to recuperate from the experience is the four star Grand Hotel in Dinard which needs no further recommendation and features in the Longshot, Cresta and French Golf Holidays programmes. Alternatives of note, namely the De la Digue in St Malo and the D'Avagour in Dinan can be found in the Cresta and French Golf

Holiday programmes respectively.

West of Dinard can be found some enjoyable but less demanding golf along the coast that will suit players of all abilities, especially those reduced to enjoying the views. From the Club des Sables D'or along to St Samson and Brest-Iroise is a journey well worth the effort and Brittany Ferries, BDH and Eurogolf have tours to suit, although again most operators can be prevailed upon to put a suitable package together.

Golf de L'Odet is arguably the prettiest course in South Brittany and the next to feature strongly in tour operators' programmes. Considerable amounts of money have been spent improving the course and it is now a fair test for high and low handicappers alike, not forgetting the resident British professional. There is a good quality Hostellerie Abbatialle close by at Benodet, featured by Brittany Ferries, BDH and Eurogolf, but those golfers preferring a more central base in this region may prefer to stay further south closer to the three most highly rated courses, Golf de St Laurent, Golf Le Val Queven and Golf de Baden.

Golf de St Laurent has played host to numerous French amateur and professional championships and the long tree-lined fairways with water hazards and strategically placed bunkers do not disappoint. There are those who would claim, however, that the number one course is now Val Queven, which despite its relative youth, has the best greens in the region and requires accurate, and often courageous, shot making. While Golf de Baden has its fair share of taxing holes, the picturesque setting and relative ease of this course by comparison has ensured its popularity with visiting golfers.

A firm favourite in the hotel stakes here is the Hotel Fairway, a three star hotel right on the St Laurent course featured by nearly all the major tour operators, many of whom believe it merits four star status if only for the excellent cuisine. Just a few hundred yards away from the hotel can be found the excellent Maeva Cottages, a collection of one and two room studio apartments favoured by Longshot, Cresta, Eurogolf and Brittany Fairways. While Brittany Fairways do include many first rate hotels in their programme, they are also recognised as specialists in the "cottage" field and deservedly so.

By way of contrast mention must be made of the Chateau de Locguenole, a four star hotel with a Michelin rosette featured in the Longshot and Cresta programmes, close to Val Queven, St Laurent and one of France's shorter championship courses, Golf Ploemeur Ocean.

Brittany Ferries and BDH both recommend the Hostellerie Abbatiale, Le Bono, an old Breton priory now a three star hotel overlooking the Baden course and well situated for Golf de Rhuys Kerver, which is renowned for its impenetrable gorse thickets but is nevertheless an enjoyable collection of 18 holes.

Brittany Fairways

Brittany has always held an enchantment for the British holiday maker. The similarities with the West Country and Celtic culture are very evident. However, in the last decade the creation of some 20 new courses has given a new treat to the discerning golfer. Distant enough to avoid the sporadic congestion experienced at those destinations a short hop from the busy Dover-Calais route, yet convenient enough to spend a few days or longer of unhurried golf on quality courses ranging from classic links, clifftop, downland and tight parkland designs, there exists an array of spectacular and imaginative modern creations, often built in the grounds of historic chateaux.

Brittany Fairways have access to a wide range of courses and accommodation ranging from the elegant Chateau de Locguenolé bordering the Gulf of Morbihan, the four star hotels of La Baule, fairway cottages on the course at St Laurent Golf Club at the heart of southern Brittany's golf pass, to rural gîtes and chambres d'hôte, offering a taste of real France and local cuisine. Who can resist a relaxed evening of regional French cuisine as the perfect conclu-

sion to a great day's golf?

Whatever your requirement in French golf, be it a weekend away, society or group visit or corporate entertaining, Brittany Fairways will match your needs to the best suited destination with integrity and first hand local knowledge. For fully inclusive packages and tailormade itineraries, please contact:

**Brittany Fairways
Summer Lane
Beaulieu
Hants
SO42 7YS
Tel & Fax: (0590) 612575**

Western Loire

Leaving Brittany for what passes as Western Loire the first course encountered is possibly France's most famous golfing landmark and certainly the course most British golfers would instantly recognise as French. Golf de la Bretesche is built around the imposing lines of a 14th century chateau, whose majesty has adorned the pages of many a golfing guide. As a test of golf the course does not disappoint with accuracy called for from tee to tree lined fairways, culminating in an unforgettable tour de force around the chateau and lake.

As the perfect partner for this golfing experience, most operators plump for the four star Manoir Rodoir at La Roche Bernard, a newly renovated mill owned and managed by the former Somerset County cricketer, Philip Slocombe. Cresta and Eurogolf also feature the cottages in the grounds of the 250 acre La Bretesche estate where peace and quiet reign supreme.

Just south of La Bretesche lie two more popular French courses in Golf de la Baule and Golf de la Sauvenay.

La Baule is rated as one of the best courses designed by Peter Alliss and Dave Thomas. The first nine holes are set amongst chestnut and oak trees, while the second nine follow the valley's undulations around the almost obligatory lake. With nine new holes due for completion in 1994 and a Jack Nicklaus Academy with excellent facilities, the La Baule complex is now one of the largest in France.

While most tour operators settle for the four star Hotel Royal in La Baule with all its traditional elegance and beautiful furnishings, Eurogolf offer a couple of alternatives equally hard to fault in the four star Hermitage and Castel Marie Louise, both situated on the sea front at La Baule, the latter also featuring with Longshot.

Golf de Sauvenay is a more recent development and typically spectacular, wandering over parkland through chestnut woods and presenting a series of interesting and varied challenges, so much so that it has risen rapidly in the estimation of many golfers.

Ranked alongside de Sauvenay and a touch further down the coast is the Golf Club St Jean de Monts occupying an impressive piece of headland with an opening hole which is definitely not for the faint hearted. The quality of the links challenge here is matched by the testing parkland course inland at Golf de la Domangere and these are just two of a number of courses featured by major tour operators in the area.

Leisure Link, Eurogolf and BDH all recommend the Hotel Altea Le Sloi, a modern three star hotel close to the St Jean de Monts course and well placed too for Golf Des Fontenelles set in scenic green countryside with a plethora of water hazards. Not surprisingly the Hotel du Golf La Domangere is also recommended by these operators as well as Longshot and this converted 15th century manor house is an exceptional three star hotel.

Those golfers tempted by the well maintained American style golf available at Port Bourgenay may prefer to select the hotel there as recommended by Longshot, Brittany Ferries and Cresta. The latter along with Touralp also promote P&V Club Apartments in Bourgenay.

La Bretesche (*Golf Resort Marketing*)

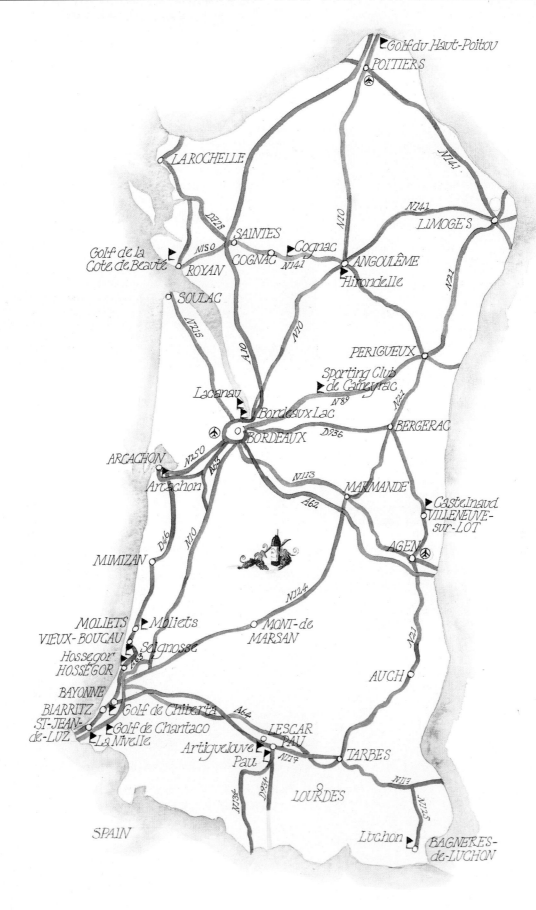

Golf du Haut-Poitou

POITIERS

LA ROCHELLE

N141

N141

LIMOGES

N70

D728

N150

SAINTES

Cognac

Golf de la
Cote de Beauté

COGNAC

N141

ANGOULÊME

N21

ROYAN

Hirondelle

SOULAC

N215

N70

PERIGUEUX

N10

Sporting Club
de Cameyrac

N21

Lacanau

N89

Bordeaux Lac

BERGERAC

N250

BORDEAUX

D936

ARCACHON

A63

Arcachon

N113

MARMANDE

Castelnaud

A62

VILLENEUVE-
sur-LOT

D46

N10

AGEN

MIMIZAN

N124

MOLIETS

Moliets

MONT-de
MARSAN

N21

VIEUX-BOUCAU

Soignosse

Hossegor

A63

HOSSÉGOR

AUCH

BAYONNE

BIARRITZ

A64

Golf de Chiberta

ST-JEAN-
de-LUZ

Golf de Chantaco

LESCAR
PAU

La Nivelle

Artiguelouve
Pau

N117

TARBES

N134

D934

LOURDES

N113

N125

SPAIN

Luchon

BAGNERES-
de-LUCHON

The Loire

Home to one of France's best and most exclusive clubs, Les Bordes, owned by the Baron Bic, is immaculately maintained and has all the features expected of a true championship course. While Eurogolf and Longshot offer accommodation at Les Bordes on the course itself, French Golf Holidays suggest day trips from their selection of magnificent magnificent chateaux-hotels which lie amongst the courses of Sept-Tours Ardée and Touraine.

The fairytale Chateau Golf Hotel Des Sept Tours and the course itself are in many ways reminiscent of La Bretesche, although the golf is not quite as demanding. The chateau is also ideally situated for the golf at Touraine and Ardrée and it is the one hotel in the region to find a place in the programmes of Longshot, Brittany Ferries, French Golf Holidays, Eurogolf, BDH and A Golfing Experience.

While the Touraine course despite a picturesque setting and a number of challenging holes, is featured only by French Golf Holidays, Ardée is more popular with tour operators. Perhaps deservedly so as it retains interest throughout the length of its 18 holes which are set in the wooded park of a Loire chateau with a river and lake enhancing the design and making for a memorable test of golf.

To match the chateaux and the excellent Hotel Alliance at Tours from the French Golf Holidays programme, Eurogolf offer the Domaine de Beauvois, undoubtedly one of the finest properties in the area and well placed for Ardrée and Sept Tours. While Longshot also commend in this area around Tours the Chateau d'Artigny and du Breuil.

Two courses which feature as prominently as Ardrée are Golf d'Avrille and Anjou Golf and Country Club. While d'Avrille has taken time to mature into an interesting test of golf with scenic surrounds, the Anjou course, designed by the British architect Fred Hawtree, has remained something of a well kept secret until now and this is a course to be enjoyed by all standards of golfer.

As for accommodation in this area to the west of Tours, Eurogolf offer two fine chateaux-hotels, Du Plessis and De Noirieux, while BDH feature the three star Grand Hotel de Solesmes as an alternative centre. Golfers favouring the Grand Hotel may also care to try out the beautifully maintained course Golf de Sable-Solesmes, which has three 9 hole layouts set between the Forest of Pince and the River Sarke and has credentials sufficient to be included by Brittany Ferries, Eurogolf and BDH amongst their top courses.

Trekking south through Cognac country where, by the way, there is a course surrounding the home of the Martell family which actually has a par 3 for a nineteenth hole, the visiting golfer with a taste for wine may be forgiven for leaving his clubs in the car. Bordeaux is the world's finest wine producing region and, while Les Golfes du Médoc may be considered one of the premier clubs, it is the premier crus of Mouton-Rothschild and Lafite that have placed Médoc firmly on the world map.

The two courses at Médoc, Les Chateaux and Les Vignes, are nevertheless worthy of their reputation, with the more established Chateaux Course to be found in most 'top ranking' compilations. The long, well bunkered fairways in the style of a Scottish links course are well maintained and the greens are superb.

In Médoc itself, Finlays, who specialise in this region, recommend Le Pont Bernet, a three star hotel with excellent facilities, and they are joined in this by Eurogolf who commend the warm welcome given by the host to English golfing visitors. Le Relais de Margaux, a chateau of impeccable quality is also included in the Eurogolf programme and is ideally situated for the golf at Médoc, Passac and Lacanau.

It is in Lacanau that most of the tour operators favour the Golf Hotel Latitudes on the actual Lacanau Course as an excellent base for touring the area. The course itself is very picturesque and hosted the French professional championships back in 1983, so it will come as no surprise to learn that accurate shot making is required around the tree-lined fairways and over the numerous water hazards.

The third course in this group at Pessac, with its three loops of nine, is equally as attractive but not quite so demanding. As an alternative to overnighting in Lacanau, Finlays offer the four star La Reserve in Pessac, while BDH feature the Hotel Mercure, five minutes from the course. Further north on the Médoc peninsula itself Longshot recommend the Chateau Cordeillan Bages, a four star hotel with great character.

Another course featured prominently in the tour operators' programmes is the Golf du Gujan-Mestras which lies to the south of Pessac. The many lakes, rough heather, trees and natural terrain combine to form arguably the best test of golf in the region.

Golfers looking to combine Gujan-Mestras with the courses to the north would be well advised to consider the accommodation available in Bordeaux itself. French Golf Holidays feature the three star Holiday Inn, although the four star Hotel Burdigala with its 18th century facade is very highly recommended as well by Eurogolf. By contrast Cresta commend the delightful two star Hotel Continental and Leisure Link propose the family run Hotel Brion just outside the city.

A golfing holiday in this area would not be complete nowadays without a visit to Les Vigiers, which lies inland from Bordeaux surrounded by vineyards. This impressive Donald Steel designed course and a magnificent 16th century chateau-hotel at the heart of the complex come highly commended by Longshot.

Bordeaux may have its wine but Biarritz is a celebrated resort with golf to match. To the north, the first course encountered on the journey down from Bordeaux is the Robert Trent Jones creation Golf de la Côte d'Argent (Moliets) which overlooks the Atlantic. Despite its location the Moliets course is another combination of water, trees and dense rough relieved by some generous fairways. A course not to be missed. Equally highly rated and the creation of another American architect, Robert van Hagge, is the course at Seignosse which has been compared in design to the Augusta National and is a favourite of Jose-Maria Olazabal. Flying the flag for Britain is the Tom Morrison designed course at Hossegor, which we shall liken to Sunningdale, courtesy of the huge pine trees which shelter the course from the sea.

Seignosse itself has a celebrated Golf Hotel which features in the selections of nearly all the tour operators, and this three star Louisiana style edifice comes highly recommended on all counts. Hossegor can offer the modern Lacotel which does overlook the lake and has one of the best restaurants in town. The hotel can be found in the Cresta and Eurogolf programmes, and Cresta also feature P&V apartments at Moliets-Plage.

In Biarritz itself Longshot recommends a former residence of Napoleon III, the Hotel du Palais, while the magnificent four star Regina et du Golf which overlooks the bay to one side and the golf course to the other is featured by Eurogolf and French Golf Holidays. In many respects the Biarritz course does not match the hotels for quality, however, when the wind blows it develops a challenging character compounded by slick greens.

A more recognised test of golf and the slightly less glamorous Hotel de la Résidence can be found on another Tom Simpson designed course at Chiberta just to the north of Biarritz, this combination of links and parkland golf, offers a well maintained variety. A slightly more demanding challenge awaits at Arlanques with its undulating terrain, though the marvellous views do compensate for what can be a somewhat ardous trek.

Biarritz

France is well known for its fine food and wine, and has been a favourite with British holidaymakers for many years. French golf courses, however, have remained a well kept secret. Now Longshot Golf Holidays have brought together over 100 of the best courses and hotels in their Longshot Golf Holidays in France brochure.

The wide range of golfing destinations in France makes choosing a holiday a challenge in itself. Why not try a weekend break in Le Touquet or at a selection of northern France's uncrowded courses? Or perhaps a longer stay in the warm sunshine of Provence? You can even combine a business trip to Paris with a weekend of golf close to the capital, at Chantilly or Versailles.

With so many options available, Longshot Golf Holidays has teamed up with P&O European Ferries, Air France and French golf specialist, Le Grand Golf, to provide you with the most flexible service possible.

Chateau des Ormes, Brittany

You may prefer to drive yourself to France giving you the freedom to stop off at places of interest en route to your holiday destination, or let the plane take the strain with a fly-drive holiday. Whichever way, Longshot Golf Holidays have the flexibility to tailor your holiday to suit your requirements.

Les Bordes International Golf Course, Loire Valley.

Longshot Golf Holidays are the leading specialist golf holidays operator with over 20 years experience, so you can be confident that you will receive knowledgeable advice and excellent service when choosing your golf holiday. Our reservations consultants will be happy to advise you on the best courses and hotels for you, and your family or friends. From the moment you pick up the phone, you will appreciate the high level of service that Longshot Golf Holidays offer. With prices starting from £129 for a short break in Le Touquet, there is something to suit every budget.

LONGSHOT'S TOP TIPS

The resorts of **Le Touquet, Normandy and Brittany** are firm favourites offering high quality golf within an easy drive of the channel ports. For the more adventurous golfer, a trip further south leads to some of Europe's finest courses where the delights of **Seignosse and Vigiers** in the Aquitaine region complement the superb provençale courses of **Barbaoux, St Endreol and Fregate**. For those seeking a luxurious retreat dedicated to rest and relaxation, the **Domaine du Royal Club d'Evian** on the banks of Lake Geneva can be described as a paradise in the heart of Europe.

LONGSHOT GOLF™ HOLIDAYS

For your free brochure call Longshot Golf Holidays on (0730) 268621

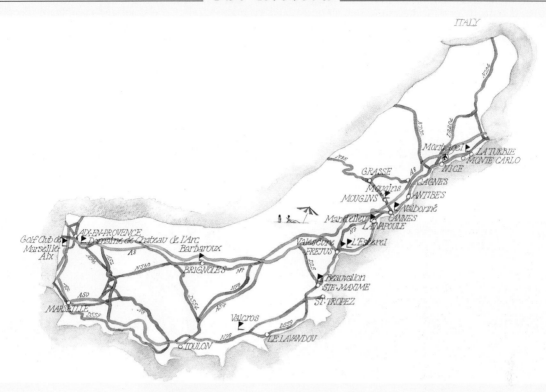

Before concentrating on the golf to the east of Marseilles and the choice along the coast, brief mention must be made of Montpellier and Nîmes in Languedoc-Roussillon. Although not generally featured by the tour operators, there is some exceptional value to be had and the choice offered by A Golfing Experience and Longshot covers the pick of the courses and accommodation.

The course Nîmes Campagne has attracted more than its fair share of accolades and is probably the course not to be missed when on holiday in the region. The Golf Club de Montpellier/Massane will be well known to those who have followed the fortunes of PGA tour qualifiers and is acknowledged as typically American in design. The same if not more could be said of Robert Trent Jones' La Grande Motte which as one would expect offers a superb test of golf. Accommodation featured by Longshot and A Golfing Experience in the Montpellier and La Motte region is purpose built and modern, although as they say themselves there is a fair selection of hotels around Arles, Avignon and Nîmes to be considered.

While there are those who would head straight for Golf de Barbaroux en route to the courses concentrated above St Tropez, the discerning golfer might opt to make first for Domaine de Fregate. This is an excellent course offering the kind of challenge expected of a Ronald Fream design. Blue Riband, a Riviera tour specialist, stress the attractions of this course and a recently completed adjacent luxury hotel, as do Longshot and Cresta.

Fregate, though is no alternative to Barbaroux, which should be experienced at all costs. This is an exceptional course both in terms of beauty and the standard of golf demanded, carrying the hallmark of the Dye Brothers (see Kiawah Island, USA). The Hostellerie du Golf de Barbaroux is a four star hotel at the heart of the course and features in the Longshot and Eurogolf programmes.

Clustered to the west of Frejus are three courses which command spectacular views of the Provence countryside and the Mediterranean. Of the three, it is the most recently completed St Endreol development which attracts most attention. Its signature hole is the 13th, a par 3 played to an island green. The testing course runs through some magnificent countryside which may be some consolation to those driven to despair by their mounting score.

Golf de Sainte Maxime, and Golf de Roquebrune offer rather limited but perhaps more manageable challenges by comparison. As beautifully situated as the course at St Maxime is the Hotel Playa Maxime, a four star hotel in the Cresta programme, while the Golf Plaza featured by Longshot in addition to the Playa impresses and is similarly rated.

In St Raphael, Homecavern recommend the Excelsior which is adjacent to the Casino on the sea front or self catering in apartments along the coast at Cap Esterel.

Either way, access to Golf d'Esterel is a prerequisite when preparing your itinerary around St Raphael. Another Robert Trent Jones creation which has played host to PGA tour events, Esterel has rapidly become popular with golfers of all abilities and has a reputation for being challenging but fair.

The Latitudes Hotel at Esterel serves the visiting golfer well. This is a modern three star hotel recommended by Cresta, Longshot and Eurogolf, overlooking the course and only five minutes from St Raphael.

Around Cannes there is definitely no shortage of quality golf. The Riviera Golf clubhouse is one of the most impressive in France while the course, again designed by Robert Trent Jones, boasts a typical combination of forest and water hazards which render it something of a picturesque challenge.

Another Van Hagge creation at Royal Mougins will not disappoint those golfers who enjoy Seignosse and Les Bordes, while the hands of Alliss and Thomas are again evident in the redesigned layout of Cannes-Mougins, host to the Volvo Cannes Open. Nearby Mandelieu has also played host recently to a Tour event, this time on the ladies circuit and proved very popular with the players. After Pau and Biarritz this is the third oldest course in France.

One final recommendation in the vicinity of Cannes goes to St Donat, which can prove a rewarding experience for high and low handicappers alike in typically picturesque surroundings.

As for accommodation in the resort, quality is the key. Blue Riband feature two luxury hotels in The Royal Hotel Casino near Mandelieu and Hotel de Mougins one kilometre from Cannes-Mougins. Homecavern dwell on the attractions of the four star Martinez on the Croisette while Longshot and Eurogolf's programmes include the equally highly rated Hotel Majestic. Self catering in Cannes is raised to luxurious levels at the Royal Mougins complex with its exceptional facilities and this option is promoted by Longshot.

There are of course those who like their golf packaged slightly differently and two Club Med villages at Dieulefit and Opio Valbonne cater for golfers.

Golf d'Obio Valbonne itself enjoys an excellent reputa-tion with two distinctly different sets of nine holes, and an excellent on-course golf hotel, originally a 17th centu-ry manor house. The hotel and course are recommended by Eurogolf, Cresta and Blue Riband and these latter two operators also point out the attraction of the Grasse Country Club course which offers fantastic views and an enjoyable round for any golfer with some notion of accuracy and placement.

Our final course to note in France and probably one of the best is Golf de Taulane. The first course in Europe to be designed by Gary Player it may enjoy a remote location on the edge of Alpes-Maritime, but this is golf at its most invigorating. With accommodation to match at the fabulous Chateau Toulane, Blue Riband offer an exceptional value for money programme.

Esterel (Golf Resort Marketing)

Portugal

Vale do Lobo (Golf Resort Marketing)

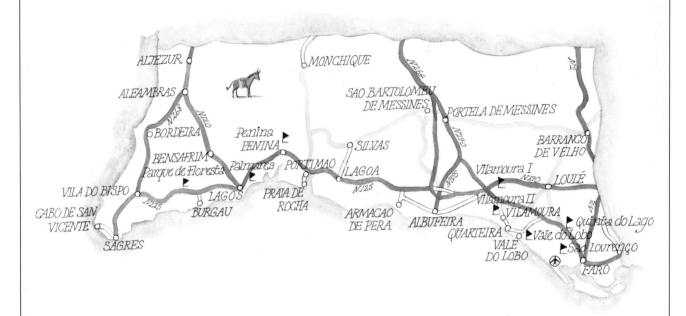

If there is one area of the world synonymous with holiday golf as far as the British are concerned then it must be the Algarve. With 15 excellent courses, quality accommodation and a genuine warmth in the welcome, Portugal's status as our oldest ally is safe for the foreseeable future. The only problems are the choices to be made, which courses to play and where to stay. There are many who will make their own arrangements but for the uninitiated this can be a veritable minefield when it comes to sorting out green fees and tee off times. Here organisations such as Golf Inc. really earn their money with their independent service selecting from the numerous programmes offered by golf tour specialists. It would, however, be fair to say that most will tailor a holiday to suit, but in this respect it does help to know what the options are first. Most operators feature the recognised golf hotels such as the Dona Filipa, Penina and Vilar Do Golf and operators such as British Airways, Thomsons, Leisure Link, Eurogolf, Select World Golf, 3D and Caravela tend to restrict their programmes to the major resort hotels. Others, notably Longmere, Longshot, Sovereign and the Travel Club of Upminster have a much wider range of properties to select from while there are those like Golf Away and Monmouth Court who concentrate on self catering.

One common denominator as far as most programmes go is arrival at Faro airport. Journeying west, San Lorenzo and Quinta da Lago are the first of a string of marvellous golfing complexes, with the Quinta estate ranking as one of the finest homes of golf in Europe.

Of the four 9 hole loops at Quinta da Lago, the B and C loops set amidst a picturesque terrain of pine trees and artificial lakes have frequently provided the venue for the Portuguese Open. The course is always maintained in outstanding condition and the greens are particularly testing.

Another Quinta estate course, San Lorenzo, this time constructed in the form of two loops, the design of the American Joseph Lee, borders fine forests and slopes along the shores of the Ria Formosa estuary and its bird sanctuary. There are a number of excellent holes, of which the sixth is one, with its lofty tee overlooking the estuary and little room for error. The final holes are very demanding and one would expect no less from a course rated amongst Europe's finest.

The standard and design of the golf here is matched by the excellence of the estate's many other facilities making it a magnificent place to stay. Elegance and luxury await guests of the five star Hotel Quinta da Lago which is a firm favourite with golfers, and each room has a terrace with views over superbly landscaped gardens and the sea. As might be expected of this hotel it is prominently featured by the likes of British Airways, Longshot, Eurogolf, Leisure Link and Longmere. Residents of Forte's Doña Filipa Hotel enjoy the privilege of golf at San Lorenzo and this is also extended to guests at Forte's other magnificent five star hotel at Penina. A reciprocal arrangement exists at the course there.

A recent addition to the Quinta estate is the Pinheiros Altos course designed by Howard Swan and Peter McEvoy and completed in 1992. The course has matured quickly into a favourite with golfers. The first nine holes

ORIENT-EXPRESS
HOTELS

The Hotel Quinta do Lago lies only half an hour from Faro airport and is set amid 1680 acres of pine woods and undulating hills in year round sunshine.

The privately owned hotel provides guests with every facility imaginable and this is complemented by friendly and attentive staff. There are 141 luxury bedrooms and 9 suites all with air-conditioning, balconies and satellite television. The Ca d'Oro speciality restaurant serves Italian cuisine and the Navegadores Restaurant offers a varied menu which includes many traditional Portugese dishes. Guests can also enjoy light meals which are available at the poolside.

The hotel has its own tennis courts and tuition is available from the resident coach.The estate also has a complex of stables with experienced instructors and the 29 acre inland salt-water lagoon forms a windsurfing centre quite out of this world. Swimmers
not only have an indoor and outdoor swimming pool but they also have a fabulous beach offering golden sands.and the blue sea of the Atlantic.

The Hotel Quinta do Lago offers two golf programmes. Firstly, the 5 days/4 nights break offers four nights accommodation with daily buffet breakfast and two dinners at

the Navegadores Restaurant, including house wine. Guests are greeted with a welcome drink at the bar and a bottle of port wine in their bedroom.The price of £408 per person also includes one complimentary golf lesson and three rounds of golf(18 hole) plus two days class A car rental (fuel not included) and use of the Health Club facilities.

The second break is the 8 days/7 nights programme offering seven nights accommodation, daily buffet breakfast, two dinners at the Navegadores Restaurant including house wine, one dinner a la carte in the Ca d'Oro Restaurant including house wine plus one themed buffet dinner with live music and Algarvian folklore dancers.. The price of £750 per person also includes six rounds of golf (18 holes), one complimentary golf lesson, use of the Health Club facilities and four days class A car rental (fuel not included).

These programmes are valid from January 6th to December 20th, 1994 except for the period from July 22nd to August 29th. The rates quoted include all presently applicable taxes and it should be noted that currency fluctuations may occur. Guests final hotel bills will be presented in Portugese escudos.

Hotel Quinta do Lago 8135 Almancil Algarve
Portugal Tel: (010 351 89) 396666
Fax: (010 351 89) 396393

are in the traditional Algarve style with fairways lined by tall umbrella pines while the back nine is water all the way. It is on the Quinta estate that Golf Away have a luxury five bedroomed villa available to golfers, typical of the kind of properties they offer throughout the Algarve. Other accommodation options of note are the Four Seasons Country Club promoted by Longshot and the Val Verde Villas from the Longmere programme.

Just along the coast from Quinta lies Vale do Lobo whose course was designed by the late Henry Cotton and there are 27 holes laid out in three loops of nine - Yellow, Orange and Green. A number of holes run parallel with the beach along the cliff tops including one of the most photographed holes in Europe, the long par 3 seventh on the Yellow course which stretches from the tee over two deep ravines to the green over 200 yards away.

Another new course to be tried before reaching the celebrated courses at Vilamoura is Vilasol whose narrow twisting fairways are again defined by umbrella pines.

Vilamoura can now be justifiably proud of all three of its 18 hole courses. Vilamoura One provides a championship test while Vilamoura Two has undergone some radical redesign to become a truly enjoyable test of golf. Both courses command breathtaking views of the Atlantic and are set amidst pine-covered slopes. Elevated tees and narrow fairways are a feature of Vilamoura One and the short holes hold the key to a good score. The telling alterations to Vilamoura Two now provide a contrasting challenge which can be enjoyed by all golfers. The same applies to Vilamoura Three which has also been subjected to fairly major reconstruction work and now features a lot of sand and water. The problems these present are in many ways offset by generous fairways, making the course an attractive proposition for high and low handicappers alike.

Further recommendations in terms of accommodation must include Quinta's Vilar do Golf, an upmarket, sports orientated complex of quality villas and apartments which features prominently with the tour operators. There are, however, many other similar developments to choose from in Quinta itself and along the coast.

The all-round excellence of Forte's Donã Filipa Hotel extends to its restaurant which is one of a number which can be commended in the resort of Vale do Lobo. Although perhaps not quite as exclusive as Quinta da Lago it has a style of its own and an abundance of villas and hotels here are featured by various tour operators. British Airways offer Acacias Apartments and the Barrington Health and Leisure Club, while Longshot, Longmere and Sovereign all offer equally good value alternatives.

Vilamoura may have the look of a typically cosmopolitan holiday resort, but there is an attractive elegance to the shops, apartments, villas and hotels which belies its relative newness. Typical of the magnificent modern hotels are the two Dom Pedros, Golf and Marina, the equally four star rated Ampalius and the five star Marinotel and there is no shortage of programmes featuring these hotels. The Olympus Aparthotel is a slightly cheaper option with self catering facilities featured by 3D, Select World Golf and Longmere. Prado Villas on the Vilamoura Estate are ideal for golfers and their families and Golf Inc. and the Travel Club of Upminster can make the necessary arrangements. Other villas and apartment complexes are offered by Sovereign, Longshot and Longmere.

To enjoy the spectacular views from the Sheraton Pine Cliffs course it is necessary to be a resident of the hotel. This will be no hardship to those who enjoy the good things in life, and the golf here is in keeping with the five star hotel rating. Apart from the excellent sport and leisure facilities, this resort now also boasts a fine golf academy, which no doubt gives advice on how to cope with par 3 holes requiring a 200 yard carry over a ravine - a problem presented at the sixth on the Pine Cliffs Course. Worth checking though if considering this hotel as a holiday base is the access afforded to other courses on the Algarve as there are numerous options available through tour operators.

And so to Carvoiero and the Quinta da Gramacho course, a rather unique Ronald Fream design comprising nine fairways but 18 tees and greens. Confused? You won't be, as the whole layout has been well thought out to provide an interesting round in a beautiful setting.

The Vale da Pinta course is also nearby and enjoys an equally scenic setting amidst orchards of fig and almond trees, although it is much more undulating. This is one of Mr Fream's more typical 18 hole creations and the quality of his work is reflected in how highly this course is rated despite only opening in 1992.

Carvoiero has a four star hotel in the Almansor with a wide range of facilities and comes highly commended by Longshot and Longmere, while Colina Village is one of those quality villa and apartment complexes to be found the length and breadth of the Algarve as well as in the brochures of Longmere and Select Golf. For those golfers looking to experience life in a more traditional Portuguese resort, then Carvoiero with all its charm and character is a most picturesque fishing village.

The last course to be designed by Henry Cotton offers somewhat different golfing fare than that normally served up by the Algarve. While the situation of the Alto club is such that panoramic views of the Atlantic and the

Vale do Lobo (*Portuguese Tourist Board*)

countryside can be enjoyed here as much as anywhere, the course plays differently with longer rough and more undulating greens just two elements to contend with, not to mention a rather untypical 661 yard par 5 hole. Golfers looking for accommodation of the luxury, self catering variety can find good value for money on the superb Alto estate with Monmouth Court and 3D.

The 18 hole championship course at Penina is another Henry Cotton creation and one that can be enjoyed by all golfers (or at least that was the intention). Penina has been beautifully landscaped and despite the relatively flat terrain, trees, shrubs, water, sand and grass all combine to create one of the most memorable courses on the Algarve.

Guests of the Penina Hotel are spoilt not just in golfing terms but by a whole array of first class leisure facilities and luxury accommodation, so much so that the beach is almost superfluous to requirements.

A total departure from Algarve style golf can be experienced on the first nine holes at the Palmares club. This is the only true links golf to be enjoyed in the region, although some golfers will probably be only too pleased to get back up amongst the orchards on the back nine.

There is no hiding though on the rolling hills of Parque da Floresta, the Algarve's most westerly golfing outpost where the fairway stroll takes in the odd ravine, a few yawning chasms, some creeks, a lake here and there, not forgetting the vineyard. To say that this course presents a tough test of both golf and character is an understatement that will be readily appreciated by all those who do (or did) take up the challenge.

Suitable establishments in which to recuperate abound, such as the five star Hotel Alvor Praiha featured by Longmere, and in Alvor, almost next door, the four star Hotel Delfim recommended by Thomsons and the Travel Club of Upminster, while the villas and apartments are well served by shops, bars and restaurants. Alvor with its casino and four mile stretch of beach is much more a resort than Lagos which, although equally popular with golfers, falls more into the quaint traditional fishing port category with cobbled streets and squares. There are two highly commendable four star hotels in Lagos, namely the Hotel Golfino and Hotel de Lagos on the beach and in the town respectively. Of the two, it is the Hotel de Lagos which figures prominently in the tour programmes while the Golfino is a Longmere recommendation, as is the Ocean Club, a rather sporty apartment complex at Praia da Luz and an obvious alternative to hotel life. Other operators have their own favourites in the region around Lagos. Golf Holidays International feature an excellent five star in the Hotel Viking with an imposing setting. Praia da Rocha is the location of the Hotel Algarve which is promoted by Thomsons and the Travel Club of Upminster and enjoys a five star rating. The Travel Club have a wide selection of villas and apartments available in the area and a wealth of knowledge to pass on to visiting golfers. Meanwhile, back out at Parque da Floresta, the resort's villas and townhouses in the exclusive village complex can be found in the Eurogolf programme.

Alto Club - Alto Golf
Alvor- Algarve

ALTO CLUB

ALTO GOLF

Set near the coast, with sunny beaches that stretch for miles and miles. Close to the ancient fishing village of Alvor the Alto Country Club offers excellent facilities for your dream holiday. Swimming pools, floodlit tennis courts, games room, à la carte restaurant and snack bar, all surrounded by sub tropical gardens.
1/2 bedroom apartments and 3 bedroomed villas are available to rent.

Alto golf was the last course designed by the legendary Sir Henry Cotton. An 18 hole Championship course which benefits from outstanding views over the Atlantic with the Monchique Mountains as a back drop. Rolling tight fairways, long rough and challenging sloping greens. A delightful Clubhouse overlooking the 18th green, a golf academy with resident professional, driving range, practice bunkers and putting green.

For full colour brochure contact: Alto Leisure
33 London Road Reigate - Surrey RH2-9HZ
Tel: 0737 222022 - Fax: 0737 226055

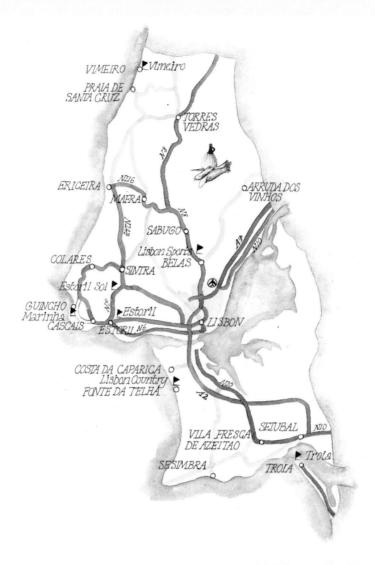

It is not so long ago that this region of Portugal barely featured on the golfing map, but today planning a golf holiday in these parts can prove almost as perplexing as with the Algarve, despite the fact there are only half the number of courses.

But what courses they are, and not all of them born of the prevailing golf boom. A prime example is the Lisbon Sporting Club course, 30 minutes drive north of the capital, which dates back to 1922. Fourteen holes are made up to 18 by four extra tees on this course set in a picturesque forestry reserve. Streams and tight fairways add to the challenge of what remains a still relatively underplayed course.

As for the Caesar Park Penha Longa course ever joining the ranks of underplayed, undiscovered courses, there is very little chance. Home to the 1994 Portuguese Open, this is a much acclaimed Robert Trent Jones creation played through beautiful country on lush green fairways and destined to become one of Europe's top courses. Situated in the foothills of the Sintra Mountains, with a 14th century monastery as centrepiece, the whole complex oozes quality. With the course, clubhouse and hotel all rating five stars in anybody's book, this is holiday golf at its best, and the resort can be found in Eurogolf, Longshot and Longmere's programmes.

These operators are joined by Select World Golf, Golf

Holidays International, British Airways and Sovereign in singing the praises of the classic five star Hotel Palacio and its Estoril Palacio course, a past venue for the Portuguese Open. The grand traditions of the hotel are carried onto the course where standards of dress must be adhered to and caddies are maintained. As may be expected the course also rewards finesse and accuracy rather than brash power.

Estoril Sol is another of the compact 9 hole variety with 18 tees. The accolades here are reserved for the beautiful setting and magnificent condition of the course, as well as the practice and teaching facilities which are second to none.

The resort of Estoril is one of the most elegant in Portugal and it comes as no surprise to learn that it is a favourite haunt of the nobility. For golfers the Lennox Country Club is particularly recommended by tour operators such as British Airways and Caravela, and there is a Britishness about the place with its golfing bias and memorabilia which is almost as endearing as the courteous staff. Alongside Lennox in Longshot, Longmere and Sovereign's programmes, more four star accommodation can be found in the Aparthotel Eden. This comprises modern well appointed studio apartments with self catering facilities,which are also highly commended by Select

Caesar Park Penha Longa Golf and Resort

Set in the historic grounds of a 14th century monastery, Penha Longa is a golf and leisure resort that is second to none. Only half an hours drive from Lisbon, its location is unrivalled - surrounded by the gentle foothills of Sintra it is one of the most beautiful, environmentally protected areas of Portugal. The resort is also only a few minutes from the long, sandy beaches of Cascais and Estoril (renowned for its international casino).

The whole estate incorporates a five star hotel, residential villages and a world class golf club. The hotel prides itself on a wide choice of rooms, all designed to the highest specification. In addition to 136 standard rooms, there are 24 garden rooms, 14 executive suites, 2 presidential suites and an Imperial suite. All have balconies commanding panoramic views of the fairways and Sintra Hills. The Jardim Primavera, overlooking the golf course, specialises in international cuisine, whilst the Midori caters for the lover of authentic Japanese food. The hotel provides unequalled banqueting facilities for up to 250 people, whilst the Cultural Centre comprising palace, monastery and gardens can accommodate up to 800 people. The beautiful swimming pool also overlooks the golf course and the indoor pool is ideal for those doing serious lap training. The hotel has its own tennis courts and a state-of-the-art health club.

The natural beauty of the grounds and gardens will be integrated with 180 luxury villas divided into five exclusive private residential villages. The first two, Village do Penedo and Village da Fonte, were released for sale in 1993. Village do Penedo occupies the most exclusive setting within Penha Longa. The villas are located either in a unique setting occupying the shoreline of the lake or sited against the spectacular backdrop of the mountains. The Village da Fonte occupies a delightful position to the south of the resort and has a communal pool which will serve as the focal point of the village.

Guests of the Cæsar Park Penha Longa Golf and Resort are just a short walk away from the first tee of the superb 18 hole par 72 championship golf course, designed by Robert Trent Jones Jr. With a total length of 6260 metres of fairways, the course was designed to provide unforgettable memories to all golf lovers. The irregular geography of the region has been masterfully used and the 1st, 2nd, 3rd, 16th, 17th and 18th holes are located in the valley between pine trees and granite rocks. For this exceptional course four specific tees were created for different levels of golfing ability - Champion, Backtee, Regular and Ladies. The club was given the ultimate accolade of hosting the Portuguese Open in March 1994 and as a result of the success of the event it will return to Caesar Park in 1995.

Cæsar Park Penha Longa Golf & Resort
Quinta da Penha Longa
Estrada da Lagoa Azul
Linhó
2710 Sintra
Portugal
Tel: (010 351) 1 924 9011
Fax: (010 351) 1 924 9007

World Golf and Golf Holidays International.

As an alternative to cosmopolitan Estoril, there is the conventional fishing village alternative of Cascais which has first class accommodation in the five star Estralgem Sra da Guia, a recommendation of Longshot and Longmere. Originally a grand manor house, the hotel is exquisitely furnished, well appointed and comes with the usual array of leisure facilities. The Hotel Village Cascais is a popular four star hotel which enjoys an excellent situation and a place in the programmes of Longmere and Caravela, who with their link to TAP offer some of the best value short stay golf holidays in Portugal. Also worthy of consideration in Cascais is another four star, the Cidadella featured by Longshot and Sovereign, and the three star hotels Baia and Ecuador, the latter offering self catering facilities commended by Longmere. The hotel Baia is growing in popularity all the time with British golfers and features with Caravela, Longmere, Sovereign and British Airways. This three star property.has been recently refurbished and offers guests extensive facilities and a superb location.

Cascais is a good base for those planning a few rounds at Quinta da Marinha, a course whose design attracts its fair share of comment. Not surprising when you consider the 18 holes include five par 5s and six par 3s, a configuration not normally associated with Robert Trent Jones. Quinta da Marinha, is in many other ways typical of Portuguese courses with lakes, pine trees and well placed bunkers. As on any course a degree of accuracy here can be a help, but Quinta da Marinha is a fair test for all golfers.

Just outside Cascais, Quinta da Marinha Hotel Villa Resort is a private development of superb town houses and villas set in a secluded estate just a few minutes walk from the course. Due consideration must be given to the facilities here when selecting holiday accommodation either direct or through one of the tour operators, all of whom seem to be united in their approval of this first rate resort.

South of Lisbon lies Aroeira and a course that is slightly more than just another designer's dream carved through pine forests and around lakes. This mature Frank Pennink creation stands comparison with Wentworth and Augusta for both quality of golf and stunning flora and fauna. One other endearing factor is the total absence of fairway bunkers.

On the new course at Montado the trees are of the cork variety and provide their fair share of problems for the wayward golfer, who will also encounter lakes and streams. Surrounded by the famous vineyards of Muscatel, the course design follows the natural terrain and there is no artificial difficulty to punish the straight hitter.

The third course to play in this area, Troia, will necessitate a ferry ride south from Setubal for those who elect to make their base in Sesimbra, renowned for the quality of its sea front restaurants and beautiful sandy beaches. Tour operators are fairly unanimous in their selection of the Hotel do Mar here but the alternative to gracious four star hotel accommodation is the equally highly rated studio apartment complex of Villas do Sesimbra which can be found in the Longmere programme. One attraction of this resort is that it is fairly equidistant from each of the three courses without being too remote.

The other realistic accommodation options for golfers concentrating their rounds in this area is Troia itself which boasts a high standard of apartment complexes at Rosamar and Magnoliamar as well as the Tulipamar Aparthotel all of which are commended by Longmere. The peninsula here comprises some 16 kilometres of beautiful sandy beaches and the Troia course itself reflects the wild natural beauty of the region. This is another very highly rated Robert Trent Jones championship course with an excellent setting combining a touch of links golf and tall pine tree-lined fairways. Troia can be a monster when the wind blows. The cavernous bunkers seem to grow before your eyes while the greens get smaller, and some aren't that big to begin with. Troia has its supporters for the title of best Portuguese golf course and certainly no occasional visitor from these shores should allow himself to be drawn into a debate on the subject if his experiences do not include a round at Troia.

Estoril *(Golf Resort Marketing)*

Madeira

Madeira cannot as yet boast courses to rival Penha Longa and Quinta da Lago but it is nevertheless developing into a very popular holiday golf destination. There may be only two clubs to keep the determined holiday golfer amused but there are a host of other sporting facilities available and few locations offer such stunning surroundings in which to relax.

The island attracts many of the major golf tour operators, such as A Golfing Experience, British Airways, Longmere, Longshot, Sovereign, Select World Golf, Carvela and Eurogolf. With the exception of Select World Golf, all include Madeira's most famous hotel in their programme. Reids Hotel at Funchal fully merits its reputation as one of the world's leading resort hotels. Everything impresses, from the spectacular setting high on the cliffs to the style and sophistication inherent in every aspect of the hotel's services and facilities. Competition to Reids at the deluxe end of the accommodation scale in Funchal comes from the Savoy, featured by Eurogolf, while Select World Golf favour the Carlton, an impressive modern development which is also included in the Longshot programme.

Sovereign commend the Hotel Raga very highly and this hotel which lies two kilometres outside Funchal offers superb views out over the island and the Atlantic. Another four star property to gain this operator's approval and that of Select World Golf and Caravela, is the Quinta da Sol where guests can enjoy luxury accommodation and first class service in a distinctly relaxed atmosphere. Recommended by British Airways and Eurogolf for hospitality and quality is the equally highly rated Madeira Palacio which is set in beautiful tropical gardens.

Golfers looking for slightly less distinguished accommodation with the option of self catering will find the Aparthotel Eden Mar very accommodating and most operators feature this hotel or can offer equivalent properties in their programmes.

As for the golf at Funchal, the Palheiro course is 15 minutes away and offers some quite remarkable views out over the bay and the Desertas Islands. The estate from which Cabell Robinson produced the course dates back to the early 19th century and the established flora and fauna have been collected from all over the world. The warm moderate climate allows golfers to enjoy the golf here the whole year round and the emphasis is most definitely on enjoyment. The layout comprises five par 3s and four par 5s and distance should not present a problem, although low handicappers looking for perfect position off the back tees will struggle over the ridges and valleys unless they produce some accurate shot making.

Madeira's second course, open since 1991, the Campo de Golf Madeira can be found at the very heart of the island. A visit to this club affords the opportunity to appreciate the fabulous countryside for which Madeira is renowned, rugged mountains rising dramatically from forests of pine and eucalyptus, springs and cascading waterfalls, exotic vegetation nourished by the myriad channels of water flowing to the sea.

The setting for the golf high on a volcanic mountainside at Santo Antonio da Serra is no less impressive and golfers will find the scenery unfurling all around them most distracting, which can be something of a problem on a Robert Trent Jones course. This one is to championship standard and has already hosted a PGA Tour event. The high altitude setting makes for a comfortable climate in which to play and all golfers will appreciate the challenge presented with Trent Jones employing the natural steep slopes and abundance of mature trees to good effect in his design. The sand traps as ever are most strategically positioned and water comes into play quite often on the Serras nine.

The message from the Campo de Golf Madeira is very much, 'watch this space' with a luxury five star resort in the offing and it is only a matter of time surely before this becomes one of Europe's premier golf complexes.

Funchal is a port of call for P&O golf theme cruisers who should not miss the opportunity to take their clubs ashore and enjoy a round at either course. Golfers looking for an alternative cruise option should consider Longshot's Black Prince itineraries which include Madeira, Lisbon and the Canaries in one programme.

Costa Verde

This region to the north of Oporto is, to coin a phrase, the undiscovered jewel in Portugal's crown. While many will know it as the home of Port and Vinho Verde, relatively few take the opportunity to either explore the beautiful unspoilt countryside with its emerald green pine forests and valleys or simply relax by the brilliant blue waters of the Atlantic on the golden beaches. Fewer still elect to pack their clubs and head for the golf courses.

As may be expected Caravela with its links to TAP cannot be faulted when it comes to promoting golf breaks to the Costa Verde. Their programme includes three Sopotels of four star quality including the Estralgem St Andre which is ideal for the course at Estela, half an hours drive to the north of Oporto. The golf is part of the Sopete development which features a number of excellent hotels for tourists and provides a wide range of sport and leisure facilities, including a casino.

Though not overlong, the 18 holes here present a genuine links challenge over a narrow stretch of land dominated by sand dunes with the prevailing breeze from the Atlantic a permanent feature.

Longmere also promote the attractions of the Costa Verde and their recommended base is the Hotel Solverde, a luxury five star hotel at Espinho, home to the oldest course in Portugal. The Oporto Club was formed by British port wine shippers in 1890 and very little of the original links design has altered over the years. This is a classic test of links golf and accurate play from the tees to the narrow winding fairways is essential otherwise the opportunity for a good score will be lost among the sea grass and sandy wastes.

The area around Oporto also includes a third course, Miramar, which is only nine holes but a genuine test of golf all the same and visitors are always welcome at this private club. Due consideration should be given to Caravela's two other hotel options for this area, the Vermac and Ofir, both of which are ideal for golfers and if the schedule permits, a journey inland to the course at Vidago is worth including in any itinerary. This is a popular spa resort with a Victorian heritage some 80 miles north east of Oporto which boasts one of the earlier designs of the celebrated Scottish golf architect Mackenzie Ross who designed Estoril and Turnberry's championship course. The layout here may not be quite as demanding, but the parkland setting among mature trees with streams all around is most memorable. Holiday golfers would also do well to consider one or two nights of therapeutic rest and recreation at the magnificent Vidago Palace.

Costa Verde

Estela Golf Course
Rio Alto, Estela
4490 Póvoa de Varzim
Tel: (52) 685567/612400
Fax: (52) 612701
18 holes, 6129 m, par 72

Miramar Golf Club
Praia de Miramar
4405 Valadares
Tel: (02) 7622067
Fax: (02) 7627859
18 holes, 5146 m, par 68

Oporto Golf Club
4500 Espinho
Tel: (02) 722008
Fax: (02) 726895
18 holes, 5668 m, par 71

Montanhas

Vidago Golf Club
5425 Vidago
Tel: (76) 97106
Fax: (76) 97359
9 holes, 2449 m, par 33

Costa De Prata

Vimeiro Golf Club
5425 Vidago
Tel: (76) 97106
Fax: (76) 97359
18 holes, 4781 m, par 67

Costa De Lisboa

Guia Estoril Sol
Linhó
2710 Sintra
Tel: (01) 9232461
Fax: (01) 9232461
9 holes, 4248 m, par 66

Estoril Palacio Golf Club
Clube de Golf do Estoril
Estoril
Tel: (01) 4680176 / 3248
Fax: (01) 4682796
27 holes, 5210 m, par 68
9 holes, 2359 m, par 34

Guia Quinta da Marinha
Estrada do Guincho
2750 Cascais
Tel: (01) 4869881/9
Fax: (01) 9240388
18 holes, 6039 m, par 71

Penha Longa Golf
Lagoa Azul, Linhó
2710 Sintra
Tel: (01) 9240320
Fax: (01) 9240388
18 holes, 6710 m, par 72

Lisbon Sports Club
Casal de Carregueira
Belas
Tel: (01) 4310077
18 holes, 5216 m, par 68

Clube de Campo de Portugal
Herdade de Aroeira
Fonte da Telha
2825 Monte de Caparica
Aroeira
Tel: (65) 2263244/1802
Fax: (65) 2261358
18 holes, 6040 m, par 72

Tróia Golf
Tróia
2900 Setúbal
Tel: (65) 44112
Fax: (65) 44162
18 holes, 6337 m, par 68

Clube de Golf do Montado
Apartado 40 Algeruz
2950 Palmela
Tel: (065) 706648/706799
Fax: (065) 706775

Algarve

Parque da Floresta Golf
Vale de Poço, Budens
8650 Vila do Bispo
Tel: (82) 65333
Fax: (82) 65436
18 holes, 5888 m, par 72

Palmares Golf
Montes Palmares
Meia Praia, 8600 Lagos
Tel: (82) 762953/762961
Fax: (82) 762534
18 holes, 5691 m, par 71

Penina Golf
Penina
8500 Portimão
Tel: (82) 415415
Fax: (82) 415000
18 holes, 6200 m, par 73
9 holes 3148 m, par 36

Alto Golf Club
Quinta do Alto Poço
Alvor, 8500 Portimão
Tel: (82) 416913
Fax: (82) 458557
18 holes, 6125 m, par 72

Quinta do Gramacho
Carvoeiro Golf
Apartado 24, 8400 Lagoa
Tel :(82) 52610
Fax: (82) 341459
2 x 9 holes, 5919 m, par72
18 holes, 5919 m, par 72

Vale de Pinta
Carvoeiro Golf
Apartado 24, 8400 Lagoa
Tel: (82) 52610
Fax: (82) 341459
18 holes 5861 m, par 71

Vale de Milho Golf Club
Rua do Barranco
Praia do Carvoeiro
Tel: (82) 358502
Fax: (82) 358497
9 holes, 970 m, par 27

Pine Cliffs Golf & Country Club
8135 Almancil
Tel: (89) 501787
Fax: (89) 501884
9 holes, 2324 m, par 72

Vilamoura I Golf Club
Vilamoura
8125 Quarteira
Tel: (89) 313652
Telex: (56914
18 holes, 6331 m, par 73

Vilamoura II Golf Club
Vilamoura

8125 Quarteira
Tel: (89) 315562
Telex: (89) 56936
18 holes, 6030 m, par 72

Vilamoura III Golf Club
Vilamoura
8125 Quarteira
Tel: (89) 380724
Fax: (89) 380726
9 holes (Pinhal), 2935 m,
par 36
9 holes (Lago), 2953 m, par 36
9 holes (Marina), 3180 m, par 36

Pinheiros Altos
Campo de Golfe
Quinta do Lago
Tel: (89) 394340
Fax: (89) 394392
18 holes, 6049 m

Vila Sol Golf
Vila Sol
Alto do Semino
Tel: (89) 302144/302145
Fax: (89) 302147
18 holes, 6183 m, par 72

Vale do Lobo Golf Club
Vale do Lobo
8100 Loule
Tel: (89) 394444
Fax: (89) 394713
18 holes, 6429 m, par 73
9 holes, 2749 m, par 35

Quinta do Lago Golf
Quinta do Lago
8100 Almancil
Tel: (89) 394529/396002
Fax: (89) 394013
9 holes (East), 3100 m, par 36
9 holes (North), 3210 m, par 36
9 holes (South), 3120 m, par 36

San Lorenzo Golf Club
Quinta do Lago
8135 Almancil
Tel: (89) 396534
Fax: (89) 396908
18 holes, 6238 m, par 72

Açores / Madeira

Santo da Serra Course
Santo António da Serra
9100 Santa Cruz
Tel: (91) 552345/552356
Fax: (91) 552367
18 holes, 6000 m, par 72

Furnas Golf Course
9675 Furnas
São Miguel
Tel: (96) 54341
Fax: (96) 34951
18 holes, 5817 m, par 71

Terceira Island Golf Club
9760 Praia da Vitúria
Terceira
Tel: (95) 25847
Fax: (95) 23827
9 holes, 6332 m, par 72

Palheiro Golf
São Gonçalo
9000 Funchal
Tel: (91) 792116
Fax: (91) 792456
18 holes, 6015 m, par 71

3D Golf is committed to making sure that customers obtain the best deals possible without cutting corners and compromising on quality. Group travel is the company's particular speciality and there are special discounts that apply. In most venues this means one in every eight people goes free!

3D have been organising PGA Tournaments, golf schools, golf weeks and group travel for the past 18 years and their mix of quality, price and professional organisation cannot be matched.

The company specialises in arranging golfing holidays to the Algarve, the Costa Del Sol, Almeria, Corfu and Tenerife. In the Costa Del Sol there is golf available at many reputable courses including Mijas, San Roque, Valderrama, La Quinta and Torrequebrada to name but a few.

In most cases start times are pre-booked and customers are guaranteed a confirmed start time before even leaving the U.K. Holidays include a minimum of four rounds of golf and in some venues there is unlimited golf.

For more information on a good deal, great golf and a memorable place to stay contact 3D Golf.

3D Golf Plc
62 Viewfield Road
Ayr
Scotland
KA8 8HH
Tel: (0292) 263331 or local call 0345 090567
Fax: (0292) 286424

Valderrama

Estoril *(Golf Resort Marketing)*

Valderrama, San Lorenzo, Penha Longa, La Manga Club. Each of these courses may seem a long way from your local club, but the opportunity to play on these and many other top European and American courses is only a phone call away.

Longshot Golf Holidays are specialist golf holiday operators who can help turn that dream into reality, without the hassle of doing it all yourself.

With more and more options for playing golf abroad, choosing a golf holiday can be a daunting prospect. Which courses best suit my ability? Can I guarantee tee times when and where I want to play? How will I get from my hotel to the golf course and how long will it take?

Penina Golf and Resort Hotel

All these questions and more are answered by the Longshot Golf Holidays brochure. If our brochure doesn't have the answer, our team of experienced reservations staff certainly will! From the moment you pick up the phone, you will appreciate the high level of service that Longshot Golf Holidays offer. Your individual requirements can be tailored to suit you - from weekend breaks to longer stays, amateur tournament weeks to personal tuition.

We can help you choose from over 100 top courses, with a wide range of hotel and self catering accommodation to suit every budget. Many hotels also offer extensive facilities for non-golfers and families, so why not combine your golf abroad with your main holiday.

Rio Real Golf Club, Marbella, Costa del Sol

When you get your copy of the Longshot Golf Holidays brochure, don't miss the "Value Plus" offers at many hotels. You can benefit from exclusive extras such as free golf and tennis, room upgrades, and free meals and drinks. In addition, each passenger travelling with Longshot Golf Holidays receives three complimentary golf balls. With highly competitive prices, Longshot Golf Holidays are hard to beat, for quality, service and outstanding value for money.

LONGSHOT'S HOT TIPS

If you want to pit your wits against the finest courses in Europe, then follow Longshot Golf Holidays' 1994 **Top Tips**. Southern Spain has fought hard to regain popularity in recent years and it is now paying off. **Valderrama, San Roque and La Manga Club** are Spanish golf at its best and with high quality and excellent value for money hotels, watch out for **the Algarve**. Year-round favourites like **San Lorenzo** and **Vilasol** still rate highly, complemented by excellent five star hotels like Penina Golf and Resort Hotel, Dona Filipa and Quinta do Lago. Best newcomer goes to **Penha Longa**. Located close to Lisbon, in the grounds of the luxurious Caesar Park Hotel, Penha Longa is set to become one of Europe's premier golf destinations.

For your free brochure call Longshot Golf Holidays on (0730) 268621

LONGSHOT GOLF™ HOLIDAYS

PORTUGAL SPAIN
FRANCE
U.S.A BERMUDA

1 SEPTEMBER 1993 – 31 OCTOBER 1994

Call Now For Your FREE Brochure on
0730 268621

Longshot Golf Holidays, Meon House, College Street, Petersfield, Hants GU32 3JN

Spain

Atalaya (Golf Resort Marketing)

Costa Del Sol

Call it what you want, a return to reality or even sanity, no matter, the Costa del Sol is back in favour. It never really went away, it just got more expensive. While golf and accommodation here have always been considered first rate, the quality of holiday golf, like any other commodity, has to be understood in terms of value for money, and this year there can be no denying that this is what golfers should find throughout the region. Of course no one can really tell what might happen if the Ryder Cup confers ultimate respectability on Valderrama and the whole of the Costa del Sol by association , so it might be advisable to pack the clubs and book flights before it's too late. There can be few arguments about Valderrama's status as favourite to host the event in 1997. It is already the regular venue for the Volvo Masters, and by general consensus the course ranks as one of, if not the best in Europe.

If Valderrama is high on your priority list of places to play then an ideal base would be the Suites Hotel at San Roque Club which is featured by nearly every major golf tour operator. This is not surprising as guests have access to golf at Valderrama, Sotogrande and Alcaidesa, as well as the resort's own course. The hotel itself is immaculate, luxuriously appointed and set in beautiful gardens, while the course here conceived by Tony Jacklin and designed by Dave Thomas, has already been awarded a PGA tour event despite its relative youth. If there is such a thing as a purpose built stadium course then this is it, although great care was taken to employ the natural terrain with valleys of trees and streams combining with open meadowland to provide a fair test of golf.

Sotogrande, like Valderrama, is a Robert Trent Jones creation, although some ten years separate their openings. The more mature Sotogrande with well established oaks, pines and eucalyptus trees bordering the magnificently maintained fairways offers as beautiful a setting for golf as any golfer could wish. On a more mundane note the par of 74 gives some indication of the challenge awaiting.

Closest to Gibraltar in this group of courses to the west of the Costa del Sol is Alcaidesa. This Peter Alliss and Clive Clark design enjoys a splendid setting and offers the nearest thing to links golf in the area.

The greatest concentration of courses lies to the east around the celebrated resort of Marbella, not forgetting La Duquessa which stands slightly apart and now boasts a four star hotel overlooking the 18th green of its own Trent Jones course. The hotel offers spacious well appointed rooms in a traditional Spanish design, while the golfers will find their rewards in accuracy rather than power. This complex can be found in programmes offered by Golf Holidays International, Longshot, Longmere, Sovereign and 3D.

Quality apartments are also to be found around the Marina at La Duquesa and along the whole of the coast as far as Malaga. The visiting golfer is spoilt for choice no matter what type or standard of accommodation is preferred. Given the wide selection of courses to play in relatively close proximity, golfers wishing to book up at the Costa del Sol often face a dilemma of chicken and egg proportions. There are those who will opt for accommodation in a preferred resort while others will select their base purely on the strength of the golf in the immediate vicinity.

Logic should dictate however, that Estepona is not the ideal base for those planning to play all their golf at Torrequebrada and Mijas, given the relative distance and accommodation options. Practically speaking unless golfers intend to play courses the length and breadth of the Costa del Sol, quality golf and accommodation do go very much hand in hand. For the record Estepona has a new course whose greens have been highly recommended.

Moving along to two popular choices for a number of years now. The first, El Paraiso has an excellent four star hotel of the same name situated on the course and is well placed for other clubs. El Paraiso was Gary Player's first design in Spain and can be enjoyed for its generous lush fairways and scenic water hazards. The natural feel does extend through as far as some heavy rough and therein lies the challenge. The hotel itself enjoys a picturesque setting amongst beautiful landscaped gardens with waterfalls. Superb new facilities reflect recent investment in the resort, which is a favourite of Golf International, Longmère, 3D and Villmar.

The Atalaya complex has two courses for guests of either the four star hotel Atalaya Park or residents of the Park Bungalows to enjoy. The comprehensive range of leisure facilities available make the hotel a resort in its own right, and as a consequence it is to be commended on maintaining the all-round high standard it does. As a test of parkland golf the Limburger course is not as demanding as some but enjoyable nevertheless, while the newer Rosner course is hilly in part. Both have splendid tree-lined fairways, water hazards and good greens. Programmes featuring Atalaya are offered by Golf International, Golf Holidays International, British Airways, Leisure Link and Thomsons.

Slightly inland from the Atalaya and set in a high mountain valley is the spectacular and testing course of Monte Mayor where a buggy is an essential accessory in overcoming the natural terrain. At Los Arqueros the natural terrain took something of a hammering from Seve Ballesteros in his first attempt at creating a championship course on the Costa del Sol. The strategic placement of trees and lakes, however, really gives Los Arqueros the look and feel of a championship course and one which, although difficult will appeal to all golfers. Hendra Holidays offer self catering in some first class townhouses and villas overlooking this beautiful course.

Hendra Holidays España

Set in rugged countryside against wooded hills, Los Arqueros is a challenging and enjoyable golf course to suit all golfers. Hendra Holidays España offers excellent, high quality accommodation in apartments and town houses overlooking the course.

You can choose from two and three bedroomed, luxuriously appointed properties featuring spacious living rooms and well fitted kitchens with conventional cookers, microwaves and dishwashers. All bedrooms have own bath or shower room. (a couple of the shower rooms aren't en-suite, apparently). Each apartment or town house has at least one large, terraced area from which guests can savour the wonderful views south and out to the sea. To the west there are dramatic views of the mountains and guests can take a relaxing dip in one of the two swimming pools.

Hendra's customers can take advantage of the glorious climate of the Costa Del Sol and enjoy a golfing holiday in an area offering more than 30 first class courses within very easy reach. For families and non-golfers in visiting parties there are many other sporting facilities, including the exceptional El Madronal tennis club close by, and there are miles of sandy beaches to explore. Two miles away the lively town of San Pedro de Alcantara offers excellent bars and restaurants, there is great nightlife at Puerto Banus just five minutes from San Pedro, with high class entertainment until the early hours and the shopping opportunities are endless at nearby Marbella.

Prices for the accommodation at Los Arqueros start at £275 low season, £350 high season, for a two bedroomed apartment. Concessionary fees at Los Arqueros, for customers booking accommodation, can be arranged at only £60 for a whole week's unlimited play, and concessions to include a minimum of four other courses for only £100 for a week.

Hendra Holidays España
Hendra Holiday Park
Newquay
Cornwall
TR8 4NY
Tel: (0637) 875778
Fax: (0637) 879017

For sheer magnificence La Quinta is hard to beat. From the clubhouse with its panoramic views over Marbella's golf valley right down to the manicured fairways this is every golfer's idea of heaven. Designed to reward accurate shot making and punish the hit and hope merchants, the course takes some negotiating and players are well advised to take stock of potential hazards lurking unseen before each shot. It is also worth noting that La Quinta also boasts a new Golf Academy with excellent instruction and practice facilities offering courses of varying duration.

Another course out in the hilly countryside well worth a visit is Los Naranjos, a Robert Trent Jones design. The first nine are played over rather rugged terrain and the second nine of what should be a quite exhilarating round wander through flat olive groves and orange trees, as the name suggests. A brief word too on Guadalmina whose courses would also not be out of place on any golfing agenda. The South Course runs out towards the sea and although it is rather flat with generous tree-lined fairways, it is still considered more difficult than the North Course counterpart which lies at the foot of the Sierra Blanca.

Selecting accommodation close to a course is always an option popular with some golfers, for example Guadalmina has a four star Golf Hotel and Los Naranjos has terraced townhouses offering self catering near its club house and beach areas, and both properties are recommended by Longmere.

And this is still only half the golf to be found around Marbella/Puerto Banus, which almost by definition becomes the natural base for a whole host of courses, which will be fine for those golfers out to enjoy a bit of the high life. Many will look no further than the five star Hotel Melia Dom Pepe with its interior elegance, first rate facilities and, set amidst the tropical gardens, three swimming pools and floodlit tennis courts. Much is also made of the hotel's association with the Aloha course, and there are those who would advocate that no golfing holiday to the Costa del Sol is complete without one round along the superb tree-lined fairways here, including the likes of Select World Golf, Golf Holidays International, British Airways, Leisure Link and Thomsons.

A typical example of an excellent four star hotel is the El Fuerte favoured by Longmere, Sovereign and Thomsons, which has undergone complete renovation recently. Longshot and Golf Holidays International recommend The Andalucia Plaza which has a most imposing facade in the classic tradition of 18th century Spanish architecture and the rooms themselves also reflect an Andalucian influence in their decor.

Maintaining the five star standard set by the Melia Dom Pepe is the Hotel Los Monteros which has long been a favourite haunt of the jet set and is justifiably renowned for its style, luxury and impeccable service. The exquisite gardens are almost mirrored in the sub-tropical vegetation to be found on the hotel's equally celebrated golf course, the Rio Real. This is one course which invites golfers to really open their shoulders, although the river itself forms a natural hazard on many holes and the mature trees are everywhere. The greens are as true and fast as any to be found on the Costa del Sol, giving the course an all round quality that makes it highly recommended. Select World Golf, Eurogolf, Golf International, Longshot and 3D all feature Los Monteros.

Well worth enquiring after is accommodation at that oasis of luxury between Marbella and Puerto Banus, the five star Marbella Club Hotel which is now contracting with operators and offering golf packages, although it is not found in many brochures. However, Golf Inc, and other leading companies should be able to assist.

Close to the nightlife of Puerto Banus is the three star Pyr Hotel which is promoted by Eurogolf, Golf Holidays International, Longmere and 3D. This is an aparthotel where guests can enjoy self catering or the hotel facilities as they choose and the Pyr has its own swimming pool, tennis courts and gardens.

Pure self catering in apartments of the highest quality can be found at the Park Plaza Suites in the heart of Puerto Banus. Immaculately appointed, the suites even provide office facilities for the executive who can't quite leave work behind, while others enjoy the private beach and watersport facilities before and after rounds.

Other apartments of note from the Longmere programme include the Plaza Del Duque, a development with beautiful gardens near the beach at Puerto Banus and the Aldeia Blanca complex behind the Andalucia Plaza.

But back to golf and brief mention of Las Brisas before moving east and away from Marbella. This is a course of some repute, very highly rated by golfers and together with Aloha and Los Naranjos makes up an outstanding group of three courses.

There are a couple of other ways to enjoy the golf around Marbella, either as a guest of the Club Med Village, Don Miguel, or coming ashore from the P&O Canaries Carousel golf theme cruise.

One five star hotel just to the east of Marbella and ideally placed for both the golf there and the courses of La Cala and El Chapparal is the Don Carlos. Situated within a 130 acre private estate and with its own private beach club on reputedly the finest beach on the Costa del Sol, the hotel's excellent sport and leisure facilities, together with a wide selection of restaurants and bars make it a popular choice with golfers and a choice selection of nearly all the major operators.

La Cala and El Chapparal together with Mijas make up the golf around Fuengirola, a beach resort where watersports are popular and with its own attractions when it comes to nightlife. There are also two highly commended four star hotels in Las Palmeras, part of the Sol group, which is a large hotel well situated on the promenade, recommended by Select World Golf, Longshot and Thomsons. Golf Holidays International and Longmere opt for Los Pyramides where the claim is four star quality at three star prices. Value for money is also to be had at the three star Hotel Sol Puerto, according to Longmere and Thomsons, again on the sea front but with a rooftop pool, and for those golfers enamoured of the aparthotel concept, 3D , Longmere and Golf Holidays International carry the Pyr, on the promenade in Fuengirola, Sunshine Golf, who specialise in this area, offer programmes including apartments at the Oasis Club and three star hotel accommodation in the typically Andalucian surrounds of the Hotel Florida.

In terms of golf the three clubs offer five courses all told and all worth playing. La Cala has two very American style courses inasmuch as the designs of Cabell Robinson employ Bermuda and Pecross grass to provide lush fairways and holding greens. But the courses are not especially tight and there is plenty of variety to be enjoyed by all golfers, especially on the South Course, while the championship designated North Course opened in 1993 requires a touch more length but the fairways are wide enough to really have a go.

El Chapparal has only the one course, designed by Pepe Gancedo and considered one of his best. Translated from the Spanish, the course would be known as "the copse" and conveys something of the wooded splendour awaiting the visiting golfer. While the course may be relatively new, the fairways which follow the natural contours of the valley floor are lined by mature established trees. The vista of pine-clad hills and sparkling Mediterranean sea renders the setting unforgettable and as unique as the combination of six par 3s, six par 4s, and six par 5s which make up the 18. Accommodation overlooking the course can be found in the complex of villas and townhouses, Golf del Chapparal , which in every way complements

La Quinta Golf and Country Club

Located in Marbella's famous golf valley, La Quinta completes the group of well established golf courses in Nueva Andalucía.

La Quinta was created by Manuel Pinero, Vice Captain and former player in the European Ryder Cup Team. Pinero is also La Quinta's touring professional. This well designed, 27 hole course requires great skill when playing, particularly on the second shots and around the greens, considered to be second to none on the Costa Del Sol.

Despite the fact that it is only five years old, La Quinta has already hosted two Spanish professional championships and three European Club Cups. It is now also the official training ground of the Spanish National team.

The club house, with spectacular views over the Mediterranean sea, is considered to be one of the most magnificent in European golf and completes the fantastic amenities available, which include a bar and restaurant, paddle tennis, swimming pool, gymnasium, turkish bath, sauna, squash courts and underground car park.

La Quinta Golf and Country Club
29660 Nueva Andalucía
Marbella Spain
Tel: (010 34 5) 278 34 62
Fax: (010 34 5) 278 34 66

The Hotel Meliá Don Pepe

The Hotel Meliá Don Pepe, in the luxury resort of Marbella, is renowned for its facilities, excellent service and the fine quality of its cuisine.

Located only 500 metres from the centre of New Marbella, the hotel is set in sub-tropical gardens and directly overlooks the Mediterranean. It is the perfect setting for incentive and business conferences, with meeting facilities for up to a maximum of 350 people.

The 18 hole golf course at Aloha is only seven kilometres from the hotel and green fees for guests are free subject to the availability of tee-off times and excluding competition days. Guests can also enjoy reduced green fees on various other golf courses in the area. Additionally there are two tennis courts and water sports (four hours per day) which guests can enjoy at no extra charge.

The most recent addition to the hotel is the new sporting club where guests can relax by taking a sauna or massage, or by participating in one of the aerobics, stretching or gym-swim lessons.

The Hotel Meliá Don Pepe
C/o José Meliá
Finca Las Marinas S/N 29600
29600 Marbella Malaga Spain
Tel: (010 34 5) 277 03 00
Fax: (010 34 5) 277 03 00

the golf, and the complex deservedly features in the Select World Golf programme.

Mijas provides two contrasting Robert Trent Jones designs. The Los Lagos championship course lives up to its name with plenty of water, eight lakes all told. Some 100 yards of bunker protect the dogleg on the 624 yard, par 5, fifth hole, which is considered one of the most difficult holes on the Costa del Sol. The greens are large and totally in keeping with the sense of openness associated with the design. However, most greens are raised and very well guarded by bunkers. Los Olivos, while not claustrophobic, is much more enclosed with plenty of trees, less water, narrow fairways and small greens all combining to provide an equally challenging and attractive course.

There are also few hotels as attractive as the Hotel Byblos Andaluz, five star opulence with a mix of European and Arabian architectural styles in a design built around typical Andalucian courtyards. The hotel, which comes highly recommended by Longmere, overlooks the two Mijas courses and provides guests with extensive leisure facilities in beautiful well appointed surroundings.

Although Guadalhorce can boast a championship course with the American-style back nine particularly well regarded, Torrequebrada is the next course to feature prominently on holiday golf itineraries. This was Pepe Gancedo's first design and the ability he showed in transforming a limited piece of rugged undulating land into a true championship course gained him, first credibility and then with time, his status as Spain's foremost golf architect. While the course itself is now both exceptionally picturesque and a great test of any golfer's abilities, note must be made as well of the spectacular views of the mountains and sea the course commands.

The Torrequebrada course is just three kilometres from Benalmadena which for the golfer is an obvious alternative to Fuengirola, given that it is also only a very short drive from other select courses such as La Cala and El Chapparal, and this is reflected in the programmes offered by the tour operators.

The most luxurious hotel in Benalmadena is the five star Hotel Torrequebrada, which has its own beach and all the associated sport and leisure facilities to be expected, not to mention a casino and nightclub which give the hotel its own niche in a resort famed for its nightlife. One advantage the resident golfer will appreciate as well is the free shuttle service to the Torrequebrada course, and this is just one of the many facilities to recommend the hotel in the opinion of Golf International, Longshot, Longmere and 3D.

Also highly recommended in Benalmadena by Longmere and Thomsons is the four star Hotel Triton with its beautiful gardens and terraces leading down to a small beach. This is a luxuriously appointed hotel with a reputation for superb international cuisine.

One three star hotel featured by Longmere offering its guests exceptional value is the Hotel Sol Patos, which has basic but exclusive facilities in keeping with the style of the resort and is well situated for most attractions. The Sunset Beach Club is an aparthotel with a difference. There are some bars and restaurants in the complex and fully equipped kitchen facilities in the elegant modern apartments, but it is the comprehensive range of sport and leisure facilities which really sets this club above other self catering options according to Select World

Mijas (*Golf Resort Marketing*)

Golf, Longmere and Sovereign.

Once upon a time Torremolinos was the definitive Spanish package holiday resort, at least for the British. Nowadays, of course it is just one of a number of Spanish resorts catering for every conceivable whim of the transient tourist population. While it may not seem the most obvious choice for a relaxing golf holiday, there are programmes which include Torremolinos with both Thomsons and Select World Golf featuring Hotel Sol Aloha Puerto, a four star hotel situated in the Carihuela district where there is still some discernible Spanish character. All the rooms in this hotel on the beach of Monternar are mini-suites, most have sea views and for sporting minded guests there are some excellent facilities.

Select World Golf also recommend, hardly surprisingly, the luxury five star Hotel Melia Torremolinos with its splendid terraced tropical gardens and excellently appointed rooms. Another Melia to gain approval is the Costa del Sol Hotel, a four star development a few minutes away from Torremolinos overlooking the beach at Bajondillo.

Besides the golf available at Torrequebrada and the other courses to the west, Torremolinos is also a good base for the Campo de Golf de Malaga which lies to the east three kilometres away. The course features in the Thomson programme and although essentially flat with wide fairways it is not as easy as it may appear, having some rather strategically placed pine, eucalyptus and mimosa trees, and plenty of them, to give visiting golfers food for thought.

Selecting the Costa del Sol above other countries, or even other parts of Spain, as the chosen destination for a golfing holiday is just the first of many choices to be made. Experienced hands will already have their favourite courses and accommodation identified, and may even have their own hit list of courses to play in the future. Although green fees have been pegged back, it is a fool and his money who takes off for the Costa del Sol without first establishing how access can best be obtained at courses he wishes to play. Some clubs can be virtually inaccessible unless part of a tour package or the golf has been prearranged, and newcomers to the area risk disappointment if when booking holidays through operators or directly they do not check which courses are included either free or at discounted rates.

Marbella Club

115

THOMSON NOW

MORE PLACES TO

Vilamoura, Portugal

Our Winter Sun brochures have always had plenty of sand in them but this year there's even more. Now there are over 40 courses to play on, ranging from the Algarve to Majorca and the Costa del Sol to Tunisia.

And you don't have to be Nick Faldo because we have courses to suit everyone. Moreover, we have the best choice of European resorts, the best choice of excellent value accommodation and the widest choice of airports to fly from.

To make life even easier we're offering specially designed packages to give you the chance to try out a variety of courses, to improve your play or even just to learn to play. And what's more, we'll give you a free green fee discount card.

OFFERS EVEN
PLAY IN THE SAND.

Atalaya Park, Costa del Sol

So for golfers who want sun and sand but perhaps only a hint of sea, no-one has more to offer than Thomson.

For more details of our golfing holidays see your local travel agent for a copy of the Thomson and Horizon Winter Sun brochures or ring the Holiday Shop on 081-200 8733, 021- 632 6282 or 061-236 3828.

Thomson

Thomson Tour Operations Ltd. ATOL 2524 ABTA A5217.

PCI is unique as a holiday company in that it has its own offices in both the U.K and Pals, near Gerona, in Catalonia. This means that clients are being looked after by PCI both before departure and on arrival. The company has its own ATOL and is able to use both charter and scheduled flights. The company is offering an introductory golf holiday in Catalonia whereby in a party of twelve golfers the twelfth person goes free!

Catalonia is gradually becoming known as one of the best and consistently good golfing areas in Spain and this is evidenced by the fact that the European PGA has chosen the area, and three of PCI's offered courses, as its base for the pre-qualifying and qualifying events for the Volvo PGA Tour for the next three years.

The company's speciality is "tailored golf holidays" for groups of any size and there are facilities to cater for everyone's needs. There are self-catering quality villas or apartments and for those who prefer hotel accommodation there is an excellent selection of four and five star hotels.

PCI are able to offer golfing holidays of varying length, on any of six courses, giving some of the most challenging and delightful playing imaginable. Club de Golf, Gerona is 72 par and 6100 metres in length. The course is located in gently rolling countryside to the north of Gerona on the way to Lake Banyoles, a noted beauty spot of the area. The Emporda Club golf course is an exciting mix of woods, water and bunkers. It is slightly inland from the coast with remarkable views. Golf de Pals is a par 73 course that is 6222 metres in length. Visitors can enjoy the beautiful scenery, carved out of what was once an umbrella pine forest along the coast of the Mediterranean. These are just a few of the courses on which clients can play.

Tee-off times can be pre-booked prior to departure but this is not really necessary. It is usually preferable to book them on arrival at the office in Pals, where the playing vouchers are handed out, as they can then be more easily arranged to suit clients requirements.

Apart from golf Catalonia has a wealth of attractions to offer the visitor. There are beautiful coastal villages and Barcelona is always worth a day visit with its wide range of architecture and culture.

Property Care International Limited
137a South Road
Haywards Heath
West Sussex
RH16 4LY
Tel: (0444) 440606
Fax: (0444) 440999.

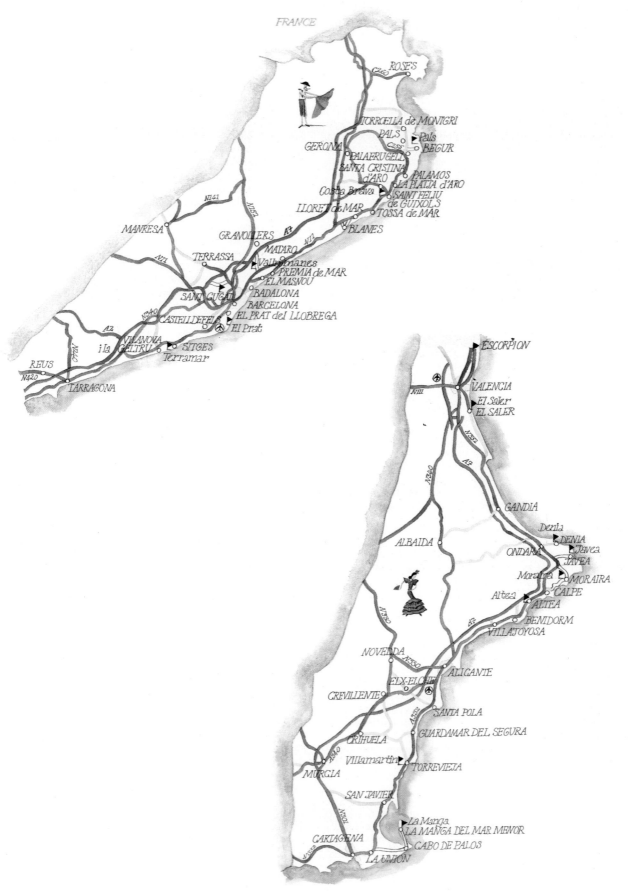

FRANCE

ROSES

C260

TORROELLA de MONTGRI
PALS
Pals
BEGUR
GERONA
PALAFRUGELL
C255
SANTA CRISTINA
d'ARO
PALAMOS
LA PLATJA d'ARO
Costa Brava
SAINT FELIU
de GUIXOLS
LLORET de MAR
TOSSA de MAR
BLANES

MANRESA
GRANOLLERS
A7
N11
N141
N152
MATARO
TERRASSA
Vallromanes
N1
PREMIA de MAR
EL MASNOU
SANT CUGAT
BADALONA
BARCELONA
EL PRAT del LLOBREGA
N340
El Prat
CASTELLDEFELS
A2
VILANOVA
i la GELTRU
SITGES
Terramar
REUS
N420
TARRAGONA

ESCORPION
VALENCIA
El Saler
EL SALER
NIII
N332
A7
GANDIA
N340
Denia
ALBAIDA
DENIA
ONDARA
Javea
JAVEA
Moraira
MORAIRA
CALPE
Altea
ALTEA
N330
A7
BENIDORM
VILLAJOYOSA
NOVELDA
N330
ALICANTE
ELX-ELCHE
CREVILLENTE
SANTA POLA
A332
ORIHUELA
GUARDAMAR DEL SEGURA
N340
Villamartin
TORREVIEJA
MURCIA
SAN JAVIER
N301
La Manga
LA MANGA DEL MAR MENOR
CARTAGENA
CABO DE PALOS
N332
LA UNION

Catalonia

There does not appear to be any obvious reason why Catalonia should be ignored by many of the operators who specialise in golf tours to the Iberian peninsula. The area has a natural beauty with mountains, ravines, forests and a beautiful coastline with long stretches of golden sand punctuated by small rocky coves. The region is rich in culture and history and Barcelona, the capital, is renowned as one of Europe's most colourful cities. As for the golf, the European PGA certainly rates the courses otherwise it would not have selected Pals, Mas Nou, Emporda and Girona as pre-qualifying venues. The region's Golf Association also cooperates with hotels and clubs to provide visiting golfers with exceptional value accommodation and access to the courses.

Thankfully one operator, PCI Golf Holidays, does work closely with the Girona and Costa Brava Golf Association to provide its clients with an excellent service in this region. PCI encourage golfers to make their base in Pals where they maintain an office to assist golfers with course reservations and tee off times. From Pals it is less than 30 minutes drive to five more of Catalonia's top courses.

The venue for the 1994 Catalan Open, Golf de Pals is an intriguing course, created by F.W. Hawtree from a dense pine forest, and the tree lined fairways provide a most picturesque setting as well as a formidable back nine. South of Pals lies Mas Nou an oasis of golf set on a plateau with forest tumbling away on every side. Also in this area is the Club de Golf Costa Brava which offers a demanding test with tight fairways and well protected greens.

To the west lies Girona, one of Catalonia's most scenic courses, while Emporda, immediately to the north west of Pals, is a course where the combination of natural and man made hazards makes for an interesting round through trees and over water to well bunkered greens. The same can be said of Torremirona which lies slightly further inland amidst the majestic splendour of the Pyrenean foothills.

The accommodation offered by PCI in Pals covers a very wide selection of well appointed apartment and villa complexes each with its own swimming pool. The programme also includes the four star La Costa Hotel which has 120 rooms with first class amenities as well as 57 self catering apartments on the sea front.

Other locations are available throughout the region. and note should be made especially of alternative hotel accommodation at the Hotel Golf Costa Brava, an excellent four star property right on the course, and the equally highly rated Park Hotel which enjoys a beautiful setting on the coast near Platja d'Aro and is within half an hour of Emporda, Pals, Mas Nou and Costa Brava.

As the PCI programme specifically caters for courses close to its featured properties, there is little mention of the golf available in and around Barcelona at El Prat, Terramar and Vallromanes to name but three. These are all excellent courses and, no doubt, PCI or Golf Inc will be only too pleased to advise on a suitable package including accommodation in Barcelona if required.

Costa Blanca

South of Catalonia lies Valencia which is only marginally more popular with the tour operators. Again this should not be construed as any kind of negative reflection on the standard of golf, accommodation and other attractions to be enjoyed in this area, and for that matter the whole of the Costa Blanca down to La Manga. Indeed it is only to La Manga, with its international reputation, that the golfer can select from the services of a significant number of operators.

Valencia features in the programmes offered by Longshot, Eurogolf and Golf International and there are some excellent courses to be enjoyed without the attendant problems popularity can bring. No one can dispute the quality of the courses themselves and of the fourteen or so in the region, there are three that really do stand out and are highlighted accordingly by the operators.

The most highly rated course and the farthest south of Valencia is El Saler, and it is there that accommodation for the area comes strongly recommended in the form of the Hotel Sidi Saler. This is very much a golf orientated hotel set in parkland next to a bird sanctuary on a stretch of beautiful coast line. The rooms have superb views out to sea over the dunes of El Saler beach, guests can enjoy a selection of leisure facilities, while the attractions of Valencia are only 25 kilometres away. Equally commended is the refurbished four star Parador El Saler, an elegant hotel with a reputation for excellent cuisine, situated on the beach next to the golf.

El Saler consistently ranks in the top ten of the various "Best Courses in Europe" compilations and deservedly so. This is a long course following the natural coastal terrain offering a classic contrasting combination of inland pine bordered fairways and a second nine of beautiful open links golf.

The next most highly rated and another top tenner as far as Spanish rankings go is El Bosque, a Robert Trent Jones design, which has like El Saler, played host to PGA tour events. This is a course where the par 3s and par 5s are considered by the designer to be some of the most demanding in Europe.

To the north of Valencia, but still only just over 30 minutes drive from El Saler is the Escorpian Club. The course here may not attract as many technical plaudits but it does enjoy an exquisite setting among groves of lemon and orange trees with the mountains as a backdrop. This is a Gary Player design, again no stranger to PGA Tour events, and though by no means a long course there is plenty of sand and water to be negotiated before returning to the elegant 200 year old clubhouse.

While the temptation may be to always head north from El Saler for alternative golf, one course to the south open since 1992, which is well worth including in any itinerary is La Sella. Some 1500 trees have been planted around the course which has quickly matured into a challenging test with well placed water hazards on certain holes.

Apartment accommodation in La Sella seems to be the popular choice, certainly as far as the recommendations of Premier Iberia and Select World Golf go. The Zarzas and Buganvilla developments offer one or two bedroom apartments set in landscaped gardens with the usual hosts of amenities close by to complement the in-house facilities, and there are also the three 9 hole courses of Javea, Benisa and Altea to provide some diversion.

Given the popularity of La Manga it is perhaps something of a surprise that the concentration of courses around Torrevieja do not receive more attention from the tour operators. Although only about an hours drive north, with beautiful beaches and lively nightlife to support the claims of the golf courses, Longmere and Premier Iberia alone feature the area prominently.

While the attractions of the major "name" championship courses for the holiday golfer are quite understandable, collecting scalps for 19th hole name dropping purposes is not the be all and end all for most golfers and those visiting this area will not be disappointed by the quality and the fun to be had out of the golf here. Not that Villamartin, for example, is a course of little repute. Designed by Puttman and opened 20 years ago, the 17th hole here has been described by no less an authority than Severiano Ballesteros as the best short hole in Spain. This is a very natural course enhanced by some beautiful surrounding scenery, and one to be enjoyed by high and low handicap golfers alike.

Las Ramblas De Orihuela is one of those shortish but exceedingly taxing courses which one day will no doubt become a championship venue in its own right. Memorable particularly for its ravines and narrow sloping fairways, each hole demands accurate shot making.

A much more open course lies between Villamartin and Las Ramblas, although it would be unwise not to underestimate the course of Real Club De Golf Campoamar. While there are only a few problem holes awaiting those golfers who really like to go for it off the tees, finishing the holes off can be a problem as the greens are normally tricky and very well protected.

Another open course at present but one which should mature into a tight test of golf once the trees that have been planted mature, is Queseda which is the farthest north of the four courses around Torrevieja.

As for accommodation, Premier Iberia feature the Aparthotel Villagolf in the heart of the Villamartin golf complex as well as a selection of villa and apartment developments all of which are equipped to a high standard and provide suitable leisure facilities, as do those recommended by Longmere.

And so to La Manga, or more accurately the Hyatt La Manga Club resort whose three golf courses are just part of the superb sporting and leisure facilities which have earned La Manga the prestigious reputation it presently enjoys. Even the setting is almost without parallel. Flanked by the unique natural lagoon of Mar Menor and the Mediterranean, in the shelter of the Murcian Hills, La Manga's 1400 acres offer such a wealth of attractions it is not surprising that a company such as Barwell can afford to specialise in La Manga almost exclusively.

Every year the courses at La Manga play host to many major events in the professional and amateur golf calendar. The South Course, an original Puttman design, was recently revised by Arnold Palmer who back in 1975 won the Spanish Open here with an eagle at 18, which may sound pretty matter of fact to those who have yet to confront this intimidating par 5.

While the South Course may be the truer championship test and has its supporters as a potential Ryder Cup venue, the North Course is certainly the most picturesque. The 18 holes sweep through ravines and along valleys, with many fairways lined by palm trees. Elevated tees and large greens make for confident shot making and an enjoyable round for any golfer blessed with a modicum of ability.

The most recently completed course, La Princesa, has matured quickly and is acknowledged as "American" in its design. Although the fairways are fairly generous in their width, accurate driving is called for, hazards are strategically placed and while the greens may be artificially receptive through watering, they are very deceptive. This is another scenic golfing challenge to the standard set by the North and South Courses and no less of an experience.

It is hard to imagine anyone returning disappointed from a La Manga holiday, given the various entertainments on offer and certainly the accommodation now available is equally unlikely to offer cause for complaint.

The five star hotel Principe Felipe is effectively the crowning jewel, maintaining the standards for which Hyatt have become internationally renowned in service and facilities. For those who prefer less formal arrangements La Manga has village complexes with apartments and villas built in typical Andalucian fashion and set amidst landscaped settings. Sport, leisure, shopping and driving facilities are always close at hand and this is one resort guaranteed to find favour with non-golfing partners and children.

La Manga (La Manga Club)

La Manga Club is set in a green valley nestling in the Murcian Hills of south east Spain, just 25kms from Murcia San Javier airport, and 90 kms from Alicante airport.

With the warm waters of the Mar Menor inland sea on one side and the Mediterranean on the other it is easy to see why this 1400 acre resort is considered the best kept secret in Spain. Olive groves, lemon trees, lakes and palm trees are just part of the beautifully landscaped scenery.

La Manga is the ultimate in sporting dreams and the last word in luxury - a residential complex incorporating multiple amenities, services and sports facilities including three magnificent golf courses.

The resort caters for all levels of sportsmanship with fully qualified coaching staff on site at all times. Advice and formal sports clinics, run by professionals, are always available and to test your skills, golf and tennis tournaments are organised each week for those wishing to compete.

Alternatively, La Manga is a peaceful and tranquil place to laze next to the pool or for stretching out on the secluded beach at The Cove. An excellent health and fitness club offers massage and beauty treatments and there are a number of bars for light refreshment and restaurants offering a variety of international cuisine.

The accommodation and properties blend in with the natural features of this superb setting and the sports and leisure facilities have all been designed with convenience as a top priority. Individual villages have been tastefully developed to provide a number of stunning residential properties on their own plot of land for private ownership - as well as a first class hotel for holiday makers.

The golf operation is quite central to the resort - no need to rush your breakfast to tee off. Choose your time and after your round you can return for a drink, stroll around the pro shop or a dip in one of the many pools.

Built in 1971 the two championship courses offer quite different challenges to the high and low handicapper alike. The North Course is some 400 yards shorter than the South Course yet, in some ways, more challenging. The premium is on accurate driving of the ball and, whilst the lakes are not in play as much as on the South Course, doglegs, bunkers and ravines mean that this is a thinking golfer's course.

From the white championship tees to the blue tees of the shorter course, both North and South courses have something to offer the professional; and the beginner. Indeed, depending on the wind blowing in from the Mar Menor, the very characteristics of the courses themselves can change by the hour.

Whatever your reason for visiting this complex, the sheer luxury and wealth of the facilities ensure it will be a visit to remember. For more information call Barwell Travel your La manga Specialists.

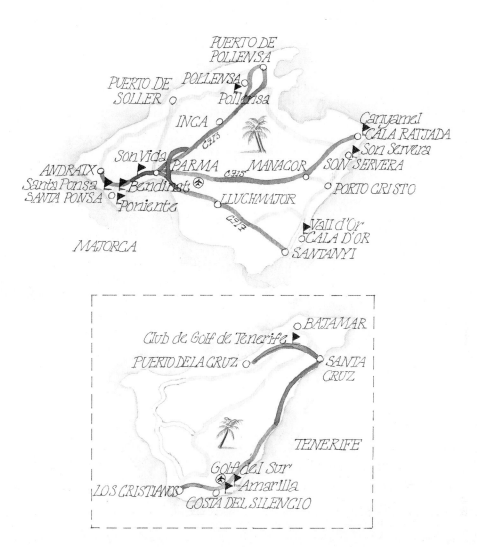

Majorca

To describe Majorca as a popular resort is something of an understatement, although it has never been quite as popular on the golfing front as some would like. Attempts to rectify the situation and attract some winter trade have given the island nine courses. This and the excellent accommodation available make Majorca an eminently acceptable selection for a golfing holiday.

Of course, for many golfers it has long been a favourite destination and for reasons mainly associated with accommodation it is the four courses on the west of the island which have been most frequented. The oldest of these is Son Vida and amidst the pleasant established surroundings something of an accurate touch is required. This is a most picturesque course with a plentiful variety of flora, fauna, water and wildlife contributing to what should be a pleasurable round of golf.

Santa Ponsa, too, has a mature feel to it, and is a championship course which hosted the inaugural Majorcan Open. Again the scenery is magnificent, and though there are water hazards on five of the 18 holes the lasting impression is always of gently sloping fairways stretching into the distance. The course does require the golfer to be proficient with every club in the bag, and its impressive nature extends to the clubhouse as well.

One course earning itself a reputation as among the best in Europe is Poniente. This is the challenging design of John Harris and is basically long and difficult with lightning fast greens. The course is immaculately maintained, which is little consolation for those golfers driven to despair by the unforgiving nature of the game as they pick their way along ravines, through greens and around lakes.

A more relaxing time may be had at the 9 hole course of Bendinat, which is one of the more recent developments but enjoys a mature setting surrounded by pine trees. The attractions of Bendinat also extend to the clubhouse which has luxurious facilities and in itself almost makes a visit worthwhile.

The Forte hotel in Paguera, Hotel Villamil, is a five star hotel which caters well for golfers with all the courses on the western side within 30 minutes drive. Paguera itself is a resort town with plenty of life and while the front of the hotel may look out onto the main street, to the rear is a sandy beach excellent for water sports. The hotel has a reputation for attracting a very select clientele to its elegantly decorated rooms and this may be due to the first class cuisine served up in the restaurant. Golf packages including the Villamil as a base can be arranged either through Forte or Select World Golf and Leisure Link who feature the hotel in their programmes.

Palma offers quite a selection of quality accommodation. Longmere recommend the five star Valpariso Palace which has the kind of facilities that keep guests happy day and night. In the Select World Golf programme there are three exceptional hotels in Palma to select from. The two hotels which enjoy a four star rating, Hotel Sol Bellver and Hotel Sol Palas Atenea cannot be faulted for their quality and the amenities they provide, but the five star Hotel Melia Victoria is probably the pick for golfers. The hotel has two pools surrounded by gardens and terraces as well as an indoor pool and gym. Views over the bay and the cathedral are as impressive as the sumptuous interior decor.

Another excellent hotel for golfers featured by Select World Golf is the Hotel Melia De Mar, which is only half a mile from the course at Bendinat. Set on the coast with a sandy bay, guests can enjoy either the extensive water sport facilities or relax in the gardens around the swimming pool. The rooms here are spacious and luxurious and both international and regional cuisine can be enjoyed.

Other hotels of repute in this general area include the Bonanza Playa and the Son Caliu. Both hotels, featured by Longmere enjoy coastal settings and provide quality sport and leisure facilities. The same can be said of the Hotel Sol Antillas which enjoys spectacular views out over the Mediterranean from its elevated position on the bay at Magalluf. This hotel can be found in the Select World Golf Programme, while the aparthotel option figures with Longmere, who also include two fine apartment complexes in the Jardim Del Mar at Santa Ponsa and the Club Galatzo at Paguera, which has the added advantage of a free bus service to the course at Santa Ponsa.

To the north of the island there are two courses which golfers based around Palma really should take time out to play. Canyamel is another of Pepe Gancedo's excellent championship standard creations and, although a fairly recent addition to the island's courses, it is likely to prove the main attraction. While Canyamel matures, the course at Capdepera is an integral part of the beautiful countryside. Surrounded by mountains and played around six lakes, the course calls for some accurate play, although there is some width to the fairways to inspire confidence.

The Travel Club of Upminster feature the rather exclusive five star Hotel Formentor at the northern tip of Majorca, which is an excellent alternative to the Palma area and their package includes golf at Son Vida. A less costly but still fine three star quality option from the same operator is the Hotel Daina in Puerto Pollensa. However, it should be noted that the major emphasis in the programme offered by the Travel Club of Upminster is placed on the "Beginners' Weeks".These are based in the Club Illa d'Or apartments which are well equipped with a garden setting, swimming pool, tennis courts and sun terrace, and beginners receive instruction at the Pollensa Club. The course here is a 9 hole Gancedo creation with water in play on four holes and is one to be enjoyed by all golfers, not just beginners.

Two other 9 hole courses on the eastern side of the island can be found at Son Severa and Vall d'Or and these are very natural courses which will not disappoint golfers out for a relaxing round. Club Med residents at Porto Petro might enjoy the diversion golf can bring and here too introductory classes are available , with golf on a 'proper' course 15 minutes away.

Canyamel (Golf Resort Marketing)

Tenerife

There may not be a lot of golf to be had on Tenerife, but that has not prevented the Golf del Sur complex becoming a very popular holiday golf choice, especially in the winter.

Ideally, the visiting golfer should also be able to look forward to some golf on the Amarilla course, but the conditions here have been known to fluctuate.

No such fears at Golf del Sur, 27 holes all told, a Gancedo design which plays host to European PGA tour events and is immaculately maintained by an army of greenkeepers and a high tech irrigation system. The setting and surroundings have to be seen to be believed, with cacti, palm and banana trees lining the fairways, a snow capped mountain in the background, hardened lava flows, and black volcanic sands. As for the golf, accuracy rather than power is the key.

Amarilla has also played host to a European PGA tour event and has a number of challenging holes especially those on the clifftops bordering the Atlantic.

Recommended accommodation tends to be split between Golf del Sur itself and Los Cristianos, a 15 minute drive away. Both are reasonably well placed for the bright lights of Playa de las Americas.

The most popular form of accommodation for golfers around Golf del Sur are the villas and apartment complexes grouped in small village style developments. 3D feature the rather prestigious Sunningdale Villas, while the slightly more obvious Golf Park Apartments are recommended by both Longmere and Sovereign. These two operators also include respectively the studios at Green Park and the Fairway Village Villas. All are equipped to a very high standard and provide a wide array of leisure facilities for guests to enjoy.

Those golfers more suited to hotel life should find satisfaction in Golf del Sur at the Tenerife Golf Hotel, a four star hotel featured in the Golf Holidays International programme, which has first class facilities and overlooks the sea. Also recommended by this operator is a three star hotel in Los Cristianos, the Princesa Daqil, which will suit golfers looking for a bit of nightlife.

Sovereign feature the slightly more upmarket Hotel Paradise Park, just outside Los Cristianos. This is a modern hotel with well furnished rooms. Guests can either relax around one of the three pools, take a sauna or indulge in slightly more strenuous activities at the tennis and squash courts or the gym.

Recommended apartment complexes in Los Cristianos, which it must be stressed is much more of a traditional tourist resort than Golf del Sur, are Tenerife Sur Apartments featured by Golf Holidays International and the Aguamar Apartments which are recommended by Longmere.

Gran Canaria

One way of enjoying golf in the Canary Islands is by means of a P&O golf theme cruise with tuition on board ship and the opportunity for a round or two at the various ports of call. Both Tenerife and Gran Canaria feature on cruise itineraries and a round at Royal Las Palmas on Gran Canaria is a must. Despite the fact that the island boasts only two courses it is, like Tenerife, a popular destination for holiday golfers and well served by the tour operators. The main course, Royal Las Palmas is coupled with the splendid Hotel Golf Bandama by Longshot, Sovereign and Eurogolf, and the link extends to the adjacent clubhouse where meals are taken. The management of what is very much a golfers' hotel organise competitions for guests and there are other sport and leisure activities to suit, while the hustle, bustle and nightlife of Las Palmas is only 20 minutes away.

Designed around an extinct volcanic crater, the course is not unduly long but it is a genuine championship test and has hosted some prestigious invitation tournaments. Accuracy from tee to lush tree-lined fairways is as important as club selection here, with good judgement of distance essential on the sloping hillside. Although the course is never crowded it is members-only on Sundays, which is an opportunity to head south to the Maspalomas Club, with its sand dunes and palm trees.

Maspalomas is not likely to be the first choice of the serious golfer taking a vacation on Gran Canaria, and the resort itself is all sandy beaches, peace and tranquillity which may, however, be the ideal recipe for a golfer after just the occasional round.

If it sounds the ticket, then Longmere offer a package including accommodation in bungalows at the Las Vegas apartment complex which has a typical array of leisure facilities and is only 500 metres from the course.

Amarilla *(Amarilla Golf and Country Club)*

European Golf

Holstebro (*Golf Resort Marketing*)

While the British are undoubtedly rather conservative in their selection of holiday golf destinations, this is not without some justification. Time is a precious commodity and a round on an unattractive or poorly maintained course represents a wasted day to the golfer on vacation. The increasing popularity of the game has also proved in many respects detrimental, with certain courses and resorts exploiting demand by charging rates out of all proportion to the enjoyment or quality provided. The British have been known to vote with their feet (and pockets) when things get out of hand, as the Costa del Sol will testify and the experience of the last few years has taught golfers to look for value for money in every aspect of their holiday golf.

It has accordingly been argued that the British look no further than the proven golf resorts when it comes to arranging their holidays and in Europe particularly show scant regard for anywhere other than France, Spain and Portugal. While there may be an element of truth in this, it may equally be argued that relatively few European countries take the trouble to promote their golf seriously as a tourist attraction and those that do target the British market often fall way short of achieving their objectives.

Denmark

Denmark is one country which has over the years invested considerable time and money in trying to woo the British holiday golfer. The nett result so far can hardly be described as an overwhelming success. Denmark is, however, very popular with German golfers. The proximity of the two countries may have something to do with this but of more relevance is the simple fact that access to the golf courses in Denmark is much easier and cheaper for many Germans than in their own country.

For obvious reasons Denmark does not have quite the same appeal to the British holiday golfer, nor does the country boast the kind of internationally acclaimed courses which in themselves are a natural draw and the miles and miles of beautiful beaches do not unfortunately come with a Mediterranean sun guarantee. In short, it is all too easy to dismiss Denmark as a potential holiday golf destination.

The very essence of holiday golf is the opportunity presented to enjoy something different, be it Fife links for the Berkshire golfer, or the hot sun on some foreign fairways during darkest winter and until now Denmark has lacked an edge to its golf promotion. West Jutland is, however, tackling the problem head on and the local tourist authority, golf clubs and hotels are working together to attract more British golfers to the region, which boasts some 22 courses.

Excellent brochures on the area and the golf have been produced which can be sourced via travel agents or obtained direct from the Danish Tourist Board. The promotional material details not only the many scenic, sporting, historic and cultural attractions of West Jutland but also the courses and hotels and the extent to which they do understand and cater for the needs of the holiday golfer. Ferries to Esbjerg and flights to Billund make the region very accessible from the UK, green fees at even the top clubs such as Holstebro are no more than at an average British course and with packages inclusive of golf being offered by hotels of all standards there is some excellent value to be had both on and off the course.

Germany

It has already been broadly hinted that Germany has a bit of a problem when it comes to golf and truth be told it is all down to image. Remarkably enough for a country where tennis was something of a 'people's sport' long before Becker and Stich began winning Wimbledon, golf is very much seen as a game for the rich and privileged. Despite the success of Bernhard Langer, and the influence he has brought to bear, the grass roots appeal will need some careful nurturing, aided by more investment in facilities and training programmes, if more Teutonic golfing superstars are to follow in his footsteps.

In many respects, however, the Germans are too sensitive to what they perceive as their golfing shortcomings and very little effort is made to associate Germany and golf in tourist promotions, particularly to the British. Statements to the effect that the clubs are very private and do not welcome visitors can be, more often than not a convenient way of saying, "Look, we don't know why you could possibly want to come and play golf here, we don't have a golf school, we don't have a driving range ..." etc, etc.

There would appear to be a number of popular mis-

 Holstebro (*Golf Resort Marketing*)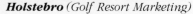

conceptions about both the general level of facilities at British golf clubs and why the British go on golfing holidays. While Germany is admittedly one of the last places a British golfer would think of in the quest for his own personal David Leadbetter, it does however have many redeeming features.

Not the least of these are the fairy tale castles to be found the length and breadth of Germany in the most picturesque of surroundings and it is possible through the Gast Im Schloss chain to plan a golf tour of Germany with accommodation in fine castles which have either their own courses or clubs nearby.

The properties featured in this European Castle, Hotels and Restaurants programme, are spread throughout Germany. Of particular note close to the Dutch border are the Parkhotel Wasserburg Anholt, a touch of Versailles surrounded by a moat, and its near neighbour the Sportschloss Velen, which fits the fairy tale castle mould very neatly and has its own course as well as a multitude of other sporting attractions. Further east the Burghotel Hardenberg's romantic setting is also ideal for golf and other more energetic pursuits.

To the south in historic Weilburg outside Frankfurt the Schloss hotel enjoys a dramatic situation high above the town and offers golf at the Braunfels club close by. From Weilburg to Boppard is a natural progression.This is a popular tourist resort on the Rhine, a starting point for cruises to the Lorelei, which also boasts the Golfhotel Jakobsberg, a former monastery now an international class resort hotel, offering panoramic views over the Rhine.

The Hotel Schloss Weitenburg is similarly well placed to afford its guests the opportunity to savour the scenic Neckar Valley, southwest of Stuttgart, and the management are only too pleased to arrange golf as well as other sporting activities.

In Bavaria, golfers may not only take advantage of the superb facilities of the Schlosshotel Egg, which dates back to the 12th century but also consider a golf programme in the Berchtesgarden area put together by Heinzelmann Reisen of Schoenau Am Konigsee. The scenery in this part of the world forms as impressive a backdrop to a round of golf as any to be found in Europe. The Heinzelmann Golf Safari programme includes golf at three or four courses and first class accommodation at prices which give the lie to the 'jet set' image.

Austria

On the border with Germany and close to Berchtesgarden lies Salzburg, where the scenery is every bit as dramatic and the attractions if anything better known. The same holds true probably for the whole of Austria, given its popularity with the British skiing fraternity and it is perhaps time that the British golfing fraternity sat up and took some notice.

When it comes to golf, Austria is most definitely equipped to service the holiday golfer, boasting a network of 100 or so Golf Green Austria Hotels, all to four or five star standard and associated with courses where they arrange tee times and organise guests' transport accordingly. A full listing of the hotels and the courses can be obtained by requesting the brochure from the Austrian National Tourist Office.

Golfers should also contact Blue Riband, who for years have specialised in skiing trips to Austria and have now turned their experience and expertise to the golf here. This British operator is well versed in the requirements of holiday golfers and its golf programmes to the French Riviera come very highly recommended.

The flag bearer of Blue Riband's Austrian venture is the Sporthotel Brandlhof in the Salzburg region which has a magnificently maintained championship standard course and the Saalach river, around which the course has been laid out, is often brought into play. The hotel is one of Austria's most highly rated and modern standards of luxury blend well with traditional decor and service.

Blue Riband Specialist Golf Tours

Austria's world of golf is a sparkling new addition to the Blue Riband's portfolio. The unique package of gloriously scenic golf includes a 5-day pass costing £125, playing the 27 holes (par 72) at Saalfelden / Brandlhof, 27 holes at Zell am See / Kaprun (par 72) and the two 18 hole courses at Küssen and Kitzbühel (pars 73 and 72). High quality courses in stunning scenery, exhilarating alpine air and sunshine and the best of traditional Austria in Salzburgerland.

The truly luxurious hotels featured include the Hotel Schörhof, where traditional elegance, exceptional cuisine and the sauna, solarium and fitness room combine to provide a memorable stay, and the Hotel Brandlhof. The Brandlhof has first-class 9 hole and 18 hole golf as well as luxury sports facilities including indoor pool and sauna, heated outdoor pool, three squash courts, indoor and outdoor tennis, indoor and outdoor riding school and a beauty salon. The decor of this spacious luxury hotel, which is used by many companies for conferences and entertaining, is the very best of traditional Austria. Other hotels who are partners in the golf package will also feature.

Tailormade holidays or events, by air or by coach for groups, are already proving popular. The ambience and charm of Austria are of course well known and loved by the British traveller and the development of golfing facilities lives up to the high standards for which Austria is famous.

Saalfelden

Enquiries and brochure requests welcome
please contact Blue Riband
Tel: 0403 258582
Fax: 0403 274504

Also in the Salzburg region at Zell Am See, the championship Schmittenhoehe course featured by Blue Riband is part of the Europa Sport Region Club and this is indisputably one of Europe's top holiday golf courses. Under the summer sun, surrounded by the densely forested slopes of the snow-capped mountains, a round of golf here is a truly memorable experience, and the course layout with its many trees, water hazards and bunkers presents a stimulating challenge to match the setting.

Another area featured in some depth by Blue Riband and by British Airways is the Tyrol and though the courses at Kitzbuehel are by no means as daunting for golfers as the Hahnenkahm may be for downhill racers, this is the golf centre of the Alps and deservedly so with first class accommodation and a good selection of local courses.

Blue Riband can offer tailormade golf holidays to any part of Austria for individuals or groups and there is little likelihood of disappointment for even the most demanding of golfers in either the courses or the resorts featured.

Switzerland

The Swiss, too, are now waking up to the potential of their courses and the country itself as a summer holiday golf destination on a par with Austria. The Official Guide to Golf Courses in Switzerland available from the National Tourist Office is a most informative publication on the subject, updated annually, detailing access to the courses, associated accommodation and restaurants as well as things to do and see in each locality.

Crans Montana through its course at Crans-Sur-Sierre and the Canon European Masters is probably the best known of Switzerland's golf regions and the three courses here provide the opportunity to play in a most rarefied atmosphere high on the plateau dominating the Rhone Valley from the Matterhorn to Mont Blanc. In Crans-Montana there is no shortage of quality accommodation to be found such as the Hotel de Golf itself, the Grand and the Royal and the region is something of a sun trap in the summer.

But there are other excellent courses and resorts to be found throughout Switzerland. The Ascona Club close to the Italian border welcomes visiting players and both the course and resort enjoy a beautiful setting overlooking Lake Maggiore, with first class accommodation on the club doorstep at the Castello del Sole, Giardino, Eden Roc and Delta hotels.

Like Kitzbuehel in Austria, the famous Swiss winter sport resort of St Moritz can also boast some excellent golf and the Engadine-Samedan Club here was founded over 100 years ago. Visiting golfers will find the club most hospitable and the course is considered amongst the most scenic of all Switzerland's alpine golf strongholds. Samedan itself has a good golf oriented hotel in the Golfhotel des Alpes, while St Moritz is only 10-15 minutes away and many of the superb hotels here such as the Badrutt's Palace, Carlton, Chelsea Guardalej, the Kulm and Suvretta House all offer golf packages for their guests.

Nearer to the Austrian border in the foothills of the Alps is Bad Ragaz, an immaculately maintained course with tree-lined fairways and very agreeable surroundings in which to relax after the round. Bad Ragaz has two hotels whose guests enjoy playing privileges at the course, the Quellenhof and Grand Hotel Hof Ragaz. Both are to the highest standards associated with Switzerland.

Italy

Golfers tempted to pack their clubs in the boot of the car and embark on a grand tour of central Europe should most definitely not consider turning round and heading home at the Italian border. The Lombardy region is not only one of the most scenic in the whole of Italy with its mountains, lakes and rivers, but the fertile plains also make for excellent golf terrain and almost half of Italy's active golfers play on the courses here. Clubs such as Marticello and Milano have hosted Tour events and others such as La Pinetina and Carimate are arguably amongst the most picturesque in Italy. One relatively new course near the banks of Lake Garda, Gardagolf, is also destined to become a firm favourite and a visit to this course combining accommodation at the Grand Hotel Gardone will prove most rewarding.

LE TRE VASELLE
★ ★ ★ ★ ★

Le Tre Vaselle is a charming 16th Century house located in the heart of the hill top village of Torgiano, a gateway to Perugia and Assisi, in Italy's green heart - Umbria. This pretty village is surrounded by the famous vineyards of the Lungarotti family, who own the hotel, their winery and wine museum are 5 minutes walk away.

Elegantly furnished in a rustic Umbrian style with beamed ceilings, stone fireplaces and terracotta floors, Le Tre Vaselle has 62 rooms, including 12 suites, all with bath/shower, air conditioning, T.V., and minibar, a highly recommended restaurant "Le Melagrane", bar and terrace. Plans are underway for a swimming pool and health club.

Only 15 minutes drive from the Perugia Golf Club, the hotel offers special rates for golfers, and can arrange many other activities including riding, tennis, cycling and country walks. Le Tre Vaselle is just two hours drive from either Rome or Florence.

LE TRE VASELLE

06089 Torgiano (Perugia) - Telefono 075/9880447 - Fax 075/9880214

Circolo del Golf
Perugia

*$\mathcal{O}$nly a few minutes drive from Perugia, and from Le Tre Vaselle,
in the village of Santa Sabina, is the Perugia Golf Club.*

*Circolo Golf Perugia was originally opened in 1959 as a private club with 9 holes.
Set in Italy's green heart - Umbria the course is beautifully landscaped
with an abundance of trees, protecting the greens and fairways.
Since 1959 the course has grown in popularity and increased to 18 holes (par 71)
with a modern wooden driving range with 12 covered positions
and a putting green with 18 holes.*

*In 1993 the club was proud to host the first Perugia open,
Part of the Professional Golf Association European Tour, attracting over 120 players.
There are golf masters always on hand to help those wishing to improve their golf.*

*The attractive club house is surrounded by ciprus trees, as you would expect to see in Italy,
with a fine restaurant, bar and pro-shop, completing this unique and friendly golf club.*

Circolo del Golf Perugia

Santa Sabina - 06074 Ellera (Perugia) - Tel. 075 / 5172204 - Fax 075 / 5172370

Piemonte, Lombardy's neighbour is home to the second highest concentration of golfers in the country and the course at the I Roveri club as well as the facilities and setting rank amongst the most memorable in Italy. Turin makes an ideal base for this course and others in the region, with the luxurious Turin Palace Hotel highly commended.

A popular tourist attraction for the British over the centuries has been Venice and this area too has its fair share of courses to note, such as the Venezia and Albarella. The Venezia is a links creation built upon the dunes of the Lido and considered one of the most difficult in Italy, while the Hotel Excelsior is one of Venice's finest and ideally situated for the course.

South of Venice is the island of Albarella. The golf here can be very testing with the prevailing sea breezes and difficult rough. The island is a resort in its own right, very lively and with many sports and leisure facilities available which guests of the four star Golf Hotel Albarella will find most agreeable.

Rimini is another celebrated holiday resort, although golfers visiting this region of Italy, Emilio Romagna, should consider a slightly removed base at Cervia, which boasts the Adriatic's finest course and a layout which will appeal to all golfers. The first nine are typical of English parkland with narrow tree-lined fairways, while the back nine with water in play on six holes offer an American-style target golf test. As a resort hotel the Grand at Cervia cannot be faulted. Both beautiful and imposing it sits on the beachfront and is only a couple of miles from the course.

Solemar International Travel Ltd of Glasgow specialise in organising golf packages to the Tuscany region where there are four courses of note, Montecatini, Casterfalfi, Cosmopolitan and Punta Ala. Solemar are able to provide golfers with a choice of hotel and villa accommodation throughout the region in resorts such as historic Florence and the elegant coastal town of Punta Ala, some 100 miles south of Pisa. Much closer to the leaning tower is another fine beach resort at Tirrenia, the ideal base for the Cosmopolitan course.

Extending the journey into Umbria, Italy's heartland, will prove most worthwhile for the discerning golfer with an appreciation of the finer things in life. Not only does Perugia boast one of Italy's most exquisite courses, the parkland design is also to championship standard and the club is developing its practice and coaching facilities to rival any other complex in Italy. Le Tre Vaselle set amongst the vineyards of the Lungarotti family estate at Torgiano dates back to the 16th century and is now effectively Umbria's most prestigious hotel. The elegant furnishings and decor are in a traditional style with many pieces from the 16th and 17th centuries and these are complemented by the tastefully integrated modern facilities. As a base to explore the many scenic and cultural attractions of Umbria, Le Tre Vaselle has few rivals and the privileges guests enjoy at the local Perugia Club make it an ideal selection for holiday golfers.

Rome has many attractions but little to recommend it as a prime golf resort, although businessmen and others who have occasion to visit the city will find two very accommodating courses in relaxed, secluded surroundings. The Golf Club Roma and the Club Olgiata are both set in the beautiful countryside neighbouring the city and Roma's Acquasanta Course meanders through some splendid scenery including the ruins of villas and an aqueduct from Augustan times. Oligiata has played host to the World Cup and features some long demanding par four holes as may be expected on a course of this standard.

Arrangements for visiting golfers to play these two courses are part of the service offered by the Hotel Excelsior and the Cavalieri Hilton. The standard and facilities of both hotels are second to none in the whole of Rome, and the combination of golf and accommodation on offer is distinctly upmarket.

Mediterranean Islands

While Majorca may be the major attraction for golfers, it should not be forgotten that Menorca has a fine course at Son Parc and Monmouth Court Holidays can offer accommodation and golf at this complex.

Belleair who specialise in holidays to Malta can arrange a programme to include golf at the Royal Malta Golf Club, a course that all players should enjoy which is surrounded by many other excellent sports and leisure facilities.

Select World Golf and 3D both feature Corfu and the Ermones Beach Hotel in their programmes. The hotel lies less than a mile from the Corfu Country Club which has much to recommend itself. All golfers will appreciate the setting and the magnificent greens, while tree-lined fairways, lakes, streams and sand traps are incorporated into a grand design which makes the best of the natural resources.

As holiday golf destinations go, Menorca, Malta and Corfu do not boast a wealth of courses to attract visitors, but what they do have is well worth making the effort to play and golfers who are not averse to sampling just the one course on their travels will find these islands most attractive.

Son Parc (*Monmouth Court*)

North Africa

Mohammedia *(Chris Lawrence/Best of Morocco)*

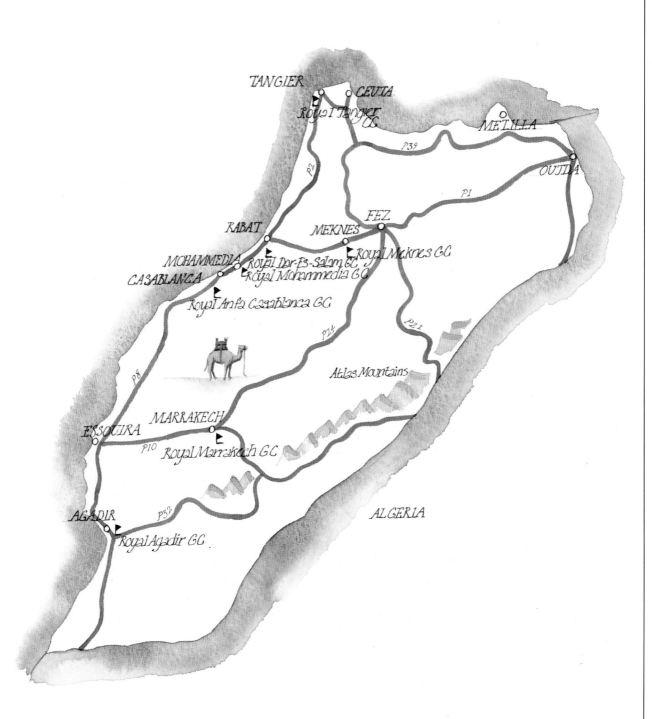

Any country boasting a course which can lay justifiable claim to the title of Robert Trent Jones' greatest masterpiece commands serious attention from the international golfing community. In Morocco's case the aspirant is the Red Course on the 45 hole Royal Dar es Salaam complex just outside Rabat. Off the championship tees the course measures an intimidating 7500 yards and every hole on this spectacular and magnificently maintained course is memorable in its own right. Tour professionals have been united in their admiration for this course since its inception and many relish the demands it makes on their game. Mere mortals will still find the course posing too many problems from the front tees which reduce the length to just over 7000 yards, but the course is fair and golfers on top of their game should return a score to reflect their handicap.

The Dar es Salaam complex is set on a 1000 acre estate, dominated by forests of cork trees and features a majestic clubhouse in keeping with the royal patronage. The facilities here are literally beyond compare and golfers can while away the time before, between and after rounds in the splendid practice area, relaxing around the pool or sampling the fine cuisine in the restaurant.

At 6600 yards, the Blue Course still represents a challeng-

ing test of any golfer's ability, though the fairways here are all the more inviting for the relative scarcity of bunkers. Many visitors to the course stay the day and enjoy 27 holes, with nine holes on the Green Course to wind down (or restore confidence) after an assault on either the Red or the Blue Course and a suitable period of recuperation.

A specialist operator when it comes to organising golf in these parts is The Best of Morocco who recommend the superb new Hyatt Regency Hotel in Rabat as the ideal base for golf at Royal Dar es Salaam. This is an exceptional hotel to the high standards associated with Hyatt throughout the world and may be a bit rich for some golfers' tastes or budgets. If so an excellent alternative is offered by this operator in the Hotel Rabat Safir.

Another operator to offer tailormade golf holidays including the Dar es Salaam and Hyatt Regency option, is FM Incentives who are actually based in Casablanca. The likes of Golf Inc. and good travel agents can always arrange a package utilising the services of FM Incentives and the scheduled flights of Royal Air Maroc. Golfers are assured of a warm welcome from FM Incentives who cater well for groups and individuals.

Casablanca lies just over an hours drive from Rabat

Royal Rabat *(Best of Morocco)*

along the Atlantic coast and Forte are quick to point out the attractions of their Hotel Royal Mansour in the heart of this cosmopolitan city as an eminently acceptable base for golf at Dar es Salaam and Royal Mohammedia which is only 15 minutes down the road to Rabat.

The five star Hotel Royal Mansour is rightly rated as one of the world's premier hotels and the cuisine, service and accommodation here match the opulence of the decor which features marble columns and exotic Moorish arches.

Until Dar es Salaam appeared on the scene the Royal Mohammedia was considered the pick of Morocco's courses, both for the test of golf it provides and the magnificent coastal setting. Although the natural terrain is too flat for the course to be described as a true links, the prevailing breezes from the Atlantic have an all too familiar influence.

The Best of Morocco and Select World Golf both recommend the inclusion of Mohammedia in any Moroccan golf itinerary. Select World Golf's programme is based around the Forte Hotel Royal Mansour while, as an alternative base to Rabat, The Best of Morocco opt for something slightly more downmarket but very acceptable nevertheless in the Hotel Miramar in Mohammedia itself.

Golf International join The Best of Morocco in promoting a new jewel in Morocco's golf crown, the Palmeraie Golf Palace which boasts a fine Robert Trent Jones designed course on its beautiful estate, just to the north of Marrakesh.

A great deal of technology and labour went into creating this green oasis in the desert of Marrakesh, with over 1,500,000 cubic metres of earth removed, grass imported from the USA and state of the art irrigation systems installed to cope with the blistering summer sun at its hottest. The result is most impressive as one would

expect from Trent Jones and there is a natural maturity and harmony to the layout which belies the resources employed. Water hazards come into play on nine holes in the form of rather picturesque lakes which blend well with the white sands of the bunkers, placed as ever to catch those errant tee shots and mishit approaches.

While the clubhouse resembles a palace in its own right, the facilities of the Palmeraie Golf Palace are truly regal. Accommodation in the luxuriously appointed rooms or sumptuous suites cannot be faulted and the hotel has a wide selection of restaurants, bars and the latest sport and recreation facilities, including bowling.

In many respects, the Palmeraie development also puts the old Royal Golf of Marrakesh course very much back on the map. This established course is situated close to a real palace, and the fairways wander through vast orange groves. The golf here and at Palmeraie together with the traditional attractions of Marrakesh, make the city an ideal choice for holiday golfers.

As for alternative accommodation, The Best of Morocco feature a number of hotels across the quality spectrum and Marrakesh also offers up the possibility of a Club Med holiday with a difference, the village lying in the heart of the city, though residents do have access to the Palmeraie facilities.

Much more typical of Club Med is their rather fine complex at Morocco's leading beach resort, Agadir, and golfers will enjoy the opportunity to play the 27 hole Les Dunes development, which many consider to be amongst the most picturesque in the world. The Best of Morocco include Agadir and Les Dunes in their programme, as well as Tangiers at the other extreme of Morocco's Atlantic coast which also boasts a Royal Club.

Royal Rabat (*Chris Lawrence-Best of Morocco*)

PARADISE FOR
THE GOLFER

PARADISE FOR
THE GOLFER'S FAMILY

T U N I S I A

THE SUNNIER SIDE OF THE MEDITERRANEAN IS NEVER OUT OF SEASON. JUST 2½ HOURS CLOSE

To arrange a holiday in Tunisia see your local travel agent. For free literature write to Tunisian National Tourist Office, 77A Wigmore Street, London W1H 9LJ. Telephone 071-224 5561.

Name: _____ Address: _____

_____ Postcode: _____

GW/12/93

Promoted primarily as the answer to every golfer's winter prayers, with temperatures rarely dropping below 17° Celsius and new courses up to European standards, Tunisia has not taken long to establish itself on the holiday golf map.

For a country which fifteen years ago had only one golf course, this is no mean achievement and it represents a commitment to golf that will, all things being equal, see a new course opening every year for the foreseeable future.

The courses lie dotted along 1200 kilometres of coastline where some of the most beautiful beaches on the Mediterranean are to be found. Not to mention superb accommodation in traditional Moorish styled hotels with modern facilities, beautiful gardens and all manner of alternative leisure attractions to hand. There is challenging and enjoyable golf to be had for high and low handicappers alike, on courses which follow the natural rugged contours of the land.

Golfers are served by the airports at Tunis to the north and Monastir to the south. Northern Tunisia is covered with woodland and the new course at Tabarka in the north western tip has been designed to blend with the natural oak and pine forest through which it runs. Tabarka will have everything from giant sandhills offering unparalleled views out over the Coral Coast to lake hazards reminiscent of America's finest.

The port of Tabarka at the foothills of the Atlas mountains has a charm which reflects a strong French influence. The choice of accommodation here can be expected to expand rapidly in the immediate future with the completion of a number of hotels around the golf complex. Presently, however, with neither the course nor the resort facilities really in a suitable state to welcome serious holiday golfers, operators such as Panorama who specialise in this area, have the resort 'on hold'.

This is thankfully not the case with Hammamet which is one of Tunisia's more established resorts and enjoys a popular and lively reputation, based on the entertainment provided in the modern hotels outside the walled 15th century Medina.

The entertainment provided by the golf courses at Hammamet is no less stimulating. At the Golf Cytrus Resort there are two 18 hole courses and a 9 hole "practice" course. The holes cover an area of some 300 acres with half a dozen lakes, some woodland, olive groves and a new variety of Bermuda grass all employed in the grand design of Ronald Fream. Of the two 18 hole courses the Olive provides an enjoyable round with few hazards and wide open fairways, while The Forest is much less forgiving, undulating fairways providing difficult lies and long carries - an ever present challenge.

Ronald Fream was also responsible for the Yasmin course just a kilometre away from Cytrus. Here the challenge of the water hazards is more a tempting series of short cuts to greens with three or four levels. Two lakes lie at the heart of this course whose rambling fairways have universal appeal.

Hammamet boasts a number of fine hotels and an excellent Moorish style Club Med village. Green fees are not included in Club Med packages but in Tunisia they are no more expensive than at an average British club. All the major specialist golf tour operators serving Tunisia offer complete packages for purchase in the UK and the accommodation on offer in the Hammamet region represents exceptional value.

Port El Kantaoui *(Panorama)*

Perhaps the most imposing, with its landscaped gardens and terraces, is the Manar, a five star luxury hotel featured by Golf Holidays International and Select World Golf. These operators together with Panorama and 3D also include the Aziza, a modern four star hotel in traditional style with spacious accommodation overlooking the sea. Another four star hotel favoured by Panorama is the Sheraton, not least for its fine cuisine, while the Phenicia also comes highly recommended by Thomsons. This award winning hotel has excellent amenities and is set in most pleasant surroundings, as is the Hotel Bel Azur which may only enjoy a three star rating, but deservedly features in the Panorama programme.

And so, to the south and its palm groves and Monastir. Home to another Ronald Fream course, this time nestling between desert and sea. Monastir is one course with a feature well known to UK links golfers, the prevailing sea breeze. Add to that, ravines to cross, water hazards to negotiate and hills to climb. This is not a course for high handicappers to play, but all golfers should at least appreciate the scenery. While most operators will arrange golf at Monastir, only Select World Golf presently feature a package based in Monastir at the Kuriat Palace, elegant and luxurious overlooking one of the area's most beautiful beaches. The course is only 10 minutes away from another of Club Med's villages set in the heart of a marina.

Like Tabarka, Monastir presently enjoys a reputation for picturesque peace which may well change, not necessarily for the better, with the Dkhila Monastir development. In the meantime, the golf at Monastir remains primarily a diversion from the attractions of Port El Kantaoui some 20 kilometres away.

Golf El Kantaoui has played host to the Tunisian Open on numerous occasions and dates back to 1979. Again designed by the Californian golf architect Ronald Fream, El Kantaoui has three loops of nine holes which take the golfer from links to parkland. The 18 hole layout is determined by daily rotation, with high handicappers restricted to the 9 hole option during busy periods. As may be expected of a course which plays host to a European PGA event it is testing, well maintained and irrigated courtesy of the functional water hazards.

Often described as Tunisia's premier Mediterranean resort, it will come as no surprise to learn that here there is the widest range of accommodation on offer. Select World Golf feature Les Maisons de la Mer, an apartment complex in traditional style alongside the marina and the beach, with waterfront cafes, bars and restaurants close by. Sovereign offer budget accommodation at the comfortable but basic three star Hotel Abou Sofiane, Panorama also feature a three star hotel in the El Mouradi which has impressive facilities. Most popular amongst the operators is the Hotel El Kanta, a quality hotel set in beautiful gardens and within the grounds can also be found the Kanta Residence. This is more competitively priced, reflecting the studio style of accommodation, but guests have full access to hotel facilities.

Other four star hotels recommended in Port El Kantaoui are the Marhaba Palace from the Panorama programme, the Hotel Riviera featured by Golf Holidays International and the Hotel Hasdrubal, a favourite of Select World Golf. All of these hotels combine comfort and elegance in traditional Moorish style with modern facilities and a wide assortment of leisure attractions.

The two crowning jewels of the Port are the five star Hotel Diar El Andalous` featured by Panorama and renowned for its excellent service, and the equally highly rated Hannibal Palace from the Sovereign programme.

Panorama Holiday Group Limited

Looking for somewhere warm and sunny to play golf in the winter? If so then Tunisia is the place to go. Whether you choose to stay in Port El Kantaoui or Hammamet, the hotels are within a few minutes walk or short taxi ride away from the resort golf courses. This cuts down on car hire costs and makes the holiday great value for money.

Port El Kantaoui - a 27 hole course whose close proximity to the hotels makes it a favourite with high and low handicap players alike. Handicap restrictions apply and segregate players over 30 handicap from lower handicap players.

Monastir - a challenging 18 hole course which has undergone major maintenance to improve fairways and greens. To encourage players, Monastir runs a shuttle service to and from El Kantaoui.

Hammamet, one of Tunisia's oldest established resorts, is fast becoming a popular golf resort. The three 18 hole courses are a welcome addition to Tunisia and offer players of all standards a variety of play.

Discounts are available to guests of certain Hammamet hotels when playing the Cytrus course.

Panorama's Golf Experience offer organised golf tournaments and learn to play golf weeks in both Hammamet and Port El Kantaoui.

Weekend breaks, schedule service from Gatwick or Heathrow, are available at competitive prices and if none of the holidays featured suit your requirements we will tailor one to meet your needs. Just call the Golf Department on 0273 746877.

Africa

Fish River (*Sun International*)

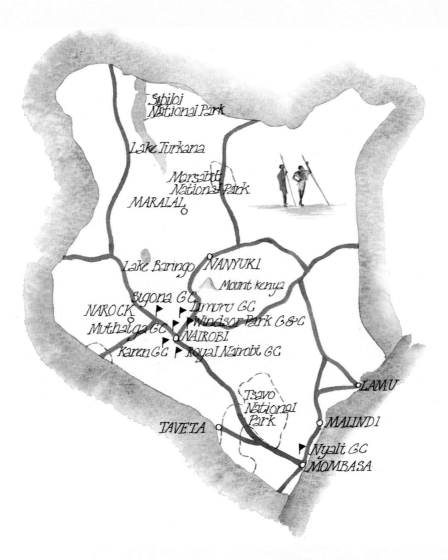

The natural splendour of Kenya has made it a firm favourite with tourists now for many years. Rift Valley with its lakes, Mount Kenya and Kilimanjaro, magnificent bleached palm beaches are just some of the attractions which draw visitors to Kenya year after year. Many will take the opportunity to see the country on safari in game reserves such as the Masai Mara, and golfers too can enjoy a holiday of a lifetime in this beautiful country.

It is claimed, and with some degree of justification, that the new course of the Windsor Golf and Country Club offers quite simply the best challenge of golf and the most spectacular surroundings in the whole of Africa. Certainly there would be no disagreements from British Airways, Golf Inc. and Sunsport who specialise in golf (and safari) holidays to Kenya. All endorse the claims of this particular resort to be the ideal base from which to enjoy not only Kenyan golf, but the countryside and the wildlife.

In many respects the Windsor development sets an entirely new standard for Kenyan resorts and certainly provides a welcome focal point for the holiday golfer. Accommodation options range from standard rooms and studio apartments to cottages in the magnificent grounds and all are well appointed and elegantly decorated. In addition to the golf, guests can enjoy the hotel's many other sporting facilities, and the restaurant has already established a reputation for fine cuisine.

The golf course is of true championship standard and meanders through mature forest and coffee plantations with water hazards a feature on the opening and closing stretch. The condition of the course is magnificent and golfers will appreciate the lush, springy fairways and fast greens.

The Windsor Golf and Country Club is only 15-20 minutes drive from the centre of Nairobi and the airport, which sees it ideally placed for some of the other major courses such as Muthaiga, Karen, Limuru, Sigona and Royal Nairobi, all of which are less than half an hour from the hotel. Nairobi's own situation, some 5500 feet above sea level, means that the climate is ideal for golf, warm but not too hot during the day and cool and comfortable in the evenings.

Muthaiga has for many years played host to the Kenyan Open and until the arrival of the Windsor course stood alongside Limuru as the two most challenging of the 36 courses in Kenya. The location of the Limuru course, on the edge of the Rift Valley amidst tea and coffee plantations, is truly one to be enjoyed, while the Sigona course on the outskirts of Nairobi is one of the most undulating.

Nestling at the foot of the Ngong Hills is the Karen Country Club (Karen Blixen of "Out of Africa" fame lives next door.). This is another championship standard test and a very scenic one at that, while mention must be made of the elder statesman, Royal Nairobi, founded in

The Windsor Golf and Country Club, Nairobi

J.Quraisby

The Windsor Golf & Country Club is set in the midst of indigenous forest and surrounded by coffee plantations yet lies just seven miles from central Nairobi.

The club opened its doors in January 1992 and has already gained a reputation as the most stylish venue in Nairobi with a championship golf course that has been hailed as the best in East Africa.

Accommodation is in one of the 80 elegant Victorian-style club rooms, or guests can choose from the 20 enormous studio suites or the 15 double cottages which overlook the fairways with breathtaking views of the Kenyan Highlands beyond. Each club room is spacious and equipped with television and mini-bar, although the special butler service provided on each club floor provides a more personal touch than regular room service.

The setting of the Windsor Course is an inspiration. It is at an altitude of over a mile above sea level, which may account for the extra distance players enjoy on every drive as the ball flies further through the thinner air. The appeal to golfers at all levels is that each hole boasts five immaculate tees. Windsor can stretch from 5580 yards of the ladies' tees to 7232 yards from the men's championship tees. The greens are immaculate and apart from the severe rough, monkeys and even leopards are the other hazards of a purely African variety that can sometimes be seen on this course!

Other recreational facilities available at Windsor are a health club with steam rooms, gymnasium with state of the art exercise machines, beauty salon, vast swimming pool with changing rooms, putting green, driving range, five floodlit tennis courts, squash courts, jogging track and croquet green.

The dining is varied and guests can choose a snack or a salad in the Conservatory, or enjoy a sumptuous buffet in the Country Room, whilst the demands of the gourmet are catered for in the elegant Windsor Room. British award winning chef, Richard Tonks has introduced his own innovative style using the wealth of fresh fruit and vegetables at his disposal together with excellent local meats and fish from the Indian Ocean.

Of course no visit to East Africa would be complete without seeing the wildlife for which the region is best known. Windsor Hotels has two luxury tented camps in the Masai Mara, just a short flight from Nairobi, from which game drives are arranged. First time visitors to the bush are always amazed at the number of animals to be seen - herds of giraffe and wildebeest, lion, elephant, cheetah and a range of plains game can all be easily found a short drive from the camp.

The Windsor Golf & Country Club are happy to arrange a weekend safari for their guests during their stay in Nairobi.

Reservations:
Windsor Golf & Country Club,
Telephone: (010 254) 2 802149/802210
Facsimile: (010 254) 2 862300   20 Lines

1906, which can boast a royal charter and affiliation with other royal clubs throughout the world.

The attractions of this area and the standard of golf to be enjoyed are such that many golfers will be happy to base their entire holiday around Nairobi. British Airways accordingly feature a suitable seven night package as well as a slightly extended ten night programme which takes in their Safari Club Trophy.

Sunsport Tours, with their links to Africa Exclusive one of the UK's leading safari operators, and Golf Inc. whose programme is coordinated with the United Touring Company (Kenya) Ltd, can both offer tailormade programmes to suit a two week or longer vacation for golfers who would like to see more of the country and experience life on safari.

Such programmes can include visits to the Serengeti, a stopover at Treetops, as well as a few days at the world famous Mount Kenya Safari Club, which has a 9 hole course of its own with another close by at the Nanyuki Sports Club.

For a two-centre golfing holiday in Kenya, though, the recommendation is to head for the glorious Mombasa coastline, and both Sunsport and Golf Inc. recommend the Nyali Beach Hotel as the place to pass some idyllic golfing days.

In addition to boasting its own championship course bordering the Indian Ocean, the Nyali Beach Hotel enjoys a wonderful tropical setting on the edge of palm fringed silver sands. Accommodation is luxurious and there are extensive sport and leisure facilities for guests to enjoy.

Just south is the lively port of Mombasa, with a 9 hole course dating back to 1911. The views from this rather testing course out over the Ocean are superb, and further golf can be found along the coast at Malindi though the 9 holes here are not among Kenya's best.

The Coast (Kenya Tourist Board)

Karen Club (Golf Resort Marketing)

Leopard Rock

Now for something really special in long-haul golfing travel.

Africa cannot be packaged. It is too immense, too diverse. Nothing can trivialise the sight of a million wildebeest migrating across the Serengeti Plains. Nobody can forecast the heavenly colours of a Kariba sunset, the hues changing by the day. Frankly, anyone trying to package such experiences is missing the point. Each of us must be allowed to discover this magnificent continent in their own way, at their own pace. For the enduring appeal of Africa is that it leaves an intense but quite different impression on every one of its visitors.

The golfing opportunities are equally varied and exciting. Imagine teeing off against a backdrop of spray from the awesome Victoria Falls. Or striding down a fairway with Table Mountain rising majestically above you. Maybe your preference is for a relaxing 18 holes just a stone's throw from the soft white sands and warm blue waters of Mombasa's sunny beaches.

This is golf in Africa. Here you will find some of the world's finest courses amid spectacular scenery and a glorious climate. Uncrowded and inexpensive, Africa is a golfing heaven.

For the best advice on the vast range of golfing opportunities that Africa has to offer, you talk to an expert. Sunsport Tours is a specialist in the sports travel field - we know sport and we know Africa. Every holiday we arrange is tailormade to specific requirements and we pride ourselves on our ability to judge the right combination of locations, activities and accommodation for each one of our clients.

Our professional and efficient personal service ensures that every aspect of your holiday runs smoothly, with attention paid to even the smallest details.

Your personal golfing encounter with Africa can begin with a simple informal chat to Sunsport Tours.

We await your call - Africa awaits your heart.

Sunsport Tours
Hamilton House
66 Palmerston Road
Northampton NN1 5EX
Tel: (0604) 31626 Fax: (0604) 31628

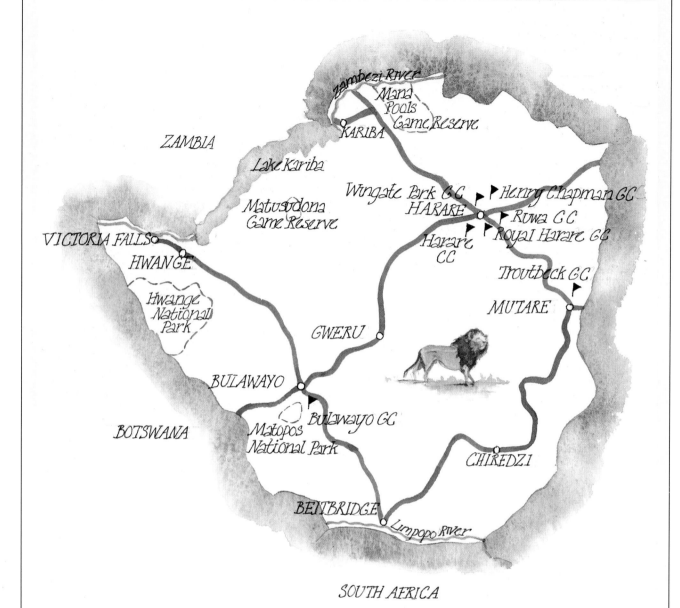

In many respects Harare, like Nairobi, boasts an ideal climate, good golf courses and enough attractions to keep most golfers happy for the duration of a normal vacation. However, in the case of Zimbabwe to restrict the holiday to the capital means not just missing out on the splendour of the Victoria Falls and other such phenomena but also some of the most exhilarating golf to be found in the country.

Sunsport's expertise in organising golf trips to Zimbabwe which incorporate all the necessary ingredients to give the holiday real flavour is, if anything, based on even greater local knowledge than their Kenyan programme, given the number of cricket tours they have organised to these parts. Sunsport are joined again by Golf Inc. and by Zimgolf in promoting Zimbabwe as an ideal holiday golf destination. All tours begin in Harare, with recommendations to include the Eastern Highlands and the Victoria Falls in the itinerary making a three-centre golf holiday.

Royal Harare and Chapman are the capital's two courses to enjoy international recognition. Of the two, Royal Harare enjoys the more prestigious reputation which may have something to do with the fact that it adjoins the presidential residence and dates back over 100 years. This is a parkland course and, although it is rather flat, an abundance of trees and bunkers conspire with difficult rough to protect the par on each hole. By contrast Chapman is much more undulating, with testing water hazards as well as trees to beware of, and this immaculately maintained course regularly stages the Zimbabwe Open.

Two other courses which visitors should find the time to play lie outside the city. On the road to the Eastern Highlands some 20 miles east of Harare is the Ruwa course with its old thatched colonial clubhouse where holiday golfers should experience some magnificent hospitality. The course itself is colourful, scenic and secluded as well as rather testing. The Wingate Park Club can be found ten miles to the north east of the capital and like Ruwa, is to championship standard and renowned for its tight tree-lined fairways.

There is no shortage of first class accommodation to be found in Harare and the city also provides plenty of cultural, recreational and wildlife attractions to keep golfers occupied off the course. Sunsport recommend the Meikles Hotel, probably the best known of all Zimbabwean hotels with a celebrated history going back to 1915. Meikles is located in the centre of Harare and guests may relax around the fine rooftop pool or take refreshment in one of the four restaurants and seven bars to be found in this elegant hotel.

For those who prefer something more in the style of a traditional country house hotel, there is the option of the Landela Lodge just outside Harare. The Lodge can only accommodate up to 20 guests in its luxurious rooms, but it is well worth enquiring after availability given its superb setting and the amenities to be enjoyed locally.

Zimgolf favour the Cresta Lodge in Harare and this operator generally selects from the Zimbabwe Sun Hotel Group properties. The group has a reputation for providing first class accommodation in well appointed rooms and the hotels themselves provide guests with wide ranging entertainment and leisure facilities.

From Harare it is a leisurely three and a half hour drive to the Eastern Highlands, the dramatic mountain ranges which run along the border with Mozambique. These are some of the most breathtaking surroundings imaginable in which to play golf and accommodation to match can be found in the Leopard Rock Hotel which comes highly commended in the Sunsport and Zimgolf programmes. The property has been recently restored in its original style along the lines of a French chateau and sits in the Bvumba Mountains surrounded by panoramic views and lush rain forests. Accommodation standards here are nothing short of luxurious and guests do not want for leisure facilities to enjoy off the course.

The Leopard Rock golf course itself has been carved from the forested slopes of the mountains. Panoramic views to the plains below and into neighbouring Mozambique add a new dimension to a round of golf on what is now, since its redesign was completed in 1991, a championship standard course.

As an alternative base in the Eastern Highlands, Sunsport and Zimgolf also feature a resort with its own course, The Troutbeck Inn, whose claim to fame might just be that the log fire in the hall has never gone out since the hotel was completed in 1950. This is a splendid hotel whose rooms look out over pine forests and a lake. Sporting facilities include many a throwback to colonial days with croquet on the lawns, billiards and clay pigeon shooting.

The pine forests figure prominently in the layout of the 9 hole course here, as do water hazards and massive boulder formations. Many holes feature challenging carries before the sanctuary of fairway or green can be found. The views here may not be quite as impressive as from Leopard Rock but that is a relative assessment to be understood in terms of magnificence.

South of Troutbeck can be found the Claremont course, which is part of the Montclair Casino complex, another fine accommodation option in the Zimbabwe Sun Programme. This is a 9 hole course with scenic views over fruit farms and Loch Mudie, with a most convivial atmosphere in the clubhouse. Closer to Leopard Rock and in the centre of Mutare, a charming town in classic colonial style as befits the provincial capital, is the Hillside Club, where members are expected to maintain proper standards of dress and etiquette. British guests who can manage this are especially welcome. The course is played over a full 18 holes with plenty of trees and water to pose questions of golfers suffering from an overdose of local hospitality.

Victoria Falls should need no introduction and, as may be expected of such a well known resort, there are a host of things for visitors to enjoy after making the two hour flight from Harare. Operator programmes obviously include traditional tourist attractions such as the Flight of Angels, a low altitude pass over the Falls in a light aircraft, visits to game reserves, the leisurely Sundowner Cruise on the Zambesi, plus the opportunity to experience some local culture and visit a crocodile farm.

As good a place as any to watch the spray rise above the falls is from the Elephant Hills golf course and there are plenty of other distractions to be found on this magnificent course. The new 18 hole layout follows an original Gary Player design and lies a couple of miles upstream from the Falls in the heart of the African bush. Small game are no strangers to the lush fairways here and elephants can often be seen grazing within a few hundred yards of the 16th. At times the golf almost seems incidental in this idyllic setting and some concentration will be called for if any kind of a respectable score is to be returned.

The Elephant Hills Hotel, to which the course belongs, offers accommodation of distinction in rooms with modern fixtures and fittings while the decor is traditional African. Sunsport include this hotel in their programme and stress the hotel's many leisure facilities which include several restaurants and a casino.

Zimgolf offer a number of options including Elephant Hills and two of the top Zimbabwe Sun properties, the Victoria Falls Hotel and the Makasa Sun. From the Falls it is just an hour and a half detour to the Hwange National Park, the largest reserve in Zimbabwe. The Safari Lodge here provides excellent accommodation and a base from which to really appreciate the unspoilt wilderness of the country and its incredible wildlife.

Troutbeck Inn (*Hotel Management International*)

Deep in the heart of the beautiful Republic of Bophuthatswana lies Sun City - a chance to escape the northern winter and find summer in southern Africa. Sun City is just an hour and a half by car from Johannesburg and daily flights operate between Jan Smuts International Airport and the airport at Sun City. There is a variety of accommodation available at this luxurious resort.

The Sun City Hotel rises out of the hills overlooking a magnificent landscape of subtropical gardens. It has one of the finest pool terraces in the world and standard accommodation features include private bathroom, radio, direct dial telephone, colour television and air-conditioning.

The Cabanas has its own swimming pool, terrace and bar. Rooms open out onto lush gardens leading down to the lake and Waterworld. Standard and de luxe rooms are available. The Cascades Hotel offers a world of fantasy all its own, with a theme of cascading water both inside and out.

Guests can take a step into the past at the Lost City - restored in 1992 as an integral part of the stunning entertainment and sports amenities of this amazing leisure resort. The Lost City pays homage to art, architecture and nature. It has recreated the marvels of an age-old, mythical civilisation, with The Palace as the focus.

The Palace is the jewel in the crown at the Lost City, with each of the 338 magnificent en suite rooms decorated with unique individuality and luxury. All have views over water, jungle or the Valley of the Waves. A royal welcome awaits every guest at The Palace. Even the architecture and richly accented decor are like no other in the world, for its lavish custom-made furnishings are complemented by unique paintings, sculptures, mosaics and other art. The dining options at The Palace are numerous and include The Crystal Court, The Tusk Lounge and Villa Del Palazzo.

Sun City is a sportsman's paradise. At Waterworld guests can enjoy just about any watersport imaginable. The Gary Player Country Club offers a spectacular spread of fairways and greens carved out of the rugged Pilanesburg Bushveld. Guests can test their skills on a course where a select few of the world's greatest players compete in the annual Sun City Million Dollar Golf Challenge. This course is probably the most demanding in the country. The design of each hole, the shape and size of the greens and bunkers and the tricky putting surfaces thoroughly test each facet of a golfer's game.

The second, and newest golf course at the Sun City Resort is The Lost City Course. The 18 hole, par 72, desert-style course covers 55 hectares and has been designed by the Gary Player Company. Each hole has four tees, giving a course length of between 5400 and 6900 metres. There are waste bunkers for the first time in Southern Africa and for the golfer who likes to live a little dangerously there are live crocodiles at the 13th hole!

Sun International
Badgemore House
Gravel Hill
Henley-on-Thames
Oxfordshire
RG9 4NR
United Kingdom
Tel: (0491) 411222
Fax: (0491) 576526

South Africa

Whatever becomes of the Republic of Bophuthatswana and other such tribal homelands in the great South African shakeup, few would bet on anything much changing at Sun City. This magnificent resort rising from the bush has always drawn comparisons with Las Vegas, another resort which seems to exist in a world of its own in the middle of nowhere.

While the delights of golf in Durban or around Cape Town suspended as far as the operators are concerned pending the resolution of the political struggle, Sun City is still very much in favour and the new Lost City development is proving immensely popular. With a second 18 hole course to complement the Gary Player Country Club, renowned throughout the golfing world for its Million Dollar Challenge, Sun City now stands very much as a complete holiday golf destination.

The recommendation is also very much a tribute to the new facilities and spirit injected into the resort since the Lost City project was completed. Inspired, they say, by the adventures of Indiana Jones, exciting waterborne rides traverse the jungle environment created by exotic forests, gardens overflowing with colourful flora and the spectacular waterfalls, lakes and pools which are everywhere to be seen and enjoyed.

The grand design of the Palace Hotel is reflected in many eyecatching features, the ornately decorated towers reaching to the blue skies above, intricate mosaic floors, murals created with semi-precious stones, all evoking the spirit of some mythical civilisation. While this hotel is now undoubtedly the showpiece of the resort, there are other hotels and cabanas from which to select accommodation and none of the properties on the estate will disappoint in terms of quality. Operators such as Whole World Destination Travel, Sunsport, Golf International, Elegant Resorts and Golf Inc. can be relied upon to offer advice on the various options available.

As for the golf, the international acclaim which Gary Player's Country Club course enjoys is fully merited. This is a championship course which will appeal to all golfers, with inviting fairways and holding greens offset dramatically by the rugged Pilanesberg scrubland. Strategically placed sand traps and water hazards add to the challenge and enjoyment.

The Lost City course is another Gary Player enterprise. The 18 holes here have a very open feel to them. However, off the championship tees the course plays very long and will prove most daunting to higher handicappers who are well advised to select from one of the three alternative tee boxes which dramatically improve the playability factor and enable all golfers to derive pleasure from the layout.

Other pleasures to be had in Sun City are available 24 hours a day and it must be remembered that facilities here are those of a small town, with theatres, cinemas, clubs, casinos and ten pin bowling all available as well as the more usual selection of sporting and leisure facilities. Residents of Sun City who tire of the resort's own attractions can also elect to enjoy day safaris to the Pilanesberg National Park, a diversion to be highly recommended to those golfers who have yet to experience something of the real Africa.

Mauritius

This island paradise edged with white sandy beaches and surrounded by clear blue sea now boasts the Indian Ocean's first championship standard golf course. Designed by Hugh Baiocchi, the development is situated in the 80,000 square metre estate of the Belle Mare Plage, one of the island's deluxe hotels. Golf Inc. are working closely in cooperation with the hotel management to bring this resort to the attention of the British golfing public and other operators such as Silk Cut and Zimgolf include the hotel in their latest programmes.

Located behind the hotel, the course is set upon a former deer reserve and there is a lush green feel to the whole area. The fairways are bordered by many different species of plants and trees while water hazards dominate the majority of holes. There are some long carries to fairways and accuracy onto the greens is often a must if a watery grave is to be avoided.

The Belle Mare Plage enjoys a most picturesque setting. The thatched roofs of the hotel buildings, shady palm trees, tropical gardens, beach and lagoon present a picture postcard impression of an idyllic retreat and visitors will not be disappointed by the high standards of accommodation, cuisine and entertainment provided.

Next door to the Belle Mare Plage is another golf course, the 9 hole design of Gary Player at the Saint Gerain, which provides a testing and enjoyable round typical of his creations. The course can be found in the estate of what is for many the finest property on the island, Le Saint Gerain Hotel, Casino and Golf Club. This hotel, featured by Silk Cut and Elegant Resorts, has long been distinguished for its luxury accommodation and excellent service. Set on a peninsula amidst acres of tropical gardens, the hotel boasts a beautiful private beach and a lagoon perfect for watersports. International cuisine is a speciality here and there is always the casino to relax in after dinner.

Le Touessrok is a sister hotel to Le Saint Gerain and is considered to be one of the most romantic hotels in the world. It has undergone extensive refurbishment and accommodation here is again to deluxe standards. While the hotel boasts its own extensive facilities, guests can also enjoy those of Le Saint Gerain, including the golf course, some 20 minutes away.

With the advent of the Belle Mare Plage course it is to be anticipated that this is the area and the hotels which will prove most attractive to holiday golfers but it must be noted that Mauritius does have other courses. Approximately one to one and a half hours from the Belle Mare Plage and Saint Gerain are two 18 hole courses, the Gymkhana Club and Le Morne Paradis, and the 9 hole Le Trou aux Biches. While the golf may not be to the championship standard of the new course nor to the same degree of difficulty as Le Saint Gerain, these are courses which can still be enjoyed and the journey will at least provide an opportunity to experience more of this wonderful island.

Belle Mare Plage
Hotel & Resort

Possibly the best resort in Mauritius

A first class hotel and resort offering fun and entertainment for a relaxed and sporty
holiday with high international standards of cuisine and comfort.
A conference room hosting up to 90 persons is among other facilities if you wish to combine work and leisure.

A perfect location:
The hotel is situated directly on one of the loveliest
sandy beaches of Mauritius, set in a well tended
tropical garden of some 80,000 square metres.
The hotel beach is protected by natural coral reef, a
superb and safe area for all watersports.

A wide range of accommodation:
86 Comfort Rooms   56 Prestige rooms
30 Club rooms   6 Deluxe suites
All rooms are sea-facing and comfortably furnished
in the same local creole style with terrace or bal-
cony, air-conditioning, bath and/or shower, television and video channels, radio and music system,
mini bar, room service and international direct
dialling telephone.
The Club rooms (33m²), Prestigo rooms (34m²) and
Deluxe Suites (68m²) all have separate bath and
shower and hair dryer.

Restaurant and bars:
The main restaurant where breakfast and dinner
are served is located along the beach.
The á la carte restaurant is located between one of
the swimming pools and the beach.
There is a beach restaurant and coffee shop.
Two hotel bars.
In the Golf clubhouse there is a restaurant and bar.

Services:
Laundry and dry cleaning are available 7 days a
week.
A fitness centre.
Three boutiques, plus a golf pro shop.
Entertainment programme and a live band.
A "COCO CLUB" for children from 9am to 9pm.
A casino and a Piano Bar.

Free Facilities:
Windsurfing - Beach volley ball - French bowling -
Chess game in the garden- Yoga - Glassbottom boat
- Kayak- Sailing - Snorkelling trips including equip-
ment - Waterski - Pedalos - 4 Tennis courts (clay) -
Table tennis - Body building equipment - Squash -
Sauna - Cold swimming pool - Aerobics - Aquagym -
a mini golf course- 9 hole golf course- 18 hole
championship golf course, handicap certificate
required.

New Championship Golf Course
Designed by BIAOCCHI FALKSON BARNARD (South Africa)
this championship golf course - the first in the Indian Ocean -
has been created on the Deer reserve. This enables it to profit by
a natural centenarian vegetarian, with numerous water sports
and lakes. These 64 hectares of prime virgin ground, are planted
with hundred year old plant species , and dotted with
bougainvillaea and flamboyant trees.
The clubhouse, in addition to the changing rooms and the individual pigeon-holes for equipment, is decorated in the East India
Company Style, and adjoins the reception at the entrance to the
building.
Two international Pro-Am Tournaments per year are planned as
from the first year. Every Saturday a tournament will be organised for the benefit of clients of Belle Mare Plage Golf Hotel and
Resort, founder members and residents of the resort only.

GOLF
INCORPORATED

For bookings and further details call now on 0959 565777

Asia

Hyatt Saujana (Hyatt Hotels)

THAILAND

KANGAR

KOTA BHARU

363

159

PENANG

Bukit
Jambul G&CC — GEORGE TOWN

PERAK.

KUALA
TERENGGANU

IPOH

Royal Perak GC

Cameron Highland GC
PAHANG

Royal Kampung Kuantan GC
Awana G&CC — KUANTAN

Kelab
Negara Subang GC
Royal Selangor GC
KUALA LUMPUR — Sanjana G&CC

487

Seremban International CC

SEREMBAN

Ayer keroh G&CC
MALACCA

95

JOHOR BAHRU

Singapore Island G&CC
Raffles GC
SINGAPORE — CHANGI
Sentosa GC — Keppel GC

Malaysia may be many things to many people but it is not a top ranking long haul holiday golf destination in the opinion of many tour operators. Not that this should deter golfers from seriously considering Malaysia, whose courses are among the best in Asia and where the game has been established for over 100 years courtesy of British traders and planters. However, given the abundance of courses and numerous quality resort locations to select from, problems can be posed when there is a distinct lack of tried and tested golf programmes available through specialist tour operators.

An approach to Golf Inc. should yield some joy, while the many general tour operators who feature Malaysia can provide details on golf at or near their featured locations. The pick of the courses can be expected to have their own associated hotel accommodation, which will accordingly be to a very high standard .

One way of guaranteeing some excellent golf while savouring Malaysia to the full in the limited time available on holiday, would involve a two-centre vacation taking in the capital Kuala Lumpur and one of the more celebrated beach resorts such as Penang.

An ideal starting point would be the Saujana Golf and Country Club which lies close to Kuala Lumpur's international airport, a magnificent estate which boasts a luxury international hotel and two championship rated courses. Saujana is one of Malaysia's most prestigious golf complexes and the two 18 hole layouts courtesy of the Ronald Fream Design Group are simply superb in terms of their condition and the challenge they present.

The sports and leisure facilities available, as well as the accommodation on the estate, are world class and the hotel has its own shopping arcade for those lacking the inclination to head into the colourful bazaars of Kuala Lumpur. Not for nothing though is this modern metropolis known as the Garden City of Lights and there are some superb restaurants and lively sophisticated clubs to enjoy at night.

From Kuala Lumpur a flight to the old British colonial resort of Penang is recommended. Often described as the Pearl of the Orient, this is a tropical paradise of swaying palm trees, sandy beaches, blue skies and friendly natives. A further cause for recommendation is the presence of a Robert Trent Jones course fashioned from land which was once considered uninhabitable not to mention unplayable. It goes without saying that the golf is to championship standard, the views from the course distractingly scenic and magnificent and the holes themselves do not give up their par without a fight. The lush undulating fairways are lined with fruit trees, 87 bunkers are to be found on the course and as in any Trent Jones design they are not there for show, while water comes into play on nearly half the holes.

The course surrounds the Equatorial Hotel which again ranks as one of the premier resorts in the whole of Asia, boasting excellent leisure facilities and entertainment day and night on the premises for guests, especially golfers who can expect to be pampered from arrival to departure.

The Equatorial is featured by Asia World Travel and doubtless many other general tour operators servicing Malaysia, all of whom with a degree of prompting either directly or through a local travel agent will be able to offer a programme including Saujana and Penang and possibly even come up with some alternatives.

Penang *(Paradise Golf Plus)*

A golfing excursion in Malaysia is never complete without a visit to Saujana Golf and Country Club - one of the 100 best golf resorts in the world* and without doubt the best golf club* * in the country.

Located less than five minutes from the Kuala Lumpur International airport at Subang, the 400 acre Saujana Golf and Country Club (popularly known just as Saujana) boasts two magnificent and challenging international standard golf courses and an excellent clubhouse with a full complement of sporting and dining facilities.

Adjacent to it, nestled in cool, green surroundings, stands the Hyatt Regency Saujana, a five star hotel positioned as the businessman's country resort in the city. A member of the internationally reputed Hyatt chain, it has luxuriously furnished rooms and suites. There are also first class facilities for conferences and conventions.

Saujana's two golf courses, the Palm Course and the Bunga Raya Course (named after the national flower, the hibiscus) are well known to golfers throughout the country, having been voted by the golfers themselves for six consecutive years as the best in Malaysia in several categories including, Best Golf Course, Best Maintained Course, Most Memorable Course and the Club with the Best Facilities.

The accolades are well deserved. Of the two golf courses, the Palm Course ranks head and shoulders above all other courses throughout the country for its challenging layout, memorable holes and pristine playing conditions all year round.

The Palm Course, respectfully dubbed 'the Cobra' for its testing and challenging play, is 6565 yards off the blue tees and 6959 yards from the black. Fringed by mature palm trees and set in undulating terrain with gaping ravines, the Cobra has the most tricky, fast and challenging greens in the country. One of its holes, the 172 yard (216 yards from the black tees) par 3 second hole is rated the most difficult hole in Malaysia. A game with the Cobra can be either satisfying and rewarding or simply deadly. Come take the challenge ... the Cobra awaits you.

Distinctly different is the 6400 yards Bunga Raya Course with its beautiful rolling landscapes and serene lakes, adding a new dimension to the game. The Bunga Raya Course has a wide expanse of undulating greenery that creates a sense of freedom and space.

Although the layout of the course, with fewer ravines and thick woods is short and looks deceptively easy, the game here too is challenging and many have regretted underestimating it.

Both courses have something to offer to the beginner as well as the professional. Selection of the tee boxes to play is important. All the various tee boxes - Black, Blue, White and Red - are open to play daily.

Saujana has the greatest number of buggies in the country and both courses have fully laid tracks. To enjoy the Palm Course, however, one should walk it and enjoy its various captivating flora and fauna.

Playing at Saujana Golf and Country Club is a privilege for the discerning golfer, We are the best. We are also the friendliest. Welcome to Saujana.

For enquiries please contact:
Saujana Golf and Country Club
PR & Marketing Department
3rd Mile, Off Jalan Lapangan Terbang
47200 Subang
Selangor Darul Ehsan
Malaysia
Tel: (010 60) 3746 1466
Fax: (010 60) 3746 2316

*"100 Best Golf Resorts in the World" published by Harry N. Abrams Inc and Golf Magazine, USA.
** Golf Malaysia Magazine.

SILVERBIRD
THE FAR EAST TRAVEL SPECIALISTS

Silverbird was founded in 1985 as a specialist tour operator to the Far East and Australasia. The company is now recognised as the specialist in the preparation of tailor made itineraries to these destinations. Silverbird's policy is to be completely flexible and as a result they do not produce a fixed price list but instead will cost your trip on an individual basis after discussing your requirements. Clients will then be provided with a quotation, for any combination of destinations, in the most practical way and at the most economical price.

In particular Silverbird specialise in golfing holidays to Thailand, which has over 50 superb 18 hole courses throughout the country, many of them up to international championship standard. Many of these courses are set in exotic locations and are beautifully maintained. Huge investment ensures that the courses are of the highest standard and the club house facilities are superb. There are strategically located drink huts every four or five holes and caddies add to your enjoyment with their expert knowledge of the greens.

Thai hospitality is very evident in the golf clubs where visitors are made very welcome. Golf courses are accessible from hotels in Bangkok, Chiang Mai, Hua Hin, Pattaya and Phuket. Hotels available in Bangkok include the deluxe riverside Shangri La and the luxurious Dusit Thani. In Ko Samui you can choose to stay at the first class Imperial Samui or the deluxe Dusit Santiburi.

Silverbird can also arrange golfing holidays to many other areas of the Far East. An exciting alternative is golf in mainland China where there are two golf courses which are readily accessible to the Portugese territory of Macau. You can either visit the course for the day or stay over in either Macau or in the Golf Club Hotel at Chung Shan Hot Spring Golf Club.

Singapore is another enviable alternative. There are six 18 hole courses on this tropical island and packages, including transport, can be arranged from most of the hotels selected by Silverbird.

Whichever destination you decide upon you will be given the best possible advice when planning your itinerary for either business or leisure.

Silverbird
4 Northfields Prospect
Putney Bridge Road
London
SW18 1PE
Tel: 081 875 9090
Fax: 081 875 1874.

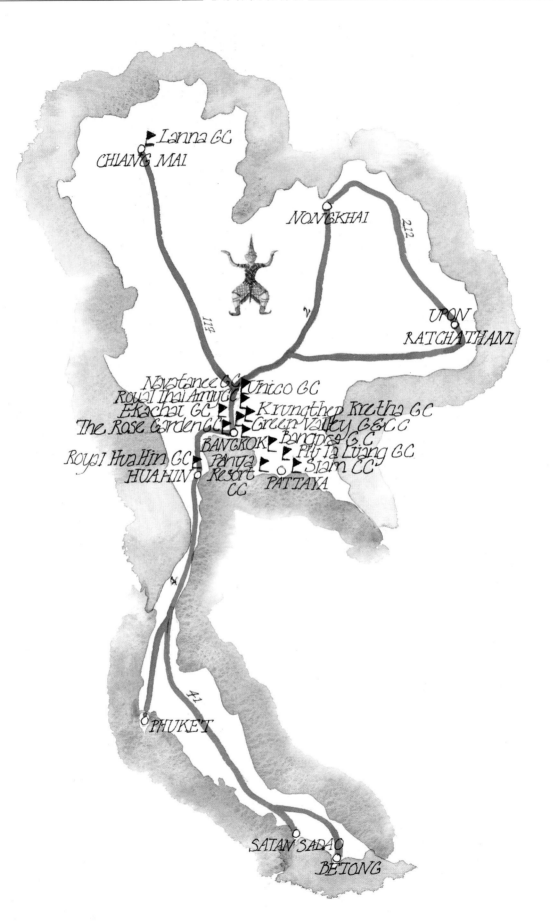

CHIANG MAI   Lanna GC

NONGKHAI   212

UPON RATCHATHANI

Navatance GC   Unico GC
Royal Thai Army GC
Ekachai GC   Krungthep Kretha GC
The Rose Garden GC   Green Valley G&CC
Bangpra G.C
BANGKOK   Phi Ta Luang GC
Royal HuaHin GC   Panya   Siam CC
HUAHIN   Resort   CC   PATTAYA

PHUKET

41

SATAN SADAO
BETONG

Now established as Asia's premier holiday golf destination, Thailand offers visitors a wealth of fine courses and excellent accommodation. Famous for its golden temples, ruined cities, deep jungle and tropical beach resorts Thailand affords the opportunity to enjoy the best of both worlds, combining golf with sightseeing and perhaps a few hours relaxation on the beach or by the pool before sampling the local cuisine and the nightlife.

Silverbird, in conjunction with Royal Orchid Holidays, offer the most extensive golf programme to Thailand covering courses and resorts from the north at Chiang Rai down to Phuket. Bangkok is included as an option for golfers determined to combine their sport with a thorough investigation of the capital's manifold and diverse attractions. In and around Bangkok there are over a dozen quality courses to choose from, of which Rose Garden, Royal Gems and Army Old are some of the most popular. Pinehurst, which came to prominence in 1992 as the venue for the Johnnie Walker Classic, is one definitely not to be missed and lies approximately one hours drive north of the city. There are three 9 hole loops here, each with a character of its own. The North Course features plenty of water, the South has a links feel and the West is well wooded. The whole complex is magnificently maintained and the clubhouse facilities amongst the most lavish in Asia.

British Airways also include the Bangkok area in their golf programme and, together with Silverbird, they recommend the Royal Garden Riverside as an ideal base for golfers. The hotel is located in Thonburi across the river from Bangkok and is renowned for its international cuisine and leisure facilities.

There are, of course, many other hotels to select from in Bangkok ranging in rank from deluxe to tourist standard and Silverbird, together with operators like Silk Cut and Asia World Travel, will cooperate in arranging a programme to suit holiday golfers' budgeted allocation of both time and money. The hustle and bustle of Bangkok does not lend itself to easy living and two-centre holidays are recommended to those hoping for the opportunity to relax as well as play the golfing tourist.

Thailand's second city, Chiang Mai, the 'Rose of the North', lies over 400 miles north of Bangkok and is well known for its history and culture, one well known attraction being the temple of Doi Suthep which stands in magnificent isolation on a hilltop with panoramic views over the impressive countryside.

Chiang Mai is also home to three of Thailand's better courses and the climate in this area is fresher and cooler than around Bangkok and the resorts to the south. The Chiang Mai Green Valley Course is one which all golfers will relish. Although at first glance the rather flat and generous lush fairways with their sprinkling of trees may not appear to pose many problems, visitors will find the many water hazards and bunkers protecting the greens all too troublesome unless they tighten up their game.

The Lanna Club can be found close to the Doi Suthep temple and is a lovely mature course to play. It is also very long and the fairways are much tighter than at Green Valley with no relief from water as the layout includes over 20 lakes, and bunkers do come into play on the fairways.

A third course in the immediate vicinity providing facilities for visiting golfers is the Chiang Mai Country Club and an excursion north to Chiang Rai can always be arranged to take in the picturesque Santiburi Country Club course.

The Silverbird/Royal Orchid accommodation options in

Rose Garden (Paradise Golf Plus)

Chiang Mai include the Royal Princess, a first class modern hotel with its own nightclub in the city centre, and a tourist class hotel, the Holiday Garden in the suburbs. Golfers looking for peaceful relaxed surroundings will find them at the quality Chiang Mai Hills Hotel which is surrounded by some beautiful gardens. This is another modern hotel with excellent facilities and its range of international cuisine includes a celebrated Japanese restaurant.

Most holiday golfers though will tend to favour the courses and resorts south of Bangkok and two of the most popular, Hua Hin and Pattaya, lie on opposite sides of the Gulf of Thailand.

It is a three hour drive from Bangkok to the beach resort areas of Hua Hin and its close neighbour Cha Am, which as yet remain more tranquil and less heavily developed than Pattaya and Phuket. Silverbird are joined by British Airways and Asia World Travel in promoting this area as ideal for golf, relaxation and recreation.

There are numerous courses of a very high standard in this region of which Royal Hua Hin, Springfield, Palm Hills and Lakeview should form the nucleus of the golf itinerary.

The Royal Hua Hin dates back to the 1920s and is set out amongst mature tree-lined fairways. The coastal setting does, however, contribute to the challenging conditions in which rounds are played and there is a definite premium on accuracy. Further inland the course is overlooked from the hills by a Thai temple, to which no doubt many golfers will have looked for divine inspiration over the years. Golf Links International use this course for their annual Thailand World Pro-Am, a very popular event around which they organise a ten day programme to the area.

The Palm Hills course is a Max Wexler design just to the north of Hua Hin and will in time be the focal point of an impressive resort complex. To isolate the 18 holes from the buildings some 40,000 trees have been planted and while they mature there is still the network of lakes and waterways to negotiate on what is a very well landscaped course.

There is work in progress too at the Springfield Club, a Jack Nicklaus project which will feature two 18 hole courses. Grass has been specially imported from the USA and as at Palm Hills there has been much tree planting. The East Course is already well established and the design very much reflects Nicklaus' philosophy that the game is all about accuracy rather than power. The holes may not be beyond the reach of the high handicappers, but some solid striking will be required to carry water hazards and find the well protected and sometimes rather narrow greens.

Lakeview may be the latest addition to the area, but it is to championship standard and the fairways here wander through an abundance of mature palm trees and, as is to be expected, water again plays a major part in the design. This is a most picturesque course which affords magnificent views of the mountains and the sea and one which will appeal to all golfers.

The magnificent Dusit Resort and Polo Club is the choice of Golf Links International as host for their tournament and the hotel is naturally recommended by Silverbird too in their programme. Surrounded by an ornamental lake, tropical gardens, sea and sand, the hotel enjoys a classic setting between Hua Hin and Cha Am and the accommodation and facilities merit their luxurious reputation.

As an alternative, set on its own private beach in Hua Hin, both British Airways and Silverbird commend the Royal Garden Resort here which includes a wide range of watersports among its leisure facilities and is well known for its cuisine. In the same area Asia World Travel also offer a wide selection of properties to suit any budget.

On the other side of the Gulf, Pattaya is less than two hours from Bangkok and enjoys a deserved reputation as one of Asia's premier beach resorts. Golf is just one of numerous options that sportsmen and women can enjoy when not soaking up the sun, while the superb restaurants and lively nightlife make for idyllic surroundings in the opinion of some golfers.

Thai Adventures concentrate their golf programme

Thai Adventures

Thailand is rapidly becoming a centre for some of the best golfing facilities at reasonable prices to be found anywhere in the world. At Thai Adventures we have considerable experience in arranging golfing holidays and base our activities in Pattaya. As the sport rapidly becomes more established in Thailand there are now 12 courses within a 20 minute drive of central Pattaya and all provide courses and facilities to a high standard. Pattaya is often considered a superior base for golfing holidays to Bangkok as the capital's traffic problems make the process of simply getting to the course far too long winded.

Some golfers like to play more golf than others, so we have based our programmes on the Pattaya Sports Club golfing section; by taking temporary membership of the club for about £11 considerable savings are made on green and caddie fees. Typically, transport, green fees and caddy fees for a round of golf will cost £15 to £25 through the club. Members are free to use their club membership for discounts as individuals or by joining the daily groups who travel to the courses together from various venues in Pattaya organised by the club.

Two local courses have hosted the Asian Open - The Siam Country Club 7016 yards par 72 and Bangpra 72095 yards also par 72. Other well known courses include Panya Country Club, the Thai Navy course at Sattahip and the Laem Chabang Country Club.

Guests are advised to avoid playing on the weekends as the courses become very crowded and some matches are played slowly with more players than would be normal in Britain.

Thai Adventures
PO Box 82
Victoria Street
Alderney
Channel Islands
GY9 3DG
Tel: (0481) 823417
Fax: (0481) 823495.

on this area as it embodies all the elements they believe necessary for a perfect golf holiday and there are few who would disagree.

Of the several courses in the area, the toughest challenge can be found at the Siam Country Club, which is a long course with undulating tree-lined fairways, problematic rough, sand and water. The course has hosted the Thai Open on a number of occasions and the 30 minute drive from Pattaya out to the club is very highly recommended.

The Panya Resort is another of Ronald Fream's fine creations and a relatively recent one. Water surrounds the 27 hole complex and often comes into play, but precision is mainly required in avoiding the sand traps and working the ball close to the hole on the deceptive greens.

Thai Adventures and Asia World Travel recommend the excellent Royal Cliff Beach Resort as the perfect base for golf in the Pattaya region, which includes other noteworthy courses to the south such as the Rayong Green Valley and the Eastern Star Country Club. This hotel is just ten minutes from Pattaya and enjoys a dramatic coastal headland setting. Guests can enjoy a wide range of sport and leisure facilities and the standard of accommodation is all that could be expected of a hotel which has earned many prestigious 'Best Resort' titles.

As an alternative, Thai Adventures are joined by Silverbird in recommending another first class Royal Garden Resort property. Ideal for golfers who wish to be close to the centre of Pattaya, the hotel nevertheless boasts ten acres of beautiful gardens and its amenities are second to none.

Among the more general operators servicing Pattaya, Asia World Travel are worth contacting for details of alternative accommodation as they specialise in arranging tailormade holidays, while the range of golfing pro-grammes on offer through Silk Cut increases all the time and this operator will always assist golfers with holidays whenever possible.

The island province of Phuket is just over an hours flight time from Bangkok and as one of Asia's most celebrated resorts can be accessed direct from many other cities in the Orient. The attraction of this island lies in the opportunity it provides for total relaxation in an idyllic setting with tropical forested hillsides sloping down to palm fringed beaches and the vivid blue sea.

While the island features with the many operators servicing Thailand, Silverbird recommend golfers combine the resort with another centre if they intend their holiday as a serious golfing expedition.

Not that the courses on Phuket are at all disappointing. The Blue Canyon course is as good a challenge as any low handicapper could ask for with the usual abundance of trees and lakes, narrow fairways and well protected greens. The length of the course can be considerably shortened by judicious tee box selection and high handicappers are advised not to overextend themselves if these beautiful surroundings are to be enjoyed to the full.

The Phuket Golf and Country Club course was designed to provide 18 holes, each with its own unique character and the layout includes doglegs and blind approach shots. Some holes have a distinct links type feel, others require precise play of target golf proportions and some wander gracefully through landscaped forest, but all provide an attractive challenge.

Quality accommodation on the island is plentiful, including Elegant Resorts' Amanpuri, which is half an hour from the Phuket course and a favourite of the rich and famous. Silverbird and Asia World Travel include the Dusit Laguna in their golf oriented programme and this is a luxury hotel with excellent

Rose Garden (*Thai Tourist Board*)

leisure facilities to be enjoyed day and night. The Silverbird programme also includes the lavish Phuket Arcadia on Karon Beach which is another lively hotel with its own nightlife and Cape Panwa which boasts a magnificent beach setting among a huge grove of coconut palms. Asia World Travel feature the Pearl Village as perfect for the Blue Canyon Course and also recommend the Amari and Diamond Cliff Hotel on Patong Beach.

Thai Golf (*Golf Resort Marketing*)

Obtaining the correct insurance cover is something that is probably glossed over in the rush to get onto the fairways and greens following the long winter. However, following a recently reported case, this must now become a top priority on any golfer's list as many golf clubs are now beginning to insist that golfers carry a minimum of third party insurance cover. There are disclaimer notices cropping up on many a golf course throughout the United Kingdom excluding liability for personal injury caused to one golfer by another.

This is a direct consequence of the judgement in a recent case where it was ruled that, "a golfer with a high handicap, who injures another player as a result of a mishit, may be liable in negligence if there is a real risk of such an event .....and such a risk could be avoided without difficulty, disadvantage or expense." In this case a golfer, who hit and badly hurt another with his ball, was held to be guilty of negligence and was ordered to pay £15,500 damages. With this threat of personal liability looming on the horizon most leading insurance companies now advise that all golfers should ensure that they are fully covered against possible incidents of this kind. Failure to be fully insured could result in a very costly court case and could, potentially, be financially crippling for the party concerned.

Third party insurance is only part of the story. Theft of golf equipment is fast becoming a major headache for golfers and many believe that this is covered by their household insurance policies. In fact, most policies only cover theft from the house and not from the car, and if they do cover car theft there is usually a set figure as to the value that can actually be claimed by the insured. A specially tailored golf insurance package would ensure that a full claim could be made in respect of loss, theft or damage to the insured's declared golf equipment and, subject to prior arrangement with the insurance company concerned, night car theft cover could also be included in the policy.

However, theft from the car is not the only problem. If there is loss, by fire or theft, to the golfer's personal effects in the clubhouse or professional's shop then this would not necessarily be covered by a household policy and it is unlikely that it would be covered by the club's insurance policy. Again, a correctly tailored insurance policy would have anticipated this eventuality and the golfer would have no problem in claiming for personal items.

One eventuality that all golfers should address is the consequence of scoring a hole-in-one. It may show great sporting expertise but it will also leave a great hole in the pocket for, tradition decrees that the player has to buy drinks all round in the clubhouse! Well, once again, that trusty golf insurance package could save your day. A correctly packaged policy will offer cover against virtually all golf related risks and will even cover expenses at the bar following a hole-in-one during a competition round. With such policies available we can no doubt expect an increase in the number of holes-in-one achieved on the golf course!

AT A GLANCE
featured Tour Operators Country by Country

		A Golfing Experience	Asia World Travel	Baruell	Belleair	Blue Riband	British Airways	Brittany Direct Holidays	Brittany Fairways	Brittany Ferries	Caravela	Caribtours	Clubmed	Cresta Golf in France	Destination Golf	Eagle Golf Tours	Elegant Resorts	Eurogolf	Finlays	FM Incentives	Forte Golf International	French Golf Holidays /Play and stay
USA	Carolinas						●								●	●						
	Florida						●						●		●	●	●	●				
	Arizona														●							
CARIBBEAN	Bermuda						●					●					●				●	
	The Caribbean						●					●	●				●	●			●	
FRANCE	Paris & N. France	●						●	●	●				●				●				●
	Brittany - Loire	●						●	●	●				●				●				●
	Bordeaux - Biarritz	●					●							●				●	●			●
	Riviera	●				●							●	●				●				
PORTUGAL	Algarve						●				●							●			●	
	Lisbon-Estoril						●				●							●				
	Madeira/Costa Verde	●					●				●							●				
SPAIN	Costa del Sol						●											●				
	Catalonia																					
	Costa Blanca			●														●				
	Majorca & Canaries																	●			●	
EUROPE	Europe				●	●	●															
NORTH AFRICA	Morocco												●							●	●	
	Tunisia												●									
AFRICA	Kenya						●															
	Zimbabwe																					
	South Africa															●						
	Mauritius												●				●					
ASIA	Malaysia		●																			
	Thailand		●				●						●			●						
	Competitions		🏆				🏆			🏆					🏆			🏆				
	Tuition		✱				✱						✱	✱				✱				
	TELEPHONE	0202 768003	0932 820050	081 397 4411	081 735 3266	0403 258582	0293 572890	081 641 6060	0345 581824	0705 751833/0752 263388	071 630 9223	071 581 3517	071 581 1161	061 929 1311	081 891 5151	0273 749661	0244 350408	0727 842256	08353 562	010 212 2 261710	0293 824040	0277 222050

HOLIDAY KEY

Tour Operators ●
Organising
Competitions/ 🏆
and/or
Tuition ✱

AT A GLANCE

featured Tour Operators Country by Country

TOUR OPERATORS		Golf Away Tours	Golf Holidays International	Golf Inc	Golf International	Golf Links	Heinzelmann Reisen	Hendra Holidays	Homecavern	Kelken	Leisure Link	Longmere	Longshot	Monmouth Court	North American Travel Service	P & O	Panorama	PCI Golf Holidays	PGA National	Premier Iberian	Sandals	Select World Golf
USA	Carolinas		●	●	●						●	●	●									●
USA	Florida		●	●	●						●	●				●			●			●
USA	Arizona			●		●				●												
CARIBBEAN	Bermuda		●	●	●								●			●						●
CARIBBEAN	The Caribbean			●	●										●	●					●	●
FRANCE	Paris & N. France			●	●				●		●		●									●
FRANCE	Brittany - Loire			●	●						●		●									●
FRANCE	Bordeaux - Biarritz			●	●						●		●									
FRANCE	Riviera			●	●				●				●									
PORTUGAL	Algarve	●	●	●	●						●	●	●	●								●
PORTUGAL	Lisbon-Estoril		●	●	●						●	●				●						●
PORTUGAL	Madeira/Costa Verde			●							●	●				●						●
SPAIN	Costa del Sol		●	●	●			●			●	●				●						●
SPAIN	Catalonia			●														●				
SPAIN	Costa Blanca		●	●	●						●	●								●		
SPAIN	Majorca & Canaries		●	●	●						●	●				●						●
EUROPE	Europe			●			●							●								●
NORTH AFRICA	Morocco			●	●											●						●
NORTH AFRICA	Tunisia		●	●													●					●
AFRICA	Kenya			●																		
AFRICA	Zimbabwe			●																		
AFRICA	South Africa			●	●																	
AFRICA	Mauritius			●																		
ASIA	Malaysia			●																		
ASIA	Thailand			●		●																
	Competitions		🏆	🏆		🏆					🏆		🏆									🏆
	Tuition		*	*							*	*	*			*		*	*			
	TELEPHONE	0628 485188	0480 433000	0959 565777	081 452 4263	0606 883070/0494 563935	010 498 652 63909	0637 875778	0843 860748	041 204 4947	0277 630720	081 655 2112	0730 266561	0626 778160	0532 461466	071 831 1234	0273 746877	0444 440606	0345 581824	0327 350394	071 581 9895	0202 701881

HOLIDAY KEY

Tour Operators ●

Organising Competitions/ 🏆

and/or

Tuition *

AT A GLANCE

featured Tour Operators Country by Country

Region	Destination	Silk Cut World Travel	Silverbird	Solemar	Sovereign	Sunshine Golf	Sunsport Tours	Thai Adventures	The Best of Morocco	The Flying Golfer	The Travel Club of Upminster	Thomsons	3D	Touralp	Villmar Holidays	Whole World Destination Travel	Zimgolf
USA	Carolinas				●					●						●	
USA	Florida				●											●	
USA	Arizona															●	
CARIBBEAN	Bermuda	●														●	
CARIBBEAN	The Caribbean	●															
FRANCE	Paris & N. France																
FRANCE	Brittany - Loire													●			
FRANCE	Bordeaux - Biarritz																
FRANCE	Riviera																
PORTUGAL	Algarve				●					●	●	●	●				
PORTUGAL	Lisbon-Estoril				●												
PORTUGAL	Madeira/Costa Verde				●						●						
SPAIN	Costa del Sol				●	●				●		●	●		●		
SPAIN	Catalonia																
SPAIN	Costa Blanca																
SPAIN	Majorca & Canaries				●						●	●	●				
EUROPE	Europe		●								●						
NORTH AFRICA	Morocco								●								
NORTH AFRICA	Tunisia				●							●					
AFRICA	Kenya						●										
AFRICA	Zimbabwe						●										●
AFRICA	South Africa						●								●		
AFRICA	Mauritius	●															●
ASIA	Malaysia	●	●					●									
ASIA	Thailand	●	●					●									
	Competitions				🏆								🏆				
	Tuition				*					*	*	*	*				

TELEPHONE: 0730 268511 · 081 780 1511 · 041 333 0533 · 0293 560777 · 0462 420271 · 0604 31626 · 0481 823417 · 0380 828533 · 0572 85791 · 0708 225000 · 021 632 6282/081 200 8733 · 0345 090567 · 0716 021952 · 071 224 2434 · 081 741 9987 · 091 389 1443

HOLIDAY KEY

Tour Operators ●

Organising Competitions/ and/or 🏆

Tuition *

For the attention of all Travel Agents

1995 Directory

The next edition of the Holiday Golf Guide to be published in Spring 1995 will contain a regional directory of Travel Agents to whom golfers can turn for specialist advice and assistance when booking their holidays.

Space in the directory can be reserved by completing the form below and returning it to Kensington West by 30.9.94. The charge for inclusion of £20 (excl. VAT) will be invoiced upon publication and all Travel Agents listed in the directory will be sent a copy of the next edition of The Holiday Golf Guide as part of the subscription package.

Order Form

Travel Agent_____

Address_____

_____ Post Code_____

Contact(s)_____

Telephone no._____ Fax no._____

*N.B. Any amendments to the above must be communicated to **Kensington West before 28.2.95***

Please enter the above data in the Directory of Travel Agents to be included in the Spring 1995 edition of The Holiday Golf Guide.

I understand and accept that the charge for inclusion is £20 payable 30 days against receipt of invoice and copy of the publication.

Signed_____   on behalf of_____
name_____   position _____

Send to: Kensington West Productions 5 Cattle Market Hexham Northumberland NE46 1NJ

The Kensington West Collection

A range of fine sporting and leisure publications

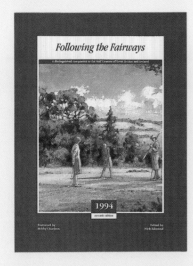

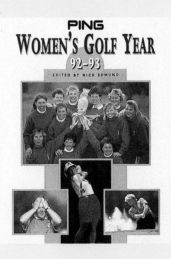

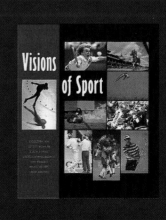

Kensington West Productions publish a range of fine sporting and leisure publications, designed to suit the interest and pocket of one and all. We are renowned for producing books in full colour, superbly illustrated with art and photography of the highest quality, to grace the shelves of any library. Our sporting annuals also provide an infinite source of reading pleasure with their informed commentary and travel guidelines. From this wealth of experience comes our new pocket series, ideal reference works for both beginners and experts which make up in price what they lack in colour. No such problem with Visions of Sport, in our opinion quite simply the best value collection of sporting photographs ever assembled.